moranthology

CAITLIN MORAN

moranthology

EBURY
PRESS

1 3 5 7 9 10 8 6 4 2

First published in 2012 by Ebury Press, an imprint of Ebury Publishing
A Random House Group company

The Random House Group Limited Reg. No. 954009

Addresses for companies within the Random House Group can be found at
www.randomhouse.co.uk

A CIP catalogue record for this book is available from the British Library

The Random House Group Limited supports The Forest Stewardship Council (FSC®),
the leading international forest certification organisation. Our books carrying the FSC
label are printed on FSC® certified paper. FSC is the only forest certification scheme
endorsed by the leading environmental organisations, including Greenpeace. Our paper
procurement policy can be found at www.randomhouse.co.uk/environment

Designed and set by seagulls.net

Printed and bound in Australia by Griffin Press

ISBN 9780091949037

To buy books by your favourite authors and register for offers visit
www.randomhouse.co.uk

www.randomhouse.com.au
www.randomhouse.co.nz

To the bit in 'Bottom' where Rik Mayall and Adrian Edmondson hit the gas man with a frying pan forty-two times. I learned so much from you.

contents

part**three**

introduction

or

I Try to Be Good

When I became a journalist at the age of fifteen, it was a matter of simple expediency.

Having been home-educated for the previous five years, I had no academic qualifications whatsoever. As a resident of a council estate in Wolverhampton, this seemed to leave me with a grand total of three future employment options:

1) prostitution
2) working the checkout at the Gateway supermarket, Warstones Drive, or
3) becoming a writer: an option I only knew of because that was what Jo March in *Little Women*, and Mother in *The Railway Children* had done, when they also fell upon hard times

Considering all the options, I immediately duffed out Gateway, on the basis that their tabards were of a green hue – which gave my ruddy skin-tone a particularly bilious tinge.

The prostitution, meanwhile, also got the ixnay – primarily in acknowl-edgement that I was, at the time, sharing a bunk-bed with my sister Caz. As she put it, quite reasonably, 'I don't want to listen to you being ridden like a show-pony three feet from my face. Plus, I think your Johns might hit their head on the Paddington Bear lampshade.'

So, writing it was. It's a choice I've never regretted – although I do have the odd, panging moment when I consider just how useful a 40 per cent discount on anything from the Gateway deli counter might have been. That is a lot of cheap crumbed ham.

I began writing. I had a list of words and phrases I loved: a collec-tion like others might collect records, or badges. Jaguary. Lilac. Catholic. Uxurious. Jubilee. Isosceles. Leopardskin. Mimosa. Shagreen. Iodine Colloidal mercury. Ardent. Attar of Roses. Corybantic. Viola. These would, surely, be useful. I knew I wanted to write intense things – write until I'd written myself new shoes and new hair and new friends, and a new life away from the inexorably compacting walls of our house. Words can be weapons, or love-spells, or just motor cars you can drive across county borders.

But what I didn't know was what to write intensely *about*, or how to write about it. I had no subject. I had no subjectivity. I was just a bundle of sprawling words.

As a bundle of sprawling words, I entered writing competitions, and, at fifteen, won one – the *Observer*'s 'Young Reporter of the Year'. In the letter announcing that I'd won, they offered me a chance to visit their offices, in London.

This was – clearly – my chance to pitch for a job. They had no teen-agers working on the paper – ipso facto, if I went down there and made the right impression, that job was mine. I was going to pitch my ass off at these guys. I was not coming home until I had a promise of further work from them in the bag.

I spent the evening before preparing for my first ever job interview in the best way I knew how.

'People like people who bring cake!' I said to myself, at 11pm. I was creaming butter and sugar in a bowl. The sideboard was covered in zested lemons.

'A lovely lemon and cream sponge! By bringing cake, I will become associated in their minds with cake, and they will think favourably of me, re: future employ!'

At the time, I was heavily under the influence of the autobiographies of actress, comedian and writer Maureen Lipman. Lipman seems to spend all her time giving her friends and colleagues in the media gifts – engraved lockets, bunches of flowers, thoughtful chocolate selections.

We didn't have any kind of cake box or cake tin for transportation down to London, so I put the sponge into a small red suitcase I had recently bought from a jumble sale, and went to bed.

The production and transportation of the lemon cream sponge – done in order to secure the job at the *Observer* – had taken maybe seven hours in total. This was six hours and fifty-eight minutes more than I had spent thinking about the actual job. Indeed, to be more specific, it was six hours and fifty-eight minutes more than I had ever considered what I would actually ever write.

So here I am, the next day, in London. Getting off the coach at Victoria Station wearing a gigantic hat – to make me look thinner – and carrying a lemon sponge in a suitcase. If I carry the suitcase by the handle, the cake will tip on the side – so I am carrying it flat, like a tray, in both hands. The time is 11.15am. I am due at the *Observer* offices, in Battersea, at 12.30pm.

'Just enough time to go to the British Museum and Buckingham Palace!' I think, having looked at the tiny map of London I have in my pocket. I am keen that this journey to London will mix business with pleasure – perhaps to create a new thing, 'plizness'.

I set off, carrying my suitcase out in front of me, like a crown on a pillow.

Three hours later, and I finally turn up at the *Observer* offices. I am trying very, very hard not to cry. All the skin has been flayed off my heels – it turns out that wearing white pixie-boots and no socks is a poor idea if you're going to walk for three hours. I am soaked in sweat, utterly morti-fied, and newly enlightened as to the scale of capital cities.

When I woke that morning, I had no idea things were so far apart in London. In Wolverhampton, if you had a reasonable jogging pace, you could touch every single remarkable building in the town in under ten minutes. Fuck it – to be honest, if you sat next to the Man on the Horse statue in Queen's Square with a tennis ball, you could bounce it off every institute of note without moving. Even the McDonald's.

London, on the other hand, seems to have endless amounts of wide, grey, straight roads, which stretch on forever, and never have the British Museum, or Buckingham Palace, or – anxiously, from 12.17pm onwards – the *Observer* offices at the end of them. I have been lost in a park, and round the back of Trafalgar Square. At one point, I tried to hail a taxi – but was holding the cake-suitcase in both hands at the time, and so looked like someone doing an impression of the wise old monkey in *The Lion King*, holding up a newly born Simba for veneration, instead. The taxi just drove past.

The kindly folk at the *Observer* have, understandably, been very worried. A fifteen-year-old girl has been missing in London for three hours – then turns up weeping and limping. They sit me down in a confer-ence room, and prepare to ask me if I've been sexually assaulted.

'I really wanted to see the British Museum's collection of cuneiform tablets!' I say, trying to satirise the idea of someone being so nerdy they kept the deputy editor of the *Observer* waiting for a job interview.

Unfortunately, they think I'm being totally truthful, and try to make me feel better by talking about their favourite exhibits – a conversation I can't join in on as, obviously, I never made it to the British Museum in the end. The only museum I've ever been in is the one at Bantock House in Wolverhampton, where they have a castle made of foil sweet-wrappers. It is a very good castle. Shiny. I tell them about the castle. They agree it sounds very special.

But still – still! Extraordinarily, after all of this, when I've drunk three glasses of water, quickly dashed a tear from my eye under the guise of adjusting my hat, and had everyone, very kindly, say 'London really IS easy to get lost in' one hundred times, there comes the moment where the deputy editor says, 'So! Now we've finally got you here, ho ho ho, would you like to work for us?'

Unfortunately, at the time, I am going through a phase of not wanting to say the right thing, or the nice thing – but the *legendary* thing instead. I imagine whole days' worth of conversations in my head, and then analyse them afterwards, from the vantage point of others, on their legendaryness-potential.

In the 'being offered a job to write three columns in a national newspaper' scenario, which I've run through 300 times, I've finally decided that the legendary response – spoken of in awe for years to come ('And then she said – hahaha oh it was brilliant …') is the one I bring out now:

'Work for you? Oh, I'd love to. I'd really, really love to.'

I pause – then pick up a paper napkin, dip it in my glass of water, and then make as if to go and wash the walls.

'First I'll do the walls,' I say, 'then the floors – that way, if I drip …'

It's a line from *Annie* – the scene where Daddy Warbucks asks her to live with him, and Annie initially misunderstands, and thinks he wants her to be his maid instead. When I imagined delivering this line, I imagine everyone laughing. 'We offered her a job – as a columnist – but she parodied her working-class background and obsession with musicals by pretending that we'd offered her a job as an office cleaner instead! Legendary!'

There is no way everyone in this room won't have seen *Annie*. This line is going to be a killer.

Everyone in this room has not seen *Annie*.

There is another awkward pause.

'Would you like to write some columns for us?' the deputy editor asks, eventually, getting things back on track by pretending what I've just said never happened. 'During the summer holidays? I think we'd be very interested to hear what you have to say about life – and cuneiform tablets! And tin-foil castles, ho ho ho!'

'Yes please,' I say, in a very simple way. I've decided to keep everything very simple from now on.

'So,' the features editor says. She's really lovely. Glossy haired. A nice lady. 'What would you like to write for us?'

I stare at her.

'What kind of ideas have you got?' she asks, again.

I keep staring. It had literally never occurred to me that I'd have to think of something to write. I thought you just turned up, said something legendary, and then they told you what to write. Like school. Papers are just … paid homework, surely? The grown-ups – a shadowy agglomeration who, in my mind, I presume to be politicians, Daddy Warbucks the billionaire and possibly John Craven from *Newsround* – decide what goes in the papers, and then farm it out to the writers. You don't have to … journalists don't … surely …

' … could do a list of the things you feel most passionately about; issues that affect you,' the deputy editor is saying. I have got nothing here. I am all out on a conversation like this. I am going to have to pull the rip-cord on this situation.

'I made you a cake!' I say, brightly. 'To have with your afternoon tea. A lemon sponge!'

I carefully place the suitcase on the table – having kept it, diligently, horizontal all day, even when I sat in that 'out of order' bus stop and cried – and open it up. People like people who bring cake! By bringing cake, I will become associated in their minds with cake, and they will think favourably of me, re: future employ!

In the punishing August heat, during a three-hour walk around London, all the lemon cream inside the cake has split, and gone rancid. An uneasy smell of vomit-cake fills the room. Everyone looks at me. In my head, I type out the sentence 'Write about this?'

Back in Wolverhampton, on the phone, my new editors suggest that I 'read the papers, watch the news – see if there's something you want to write about'.

I assiduously research every high-profile current affairs story in the media for two weeks straight – then write 600 words about my brother getting lost on Ynyslas beach last year. The week after, I file 600 words about going to the library with my brothers and sisters ('We are in the "Books So Boring They Should Have Won The Booker Prize" section'). My third, and last, piece is about the family going on a picnic.

And then that's it. That was all the *Observer* offered me, and it's finished. I'm unemployed again. I'm going to have to try and find some work.

Six months later, I'm on the phone, pitching ideas to the *Guardian*. I know they want 'teenage-y' things, so I'm doing my best, but I don't really know much about teenagers, to be honest: being home-educated, the only teenager I know, apart from myself, is my sister, Caz, and she's currently not speaking to me.

When I go into her room, she makes me stand in the corner, facing away from her, while I talk. Years later, I see the serial killer doing exactly the same thing to his victims in *The Blair Witch Project*.

'I could write about, erm, keeping a diary, or, erm, fashions,' I say, dubiously. 'Or, erm, buses?'

I spend a lot of time on the bus. I've noticed a pecking order in the seating arrangements, and am keen to share my theory that the true visionaries always sit top deck, front left, because that's the position Dan Aykroyd assumes in the car in *The Blues Brothers*, and he is my favourite Brother. I have a lot of bus observation ready to roll.

'You can be as hard-hitting as you like,' the editor says, kindly, as the word 'buses' still hovers in the air. Buses.

'Errrrr …' I say – the commission slipping away from me. I need to say something. I need to say something ear-catchy. In a panic, I blurt: 'Anorexia?'

'Yes!' she says, instantly.

It's funny because, at the time, I spend most of my free time eating cream crackers covered with Shippam's Ham & Chicken paste. I am so in love with food that I get excited when the paste squirts up through the tiny holes in the crackers, like worm-casts. If I've ever had anorexia, it lasted less than forty-five minutes. I've not been very committed to it.

'I'd love to!' I say, before modulating down into my 'issues' voice. 'It's a terrible disease, and I can't believe I'm watching my generation being laid to waste by it.'

I know nothing about anorexia. But now I've got 500 words to file by 5pm so I do what anyone would do: just make up any old shit.

'Lolita didn't diet. But today, children of twelve or younger are conscious of the width of their hips, the length of their legs, even the slight curve of their stomachs,' I started, cheerfully, although God knows why – I hadn't actually read *Lolita*. She was the only twelve-year-old I could think of, I suspect; apart from Marmalade Atkins, who wouldn't really have been appropriate in this context. I just knew Lolita was generally 'victim-y', so chucked her in here. This is what you do, when you know absolutely fucking nothing.

'I had a mini-skirt like Julia Roberts. I thought I should have the legs to go with it,' said Eloise, who I'd just totally made up.

I'd also seen an episode of *Casualty* where a ballerina eats toilet paper, so I put that in there, too.

The piece ran in March 1992, and astonishingly did not change anyone's views on anorexia – not even the quote from 'a GP' (who I'd made up) going, 'These nineteen-year-olds come in here and ask to be put on the Pill, and I'm inclined to pat them on the head and give them Smarties instead,' which is obviously what I, deep down, thought would cure anorexia at the time. Smarties.

Or here's another piece I managed to blag at the *Observer* around the same time – 1993 – entitled 'We've Never Had It So Bad'.

'What's so great about being a teenager in the material world of the nineties?' asks Caitlin Moran.

This really was a symphonic piece of bullshit. In the piece – 600 words long – I lamented that I and my friend ('She's sixteen – six and ten years on the planet, four leap years – and says her life terrifies her because it seems so long until she'll die') were being culturally crushed by the Baby Boomers.

'Sometimes we climb up onto the five-storey car park, and throw bits of gravel at the people below, and my friend will shout "WHO AM I?", and I laugh until I cry because no one can hear us, and no one can tell her.'

It's specious toss from beginning to end. For starters, you can't get access to the roof of any five-storey car-park in Wolverhampton: they're all completely sealed off, clearly to prevent health and safety issues exactly like the one I'm lying about here. And I honestly don't think any teenager has ever shouted 'WHO AM I?' to the sky, except on dramas on Channel 4, which is exactly where I'd got this from.

'She has no identity, save that which advertisers sell her,' I continue, piously, castigating the whole advertising industry; wholly ignoring the fact that I love the song from the Bran Flakes advert ('They're tasty/ Tasty/Very very tasty/They're very tasty!') and am quite emotionally invested in the romantic plotline of the Gold Blend couple.

I'd like to quote you more of the terrible pieces I wrote around this time – thrashing around, desperately, for something, anything, to write about – but I can't, because this is where my Fleet Street career ground to a halt for a while. A sum total of five pieces before everyone realised – including, finally, me – that I had absolutely nothing to write about. Or, more truthfully, that I did – but I just didn't know what it was yet.

I went underground (back to bed) and tried to work out how I could get a job writing when I knew – and I'm being generous here – absolutely nothing about the world. It took a while, but by the time I was sixteen, I had a plan.

So I'd finally figured out I couldn't write about my own life, because I hadn't done anything. I was going to have to write about other, older people, who've actually done stuff, instead. I was going to become a rock critic – because I read *NME* and *Melody Maker,* and they are publications where writers will use words like 'jaguary' and 'jubilee' and 'shagreen' whilst describing why they do or don't like U2, and I think this is probably something I could have a go at.

I write test reviews of my five favourite albums – *Hats* by Blue Nile, *Pills 'n' Thrills and Bellyaches* by Happy Mondays, *High Land, Hard Rain* by Aztec Camera, *Reading, Writing and Arithmetic* by The Sundays, and *Nothing's Shocking* by Jane's Addiction – and send them to the reviews editor at the *Melody Maker*, in an envelope that I carefully scent with lemon essence from the kitchen cupboard, to act in lieu of a lemon sponge in a suitcase. I am still working on the presumption that people will only give me work if they somehow associate me with bakery. Perhaps it's this kind of erroneous assumption you get educated out of you at Oxbridge.

The reviews editor calls me the next day and asks me to do a test review of a local gig. When it's printed, I get £28.42, and become the freelance stringer for the Midlands area: Birmingham, Wolverhampton, Dudley and Derby. If there's a band who've sold around 2,000 records playing in the backroom of a pub within twenty miles of Spaghetti Junction, I am all over it. I am now, vaguely, in charge of indie in West Mercia.

After I had been working at *Melody Maker* for just seven months – working my patch, filing my reviews, stacking up those £28.42s – I wrote a review of Ned's Atomic Dustbin's new album, entitled *522*.

In the hipster pecking order of the time, Ned's – as their fans called them – were pretty much the lowest of the low: a group of lads from Stourbridge – the Midlands! My patch! – barely in their twenties, who made amiable, slightly slack-jawed, very white rackets for amiable, slightly slack-jawed, very white youths to leap around to. In terms of funk, or glamour, they rated level with Bovril, or the clog. Additionally, their career was past its best. They were on the wane.

Nonetheless, a lack of funk, hotness or success is not, and never has been, a crime. It's not even against park by-laws. Therefore, the thermonuclear savaging I proceeded to give that album, over 480 words, was as unnecessary and unprovoked as Chewbacca strafing the local duck pond with the Millennium Falcon.

Actually, I wasn't using weaponry a quarter as sophisticated as the Millennium Falcon. It was more like Chewbacca falling out of the Millennium Falcon, then wading into the duck pond and kicking the ducks, then stamping on the ducks, then punching the ducks – alarmed, innocent ducks, now all quacking as the Wookiee flailed at them, wholly unprovoked, and who didn't leave the pond until the water was covered in tail-feathers.

'Hello, boys,' I opened – addressing the band directly. 'Funerals are a bummer, aren't they? Career in a coffin, all we have to do is chuck a bit of earth around, and troop through a thick grey gauze of rain to the wake, and get pissed. I have been chosen to stand, blearily, at the wake, and say a few words at the passing of your ability to ever sell records again. What can I say? The words of one of the great poets – Liam from Flowered Up – seem appropriate: "FUCK OFF! FUCK OFF AND DIE!"'

Eighteen years later, and I am still so mortified by what I wrote, I can only look at the middle section through my fingers: 'Putrid … anthems to nothing … stink … dirges … nasty scribbles … no one gives a flying fuck …'

I accused them of being sexless, tuneless, fuckless, revolting: responsible for a musical climate where bands crawled on their bellies with three chords, rather than flying with the aspirations of gods. I was a total wanker.

I ended with: '1994 was the year we waved goodbye to Kurt Cobain and That Bloke out of Doctor Feelgood. Feel like making it a hat-trick, Jonn(nnnnnnnnn)?'

Yes, that's right – I ended an album review by wishing death on the lead singer, either by the methodology of Kurt Cobain, who'd shot himself in April, or the lead singer of Doctor Feelgood, who'd died of cancer in August. And spelt his name 'sarcastically', to boot.

The review itself was sub-headlined 'Jesus, Caitlin – there are gonna be repercussions about this one'. As if the magazine itself was alarmed by what I'd written.

Looking back now, I can see what I was doing. I was, by now, a seventeen-year-old, working in an office otherwise full of adults. I was a cub, savaging some prey, and bringing back the carcass to the pack elders, to impress them. I wanted to make my mark.

However, even the most cursory examination of the situation shows us that I was not bringing back a mighty Arctic fox. I had just come back with a couple of sad, surprised ducks instead.

And, of course, we can also see that I was not a white-toothed wolf-cub, either, but a puffin, or a penguin, or a giant hen: some perambulatory creature not built for pugilism. I would never go up to someone at a party and be horrible to their faces – so why was I doing it in a magazine? I was just thinking of what I wrote as 'some copy' – some space filled on a page, with whatever came into my head at the time.

But of course, it's not just 'copy'. There's no such thing as 'copy'. Putting things on paper doesn't make it matter less. Putting things on paper makes it matter *more*.

The bottom line is, I believed I was a nice person – the kind of person who brought a lemon sponge to the *Observer* and would pick worms off the pavement and put them onto the verge with a cheerful 'There you go, mate' – but I appeared to be pretending to be a cunt. Why was I doing that? There are enough cunts in the world already. We don't need any more. The only kind of person who would *pretend* to be a cunt probably *is* a cunt. This faux-cuntiness was a cunt's game. I decided I was going to stop.

I'd like to pretend I worked all this out myself, in the weeks after the Ned's Atomic Dustbin review was printed. That I quietly figured out what my principles were, and who I wanted to be, in a determined, intellectual re-imagining of myself: a rebirth through philosophy, and reason.

In reality, the man who was to eventually be my husband took me to one side at a gig a week later and said, in his mild way, 'That review was a bit … off.'

And that was when I realised – in a huge, anxious rush – that I couldn't do what so many of the writers I enjoyed – A A Gill, Julie Burchill and Hunter S Thompson – did. That gleeful arson, those cool assassinations.

I was not, like them, crouched behind my typewriter, picking off marauders with a pearl-handled pistol. I couldn't manage the daily rages of the columnists who despaired over the parking restrictions, and their tax bills, and the immigrants, and the gay dads, and the BBC, and women's fat arses in the wrong dresses, and the health and safety regulations. I couldn't handle the grief.

What I was built for, I felt, was something a bit more ... herbivore instead. As I started to reassess my writing style, I thought about what I liked doing – what gave me satisfaction – and realised the primary one was just ... pointing at things. Pointing out things I liked, and showing them to other people – like a mum shouting 'Look! Moo-cows!' as a train rushes past a farm. I liked pointing at things, and I liked being reasonable and polite about stuff. Or silly. Silly was very, very good. No one ever got hurt by silly.

Best of all was being pointedly silly about serious things: politics, repression, bigotry. Too many commentators are quick to accuse their enemies of being evil. It's far, far more effective to point out that they're acting like divs instead. I was up for div-revealing.

'I am just going to be polite and silly, and point at cool things,' I decided. 'When I started writing, I would have killed to have one thing to write about. Now, I have three. Politeness *and* silliness, *and* pointing. That's enough.'

So, yes. If this collection is anything, it is, I hope, either silly, or polite, or pointing at something cool. There is some vaguely serious stuff in here – recently, I have enjoyed taking to my writing bureau and writing about poverty, benefit reform and the coalition government in the manner of a shit Dickens, or Orwell, but with tits. T S Eliot's quote, in 'Little Gidding', is true: 'And at the end of all our exploring/Will be to arrive where we started/And know the place for the first time.'

The fifteen-year-old wannabe journalist in Wolverhampton, who was desperately looking for something to write *about*, actually had a million things to write about, all around her: council estates, and life on benefits, and friends with mental illness, and the wholly altered state that is being grindingly, decades-long poor – too broke to travel to another town, or escape from lingering, low-level dampness, fear and boredom.

But – perhaps in reaction to all this – my underlying, abiding belief is that the world is, still, despite everything, a flat-out amazing place. This book is a collection of instances of how brilliant the world often is – written by a life-long fan of existence, and the Earth. Yes, there might still be speed humps, and paperwork, and Innocent Smoothie bottles going 'Hi! My name is Graham the Smoothie! Please drink my goofy fruitiness in as maverick a manner as possible! SLURP ME WITH YOUR HIPSTER STRAW'. This world can be irksome, and even I – essentially Pollyanna, with a C-section scar – have had a couple of rants in here. I will be honest with you: there is not much in here to increase the pride-levels of Nazis, internet trolls, or Lola from *Charlie and Lola*. That crayoned harpy must die. And I will actually stand by that death-wish. Unlike the one I levelled at poor Jonn from Ned's Atomic Dustbin, to whom I now – eighteen years later – apologise to, whilst lying on my belly in abject prostration and mortification. I am so, so sorry. Tell your mum I'm sorry, too. She must have been dead upset.

But, generally, this is a manifesto for joy. When I got my second chance at being a journalist – being taken on by *The Times* as a columnist when I was eighteen, in my new persona as the 'pointing cheerful person' – I determined to use the opportunity to racket around as many exhilarating things as possible. As a consequence, in this collection, I get into the TARDIS; go to a sex club with Lady Gaga; get drunk with Kylie; post a picture of a squirrel's gigantic testicles on Twitter and make an international news story; smoke fags with Keith Richards; blow my chances of marrying Eddie Izzard for the third time in ten years; walk twenty-six miles in the rain, eating cake; become an internet dwarf called 'Scottbaio', then accidentally die, on air, on the *Richard & Judy* show; pay my income tax whilst shouting 'Hurrah!'; and confess to, once, having trapped a wasp under a glass, then got it stoned.

The motto I have Biro'd on my knuckles is that this is the best world we have – because it's the only world we have. It's the simplest maths ever. However many terrible, rankling, peeve-inducing things may occur, there are always libraries. And rain-falling-on-sea. And the Moon. And love. There is always something to look back on, with satisfaction, or forward to, with joy. There is always a moment where you boggle at the world – at yourself – at the whole, unlikely, precarious business of being alive – and then start laughing.

And that's usually when I make a cup of tea, and start typing.[†]

[†]Actually, it's not. I usually leave it for at least another three hours of pissing around on the Topshop website, attacking in-growing hairs on my leg with tweezers, and looking at dream apartments in New York, before panicking, and beginning to hammer out stuff a scanty hour and thirty-seven minutes before deadline – but that's not as inspiring a sentence to end on. It kind of ruins things, tbh.

part**one**

Caffeine, *Ghostbusters*, Marijuana, and a C-3PO Made of Ham

In which I explain why Ghostbusters *is the greatest film in the world, dismiss David Cameron as 'a camp gammon robot', watch Michael Jackson's memorial service in a state of some astonishment, and keep the Prime Minister waiting.*

But I start where I always end: in bed, confusing my husband.

I thought long and hard about what the first piece should be in what is the nearest I will ever get to releasing a The Beatles Blue Album, *or* The Beatles Red Album. *Some incredibly righteous piece about the welfare system? A rhapsodic eulogy to how much I want to bang Sherlock in* Sherlock? *Or a carefully weighed take-down of trans-phobia, sexism and homophobia, as mediated through the unlikely, yet ultimately fitting, imagery of the Moon Landings? Don't worry – they're all in here. Especially the Sherlock thing. There's a lot of Sherlock love in here. In many ways, this book might as well be called 'Deduce THIS, Sexlock Holmes!' with a picture of me licking his meerschaum, cross-eyed and screaming.*

However, in the end, I ignored all the more worthwhile, culturally valid and heartfelt stuff in favour of a ratty, decades-long, rumbling semi-feud with my husband instead.

Call Me Puffin

00.17am. We are just going to sleep. I can hear Pete's breathing is modulating into REM. In the loft, the boiler powers down into standby mode. The duvet is perfectly snugged in. The day is done.

'I love you, Bear,' I say.

'Mvv mmo too,' he replies. There is a silence. It is followed by a second silence. Then:

Me: 'Bear. It's funny, isn't it? Bear. I call you Bear.'

Pete: 'Mmrg.'

Me: 'But you … you have no nickname for me. It would be nice if you had a nickname for me.'

Pete: 'Marrrp.'

Me: 'Because, you know, it's been sixteen years now. I've had lots of slightly noisome nicknames for you – Bear, Pie, Mr Poo, The Wurbles – but you've never had a nickname for me.'

Pete: 'Mrrrrrb.'

Me: 'I mean, a nickname arises out of a need, doesn't it? To rename something in order to display ownership; or indicate that you see in someone an aspect that no one else can, and which demands unique acknowledgement. So not having a nickname for me kind of suggests you would quite happily let me be stolen by tinkers; or that you can't really tell the difference between me, my sisters and Moira Stuart.'

Pete, unhappily: 'Mrrrrrp.'

Me: 'Seriously: I think I really would quite like a nickname. It would make me feel more loved. I would feel a lot more loved if you could come up with a nickname for me. Now. Do it now.'

Pete, turning over in bed: 'I'm asleep.'

Me: 'I'll help you brainstorm. It needs to be playful – yet tender.'

Pete, disbelievingly: 'Playful yet tender. Is this actually happening?'

Me: 'Yes. And, ideally, it would be reflective of the unique insight you have into me, after all those years. What comes to mind when you think of me?'

Pete: 'The word "me".'

Me: 'Do it properly!'

Pete: 'Seriously. The word "me". You say it a lot. That, and "serum". But I don't really know what that means.'

Me: 'Not what *I say* – it's got to be what *you think*. WHY DO YOU LOVE ME?'

Pete, vaguely: 'You're a woman?'

Me, firmly: 'My nickname can't be "Woman". All my feminist friends will write a petition against me. What else is springing to mind?'

Pete: 'You're wholly unaware of how much work I have to do tomorrow.'

Me, helpfully: 'I'm unexpectedly practical, aren't I? Like, I mended the stereo on that hire-car that time. Something along the lines of "MacGyver", or "John McLane" – that's the character Bruce Willis plays in *Die Hard*. But with a sexy twist. Maybe "Bare Grylls". But that only really works on paper. We need something more … aural.'

Pete: 'You should call a friend to talk about this. One of those chatty gays. They'd love something like this.'

Me: 'What loveable quirks do you notice about me?'

Pete, despairingly, after a minute: '… you eat a lot of yoghurt.'

Me: 'I eat a lot of yoghurt?'

Pete: 'You eat a lot of yoghurt. I could call you "Yog".'

Me, indignant: 'Yog? You can't call me Yog – that's George Michael's nickname. You can't give me a nickname that's already being used by a celebrity. You might as well call me "Brangelina", or "The Pelvis". You're not really trying here, are you?'

Pete: 'I'm so very unhappy.'

Me: 'What about "Puffin"? It is my favourite bird – a small, round, gothic bird with a large nose. Plus it punningly acknowledges my stoner years, proving you knew me right back in the day, when I still thought there were eight days in the week, because of The Beatles. Puffin.'

Pete: 'Puffin! That is good. That is very, very good. Yes. You are Puffin to me now, for ever. The matter is settled to mutual satisfaction. I am wholly joyous. Do I sound sarcastic?'

Me, happily: 'No. I am happy now. Bear and Puffin. That is us. We are Bear and Puffin. Good night, Bear.'

Pete: 'Good night.'

Small, angry silence.

Me, eventually: 'Puffin.'

Pete: 'What?'

Me: 'Good night, Puffin. Say, "Good night, Puffin".'

Pete: 'Good night, Puffin. You demented fucking bitch.'

As you can see, my domestic life now is one of joyous fulfilment. Should you ask me how this has come to be, I would quote the words of one of The Muppet Show's *greatest acts, Marvin Suggs and the Muppaphone. As Suggs plays 'Witch Doctor' on the Muppaphone – a living xylophone made of Muppets, which he repeatedly bashes with small hammers, eliciting screams – he talks about the public reaction to his act.*

'People ask me – what is your secret with the Muppaphone?' he says, in his strangulated, high-pitched voice. 'And I say – MUTUAL LOVE AND RESPECT.'

For me and Pete, it has been much the same. And so we sail on in the deep blue bliss of marriage. But it has not always been like this. I came from a radically different background. In many, many ways, my early life resembles Angela's Ashes, *or* A Child Called It. *This searing account of what it was like to reach adulthood having never had a cup of tea amply illustrates the deep mental scars I still bear, bravely, today.*

Note how the piece dates from a time when one still paid for the Evening Standard, *and how accurate my assessment of its future proved to be. I am like some kind of media scrying bowl.*

Caffeine – Lifeblood of the Twenty-first Century

As I write this, I'm sipping at a lovely cup of tea. Obviously, in many ways, and discounting the sundry opinions of Tony Parsons, this is the least print-worthy sentence of the week. A brew is not news. Everyone drinks tea. Of course they do.

Except, until recently, me.

Yes – until last summer, I had had three cups of coffee, and maybe ten cups of tea, in my life. My whole life. I know. *I know*. Reading my words must be like reading the musings of a MoonMan from Mars. But what can I say – hot drinks never really happened for me. I guess I never met the right person to introduce me to tea. Or perhaps I never really felt confident enough in myself to believe anyone would want to make tea for me.

Last summer, however, we had a new kitchen fitted, and as the kitchen is also where I work, I had to decamp for five weeks to the coffee shops of Crouch End with my laptop. Being sensitive, I noticed within weeks that it was the custom of these places not to ask for 'a big cup of tap water, please', but to drink their expensively vended tea, or coffee, instead. Within two weeks, I had gone from a caffeine virgin to someone who could easily knock back four lattes and as many teas in an afternoon, and I tell you this: it made me see everything in a whole new light.

Friends, we live in a caffeine world. We think in a caffeine way and we live caffeine lives. Our problems are the problems of people addled with popular hot beverages, and our thoughts are half our own, half the product of our cups. So many aspects of modern life I'd never understood before – things that had completely baffled me about society – suddenly became obvious, once I'd spent a month off my face on tea.

Take, for instance, headaches. Until I became a tea addict, I presumed that people saying 'I have a headache' was simply a euphemism for wanting to opt out of an impending activity – like my father saying 'I can't – I've got a bone in my leg' when I was little, and wanted him to play hide and seek.

Enter the world of caffeine, however, and you live in a world where your skull suddenly becomes very weak and porous, into which vexing low-level pain can seep at any minute.

Likewise, insomnia. Usually, my average span between 'lights off' and dreaming of *Doctor Who* was under five minutes. Late at night after a busy day = going to sleep. It seemed quite basic. Now in the post-tea world, however, any cup after 4pm provokes an unwelcome wakefulness in the centre of the brain, present long after the non-caffeinated would be woozily stumbling to bed. When found in conjunction with caffeine problem three – low-level anxiety and restlessness – what Thom Yorke of Radiohead once so accurately described as the 'unborn chicken voices in my head' can cluck on until 1 or 2am. Just from tea! I tell you, it's put me right off the idea of crack.

The main thing I've noticed, however, is how unreasonable, self-absorbed and permanently outraged caffeine has made me. The bottom line is, hot drinks turn people into pigs. Simply walking along with a take-away coffee in your hand turns you into a belligerent fantasist. You really feel like you're a vital cast member of *Sex and the City*, or *The West Wing* – when, of course, really, you're just a schmoo with a brew heading for John Lewis. Knowing all this doesn't make me any more pleasant. In the last few months, I have started arguing with people in my head.

Instance: yesterday, at Oxford Circus, I wanted to buy an *Evening Standard*, but only had the money in coppers. As I hovered to the side, counting my change, I had an absolutely apoplectic row with the 'EenSaad!' man – but wholly and solely in my mind.

'What you giving me all this brahn money for?' he asked me, in his Cockney way, in my imagination. 'I've got a wallet – not a sack.'

'This is exactly why the *Standard* is going out of business!' I shouted back, as interior monologue. 'This is fifty brown pennies more than I'm paying for the *Metro*, or the *London Paper*. I *work* for a newspaper! I *know* which way the wind's blowing! It'll all be online in three years' time, trea-cle, and you'll be in a cardboard box being weed on by foxes! Screw you, man. SCREW YOU!'

This furious spat was cut short by, in the actual physical world, me giving the *Evening Standard* man 50p in loose change, and him saying 'Cheers, love' and giving me my paper.

I had had three lattes before 11am.

There is a plus side to caffeine, of course. I've lost nearly a stone, can write a blog entry in nine minutes flat, and feel a previously undiscovered connection with the world, simply by being able to say 'I could murder a brew. Tea, anyone?' to a room full of nodding people. Indeed, I would say that this feeling of finally being like everyone else is the most attractive aspect of having become a caffeine drinker. Irritable, tired, anxious and sporadically unable to see out of one eye due to migraine, I finally feel normal.

Having been born to an ardent Trade Unionist father – 'You come back here telling me you've voted Tory, and you can spend Christmas Day on the fucking doorstep' – I have always been 'wary' of Conservative leaders. This is, perhaps, fairly clear in the following tirade of derision against the then-prospective Chancellor and Prime Minister, George Osborne and David Cameron – thinly disguised as a review of Andrew Rawnsley's documentary Dispatches: Cameron Uncovered.

For a while, inspired by this review, there was a Facebook group called 'David Cameron Is a C-3PO Made of Ham', which is probably my second-favourite achievement of my career – after being able to tell Keith Richards that Noddy Holder from Slade was telling everyone he wore a wig (later in the book. Near the end of Part One).

A few weeks after this review ran, I met David Cameron at a garden party held by News International, publishers of The Times. *Chatting with fellow* Times *columnist Giles Coren next to a table bearing cheeses – 'Always set up camp next to the cheeses,' Giles said, wisely – we noted that David Cameron had noticed us, and was drawing near for a chat.*

'Oh, I do so enjoy YOUR writing,' Cameron said to Giles – planting himself between me and Coren Jr, with his back towards me.

I was amazed. I thought the whole point of posh people was that part of their incredibly expensive private educations was to behave graciously toward red-faced Hogarthian peasants such as myself. It seemed not. £100,000 at Eton and he was still an asshat. Still – little I cared. With Coren now other-wise occupied in talk of property prices in Ladbroke Grove, I had a full run on the cheese table, and subsequently managed to decant half a Reblochon into my handbag before ordering a taxi.

Three short months later, David Cameron was the Prime Minister of Great Britain and Northern Ireland, with access to nuclear weapons, and the Queen.

David Cameron: Gammon Robot

George Osborne's the thing, isn't he? George Osborne is the thing. You can have all the footage you like of David Cameron being 'modern' and 'quotidian' – riding a bicycle, wearing shorts, drinking tea out of a mug instead of the Eton Tea Goblet, traditionally awarded to the best Oik Basher from Turret Six – but really, his poshness and uselessness is but a foothill compared to George Osborne's. Osborne is your go-to guy for posh and useless. He's like Hugh Laurie's Prince Regent in *Blackadder,* but with an iPhone.

You can imagine early Victorian explorers discovering a Pacific island full of huge, delicious, hapless George Osbornes, and clubbing them into extinction in three months flat. This is, let us not forget, an Etonian baronet who only went into politics because he failed at becoming a journalist.

Failed at becoming a journalist? HAHAHA! No one fails at being a journalist! Have you seen who gets in on this gig? Children, freaks, idiots, perjurers, wenchers, preternatural fornicators, slaves to the opium pipe. Tony Parsons. Shoot a baboon, get into fist-fights at the Press Awards, make up stories wholesale – no one cares. Seriously, if an Etonian baronet can't put on his blagging boots, pull some strings and score some half-arsed 'society' column in the *Evening Standard,* then you suspect he couldn't blag his way into his own house with his front door key in his hand, and his address written on a label round his neck.

Andrew Rawnsley's *Dispatches: Cameron Uncovered*, then, gave us another chance to marvel at the miracle of the man being seriously proposed as the next Chancellor of the Exchequer, literally of our country. Yes, it was really supposed to be a profile of David Cameron – but, as anyone who watched it will know, Rawnsley didn't really get anything on Cameron. Unlike his current, talking-point book on Gordon Brown, *The End of the Party,* there were no '24-carat' stories here of Cameron going stark, staring mad, and jostling someone in a corridor, once. The nearest we got to a revelation was some political analyst's assertion that Cameron's target voter was in fact his wife, Samantha.

'She *might* have voted for Blair in 1997. This time around, she's thinking of voting Tory – but wonders if they've changed enough,' he speculated.

Blimey. Cameron's not really busting a gut here, is he – if his main ambition is to get his wife to vote for him. Two lie-ins and the promise his mother's not coming for Christmas this year, and that vote is in the *bag*. If all elections only consisted of a single vote, cast by your missus, Cameron would storm it. Cameron would additionally storm, one realised, whilst watching the programme, any fancy dress competition that involved guests rigging up as 'a C-3PO made of ham'. His resemblance to a slightly camp gammon robot is extraordinary. You can practically see the breadcrumbs in his hair.

But it was Osborne who really stole the show – his every appearance prompting whoops of disbelief from the viewer. In the House of Commons, railing against Brown and Darling, Osborne's fists were clenched, pugilistically – save for his pinkies, which stuck out, on auto-posh. Amazing. Why has no one noticed this before? He might just as well have ended the speech with, 'And Nanny agrees with me, too.'

The recurring theme amongst the talking heads was a barely disguised horror at the Tory party's economic plans. Despite having recently come out of recession, Britain apparently remains very vulnerable to the 'double dip' – not the fear of contracting herpes simplex from a party tub of salsa, but momentary economic relief, followed by, if public sector spending is scaled back, 'a massive depression'. A gigantic fiscal cold sore, if you will.

'Ask the Americans about 1937,' David Blanchflower from the Bank of England said, drily.

As Rawnsley pointed out, if the Conservatives get in, George Osborne will be overseeing the biggest spending squeeze since 1945, as they engage in their traditional pastime of scaling back the Welfare State. Over the decades, the main task of any Tory administration has been to come up with a new, euphemistic way of describing how they'll scale back the Welfare State. Cameron's pop is the coining of the phrase, 'Big Society'.

In the 'Big Society' charities and voluntary organisations will, apparently, step in and pick up the slack in areas where once the Welfare State existed.

For anyone wondering if this might work, Cameron's former tutor at Oxford, Vernon Bognador, appeared to explain.

'That is the philosophy of the nineteenth century,' he said, briskly. 'What does "Big Society" really mean? That if you become destitute, the Salvation Army will step in? It doesn't work. That's why we invented the State.'

Later on, Rawnsley asked everyone what 'Cameronism' means.

'I don't know,' replied Vince Cable – Britain's de facto tribal elder, in the continuing absence of Merlin. 'And I don't think he does, either,' he added.

I know what 'Cameronism' is, though. It's that thing where George Osborne might become Chancellor of the Exchequer. Brrrrr.

David Cameron and George Osborne aren't the only Tories I've been mean to. In this 2008 column, I make the argument against Boris Johnson as putative London mayor as vociferously as I can. I felt I had sensed his key weakness.

Boris Johnson: Posh Albino Fanny-hound

Now, I am no political ingénue. I have read books (one) by Will Hutton, voted in every election (they give you a free biscuit at the Stroud Green polling station! Gigantic swing to me!), and know the difference between Geoff Hoon and Chris Huhne. I think. Other than the spelling.

So this is why I feel more than qualified to talk about the forthcoming mayoral election in London. Indeed, to be honest, in many ways my awesome political knowledge is a positive hindrance when it comes to talking about the mayoral election. Or, indeed, any elections. Let's face it: these days, people don't vote for political reasons. Hahahaha – of course they don't. I imagine there are, literally, more people who have had sex with Boris Johnson and Ken Livingstone than have read either of their manifestos. Literally. Perhaps this accounts for their 'modern lifestyles'. Maybe's it's all 'horizontal campaigning'. They're just getting 'ticks' in 'boxes'. Brrrr.

Those who vote do so for dozens of different reasons, hardly any of them political. They vote for someone because they're bored with 'the other one'. They vote because they like someone's hair. The great majority of voting is done, I suspect, on a simple, hereditary basis. Certainly, my four-yearly vote for Labour was passed down to me from my father – who, in turn, had it passed to him from his father.

'And before him, there wasn't a Labour to vote for. Which is why the poor bloody Irish were all forced to live in caves, under the Englishman's colonial mansion, eating mud, sleeping on mud, and making statues of Brendan Behan out of the mud,' as my father explained, in my formative introduction to the British political system. Continuing this tradition, I have explained politics to my children in a similarly biased manner.

'The Tories don't believe in the redistribution of wealth by the State,' I told them, on the way home, eating my voting biscuit. 'They think that middle-class people just kind of … give their money to the needy, anyway. But let's face it: we don't, do we, darlings? So vote Labour.'

Voting isn't about politics, analysis or clear, rational thought any more. It has become an odd cross between family tradition, belligerence and whim – the same kind of basis on which the British choose a picnic spot, only with radically greater consequences. So having got that clear, here, then, is the full, truthful reasoning of my voting on Thursday. This comes with apologies to everyone who doesn't live in London, couldn't care less about the mayoral election and might very well be 4ft under a gigantic, unreported flood, for all we know, in our self-important, London-centric frenzy. Sorry, provincial guys.

I will NOT be voting for Boris. Quite aside from being a ditzy, posh, albino fanny-hound, he has a far greater impediment to running one of the greatest cities in the world: he is disabled by his own funniness.

I understand Boris's weakness. I understand it only too well. As someone who spends most of her life trying to be funny, I know just how much effort it takes. It's like running a quiet heroin habit on the side. It's a full-time commitment. It makes you fatally, fundamentally unsuitable for a job with genuine responsibilities and consequences.

In the past, I have totally ignored people who have admitted that they are pregnant, in love with me or have increasingly suicidal feelings – simply because I was too busy trying to think of a pun off the back of something they'd said five minutes previously.

Suicidal friend, counting out pills: ' ... and that's why I am going to put an end to this. I can't do anything right any more. I'm ruining other people's lives now. I just want to stop this existential madness.'

Me: '... so that short guy in the cafe, right – you could have called him Leonardo Dave Inchy!!!!!'

Any effective politician shouldn't be making more than four jokes a year, tops – and at least three of those should be made quietly, at home, among friends and family. The distressingly large number of people who seem set to vote for Johnson simply because he's 'funny' – what we might term the 'BorisROFLMAO' vote – don't realise that Boris is ideologically committed to something that will always take precedence over budget meetings, and the city's security, which is: Boris being funny.

Voters! This isn't *Britain's Got Talent*! This is the bit when we decide who's emptying the bins, booking the buses and moving on the tramps for the next four years. Boris wants an audience, not an Assembly. We might just as well vote in *The Friday Night Project*'s Justin Lee Collins as Boris.

I AM voting for Ken, on the basis that he's done the job for so long, no one's going to be able to come in and work that filing system now. No one. There's probably a way of flushing the tricky toilet on the third floor that only Ken knows. The whole housing department's lottery rota could go to pot if he gets the boot.

Seeking his third term, Ken is suffering the same problem that Tony Blair did last year – people are just a bit bored with him, and want to try something a bit different. But everyone should remember that this is the very same reasoning that led more than 60 per cent of the female population to get Alexa Chung-style fringes last year – fringes that we all regret now, don't we, ladies? We wish we'd just stuck with what we knew worked. And London is – and I genuinely do believe this – even more important than hair. We don't want the metropolitan equivalent of eighteen months in hair grips, growing out an unwise choice of mayor. We should stick with what we know. Vote Ken!

Having three columns a week in a national newspaper is a bit like having three children: you're knackered and grumpy all the time, can't shift that final stone, and you don't understand why they can't just crack on with it on their own and get out of your FACE.

Haha, not really! I don't mean that! What I really mean is that it's hard to decide which one you love the best.

The TV review allows me to have a good old natter about what we all saw on telly that week – one of the great pleasures of living on a small island that still generally tends to watch one of four channels. The magazine column, meanwhile, allows me the kind of monologue that one might deliver, in a slightly slurred yet impassioned way, to a minicab driver who is doing their best to ignore you and turn up 'Alone' by Heart on Magic FM at 3am.

'The thing about my hupsand, right, is that his never, never gived me a nickname, razzer plazzer mazzer fazzer TWO CHILDREN AND SEVENTEEN STITCHES!!! I've done a small sick on the seatbelt but it's fine don't worry I've got a hanky, I'm just WIPING it away. Don't look.'

Sometimes, however, despite trying to be impartial, I think that my Friday column on celebrities – the innovatively named 'Celebrity Watch' – might be my favourite. It's essentially a weekly stand-up routine about the contents of OK! magazine. It is the alternative career as a comedian I could have forged, had I not had such grave 'sweating' issues that my damp underarms are visible from over fifty feet away within seconds of talking in front of more than nine people. Really, I'm just like Lenny Bruce, but shy.

This Celebrity Watch was devoted entirely to the outright honking clown-car insanity of the memorial service for the late Michael Jackson – an extraordinary event which, for all who saw it, will live on in their unhappy, gibbering minds for ever. For those who haven't read Celebrity Watch before

– a massive demographic that includes my mother and at least one senior management figure at The Times, *who refers to it as 'that number thing' – it takes the format of a Top Ten countdown, simply because it requires far less structure and skill to write something as a Top Ten countdown. And I refer to myself throughout in the third person as 'CW' – short for Celebrity Watch – because I like giving the impression of being a mysterious, powerful celebrity-judging organisation ratifying all this stuff in a scientific manner, rather than the reality: someone in their dressing gown typing away whilst eating endless amounts of Celebrations. Snickers for preference. The nuts are like a healthy protein.*

Celebrity Watch Special: Michael Jackson's Memorial

Ten. UP. The Jackson Four. It was the first suggestion that not only was this going to be an unusual memorial service, but one so gigantic, random and barking that the viewer at home would often have to touch their legs, say, or look at a kettle – saying, 'These are the normal things. I must remember what the normal things are.'

Michael Jackson's $15,000 golden casket was carried into the arena, on the shoulders of Jackson's brothers, as a choir sang – perhaps ominously, in the view of the open-casket funeral tradition – 'We will see the king.' Jackson's brothers, you couldn't help but note, were all wearing a single, white, rhinestone-studded glove – Jackson's signature accessory-motif, aside from a full face mask, and/or enraged chimp. To put this into context, it's a bit like if all the pallbearers at Elvis's funeral had been wearing big plastic quiffs and doing that wobbly thing Elvis did with his legs. Amazing.

Nine. DOWN. Congresswoman Sheila Jackson Lee. In the ultimate 'Good luck with that!' moment of 2009 so far, Congresswoman Lee took it upon herself to be the one who would mention both Jackson's $22m out-of-court settlement to Jordy Chandler, *and* 2005's seven counts of child sexual abuse, and two counts of administering an intoxicating agent in order to commit the felony. *But in a good way.*

'As a representative of Congress, we understand the constitution. We know that people are innocent until proved otherwise!' Lee said, trying to sort out that whole 'persistent paedophile rumours' thing in a couple of breezy sentences, in front of Jackson's children.

Personally, CW would have played it marginally safer, and done a nice reading of 'Stop All the Clocks' instead.

Eight. UP. Kentucky Fried Chicken. Magic Johnson – helpfully described to we Limey viewers by Paul Gambaccini as 'playing for the Lakers, the Manchester United of America' – appeared to walk up to the podium with two agendas: 1) To respectfully honour the life and times of the late Michael Jackson. 2) To try and mention Kentucky Fried Chicken in a positive manner as many times as possible.

'I went to Michael's house – and the chef brought Michael out a bucket of Kentucky Fried Chicken. I was like, Michael – you have Kentucky Fried Chicken! That was the greatest moment of my life ... we had such a great time, sitting on the floor, eating that bucket of Kentucky Fried Chicken. God bless you, Michael!'

Seven. DOWN. P Diddy. P Diddy – who some of we more old-fashioned types may insist on still referring to as 'Puff Daddy'; his original, stupid made-up name – also attended the memorial. Being a man of the twenty-first century, Diddy [@iamdiddy] keeps Twitter up to date with his movements at all times. The entry for the day before the funeral read 'I haven't been to sleep yet! LOL. I'm still at the after-party from last night! No sign of quitting!' There was a quick tone change with the subsequent two tweets: 'I'm at the memorial. RIP Michael Jackson' and 'Just left the funeral. So sad!! RIP MJ!!!!' The next day, however, it was very much back to business as usual, with the – presumably lunch-inspired – 'I love sweet tarts!!!'

Interesting Diddy point: both 'sweet tarts' and the burial of the King of Pop warranted three exclamation marks.

Six. DOWN. Brooke Shields. Giving a weeping testimonial that appeared to go on for nearly three days, Shields' aim was to try and convey to the audience what the man she had known was like. Unfortunately, the man she had known was Michael Jackson, and every anecdote she had sounded like a cross between the kind of dream you have when you've got chickenpox, and something she was making up in order to get him into even more trouble.

A case in point was the story of how, the night before Elizabeth Taylor's wedding, she and Jackson broke into Taylor's room as she slept, to look at the wedding dress, as Michael – a thirty-three-year-old black, straight man – was too excited to wait until the morning. The next day, at the wedding, Shields and Jackson 'pretended to be the mother and father of [Elizabeth Taylor]. It sounds weird,' Shields concluded, looking rather wild-eyed, 'but we made it real!'

You think? Like CW has said once before today – good luck with that!

Five. UP. Diana Ross and Elizabeth Taylor. Both the pivotal gay icons in Jackson's life were absent from the memorial service – preferring to issue personal statements on the day, instead.

Taylor's commented that she did not want to be part of the 'Whoopla' – an important coining of a new word, given that mankind did not previously have a term for 'Memorial service where the corpse's daughter will "close the show" by being herded onto a stage, weeping, whilst her uncles comfort her by stroking her with rhinestone gloves.'

Ross, meanwhile, had different fish to fry. Following the unexpected revelation that Jackson had wanted custody of his children to go to her – inspiring thoughts of some screwball Motown version of *Baby Boom*, with Ross as Diane Keaton – it seemed as if Ross's message made her position on the matter very clear.

'I will be here [in her own home, not at the funeral, very far away from everything, particularly the children] whenever they need me [to lend them $20, or give them advice on floor-length, fishtail cocktail dresses and backcombing],' Ross clarified.

Four. UP. Paul Gambaccini and Trevor Nelson. As the BBC's commentators for the memorial service, Gambo and Nelson were put in a slightly invidious position – given that what they were commenting on did, more often than not, prompt the simple, straightforward reaction, 'Holy moly, have I really just seen an "In Memoriam" photo-montage where a shot of Michael Jackson shaking hands with Nelson Mandela was immediately followed by a picture of Michael Jackson shaking hands with Kermit the Frog?'

In the event, Gambaccini and Nelson managed quite well – even filling the half-hour technical difficulties with this peerless piece of speculation, on which celebrity would cry first: 'Either Jennifer Hudson [who recently had three members of her family murdered by her estranged brother-in-law], or Usher. He's very *young*,' Gambaccini said, wisely.

Three. DOWN. Usher. Well, in the event, Paul Gambaccini turned out to be a veritable Nostradamus of celebrity grief: Usher *did* cry during his version of 'Gone Too Soon'. Usher – who, ironically, was not cast as an usher during the event – appeared to have some manner of odd, compulsive moment during his number: leaving the stage, he walked down to Jackson's coffin and touched the side of it briefly, before, in some manner of trance, he kind of *jiggled the lid* a bit. Almost as if he were checking the quality of the hinges.

Ironically, Celebrity Watch can imagine Usher using 'Jiggle the Lid' as the title of his next album. It has a tone of urban suggestiveness.

Two. UP. The *Mirror*. In a week where the entire media went, 'Right, he's dead now, and none of his relatives have the time, money or inclination left to sue us, so we can just print absolutely anything that comes into our minds. Any old crazy s**t. Chimps, sperm, drugs, ghosts. The lot.

Woot!', the *Mirror* won a close-fought battle for 'Most wholly unnecessary and ancillary bullet point'.

Relaying how Jackson was to be buried without his brain, due to the
requirements of the autopsy, the *Mirror* spared no detail – including, with
no little relish, the phrase, 'The brain will be placed in a plastic bucket.'

At the end, on a separate line, the report concluded: 'Michael Jackson
starred in the 1978 musical *The Wiz* as the Scarecrow – playing the character without a brain.'

One. DOWN. Shaheen Jafargholi. If Michael Jackson died 'of' anything,
it was – and I think we're all in agreement here – a combination of being
treated as a cross between a sideshow and a demi-god for possessing such
unearthly talent, working an adult career from the age of six onwards,
fetishising his own ruined childhood to the point where it drove him
insane, and then having that insanity in a media spotlight so remorseless,
there are entire wars that have been given less coverage than the changing
colours of Michael Jackson's skin.

If there was *one single thing* we could learn from the life of Michael
Jackson, it would seem – other than that sequin-appliquéd military-wear
dates unexpectedly well – it is that child stardom is a terrible idea.

So at Michael Jackson's memorial on Tuesday, it was interesting to see
that one of the twelve live performances came from Shaheen Jafargholi –
the Welsh twelve-year-old semi-finalist from this year's *Britain's Got Talent*.

Introduced on stage by Smokey Robinson to sing 'Who's Lovin'
You?' – a song which, as Robinson helpfully pointed out, a nine-year-old
Jackson had sung with 'such knowingness and pain' (HELLO! THERE'S
A CLUE THERE!) – Jafargholi had to face down a worldwide audience
of millions and, right in front of him, the entire Jackson family, Stevie
Wonder, Mariah Carey, and Michael Jackson, dead, ten feet away from
him. So no pressure or crippling emotional resonance there then.

It's impossible to think of a single aspect of it that wasn't dazzlingly
inappropriate. It was a supernova of wrongness. It's almost the next
evolutionary stage in incorrect action. Performing children at Michael

Jackson's funeral? Why would you do that? It's like getting Slimmer of the Year to do a reading at Lena Zavaroni's memorial.

The next day, chat-show host Larry King said that, when he'd asked Motown founder Berry Gordy who Shaheen was, Gordy replied, 'I have no cotton pickin' idea – but if I were still in the business, I would sign him tomorrow.'

Of course he would. Because whilst Michael Jackson might have been lying before him in a coffin, dead at fifty, it was in front of an audience of *millions*. And that's the bottom line.

Of course, the late Michael Jackson wasn't the only person to have had a problem with drug abuse. I, too, had a dark past of substance abuse that I wished to confess to Times *readers – prompted by the 2009 press hoo-ha over Julie Myerson's controversial book,* The Lost Boy: A True Story, *in which she explained she'd kicked her teenage son out of her house when he refused to give up smoking dope.*

As I explained in the following piece, during my stoner years, I should have kicked myself out of my own house – except I was too stoned.

I am Caitlin Moran, and I Was a Skunk Addict

I was addicted to skunk weed for four years. That it's taken me three weeks of shouty headlines about Julie Myerson's son to remember this tells you pretty much everything you need to know about dope-smokers.

But then again, 'addicted' is quite an extreme word, isn't it? It's quite … *final*. Was I 'addicted'? Yes, I smoked every day, twice as much at weekends, could neither watch TV, listen to records or have my tea without a 'bifter spritzer', made a bong out of a Coke can, then another one out of an old fish tank, had three dealers, didn't really have any friends that weren't stoners, chose which bands I was going to interview on the basis of whether I could get stoned with them or not, and, once, gave a wasp a blow-back. But is that really 'addiction'? You could just say that I liked it a lot. To be honest, I behaved almost identically when I first got into couscous. That stuff is so fluffy.

This, of course, is another problem with dope-smokers. They can't really take a strong line on anything because everything's relative, their mouth's too dry to argue, and their synapses look like an Upside-Down Pudding that's been smashed about with a stick.

I want to make it clear that I don't smoke now. I haven't taken anything since I was twenty-two because, and I will be honest with you here, I eventually went stark raving mad, and ended up riding a bicycle up and down Holloway Road, trying to 'sweat the poison out'. At the time, I was so fat from a stoner-diet of deep-fried crispy beef and Mango Soleros that I had bought the bicycle – the chunkiest, most industrial mountain bike in the shop – on the basis that it made me look 'thinner' than all the other, smaller, more aerodynamic bicycles available. As a consequence, I could scarcely pedal it more than 50 yards without having to lie down in someone's front garden, for a rest. I was operating on some pretty exciting and innovative logic at the time.

I started smoking weed when I was seventeen, because that is just what you do if you like The Beatles. If this were America, I could probably now sue Paul McCartney, wholly on this basis.

From the very start, I was a terrible stoner. Not in any sense of being hardcore, and wild, like some crazy-eyed loner on a voyage to Valhalla. I mean literally terrible. Every time I smoked I passed out. I once got so stoned interviewing Radiohead that I had to be put to bed in the bass player's spare bedroom. Except I was so stoned I missed the door to the spare bedroom, kept walking up the stairs, and went and slept in the loft instead – where a wasps' nest had been recently fumigated, and the floor was covered in crunchy, dead wasps. In the morning, my lovely millionaire genius host was distraught.

'You slept in the waspy loft!' he horrored.

'Oh, it's OK,' I said, cheerfully. 'I was stoned!'

I did a kind of 'We *all* know what it's like when you're so stoned you interview the biggest band in the world by just nodding at them, then break into their loft and sleep on some insects' faces'. He just stared at me like I was mad.

Of course, it's a miracle I had a job at all. Work-rate wise, a ferocious skunk habit suits someone who can survive on the proceeds of six, maybe seven, hours of work a week, tops. You're looking at musicians 'between albums', pre-school children, royalty, etc. Despite Michael Phelps' admirable efforts in this area, it is not really the ideal drug for Olympic athletes – or, indeed, anyone who really needs to get a jiggy on in furthering their life. Everything grinds to a halt when you start smoking. In the four years I was chonged off my num-nuts, there was one, sole innovation in my life: the invention of the Shoe Wall – a wall in the hall where I banged in twenty nails, in dispiritingly uneven lines, and then hung up all my shoes. Needless to say, when I finally did stop smoking, I remodelled the entire house, lost four stone, took down the Shoe Wall and quadrupled my work-rate in six months flat.

Towards the end of my four-year skunk-in, signs of the End of Days started to accumulate. A friend who had been smoking since he was thirteen totally wigged out, and developed schizophrenia. Although sympathetic, my main reaction was to think, 'Some people can handle it, and some people can't,' and then smugly light up a big fat jay. I was also starting to notice that it was taking huge amounts of skunk to get half as wasted as before – necessitating the invention of first the Coke-can bong, and then the fish-tank bong, as my smoking took on a borderline industrial intensity. Paranoid I was being ripped off, I 'tested' the potency of the skunk on a wasp, by trapping it under a glass, and giving it a blow-back. The wasp just lay on the floor, clearly considering buying a chunky bicycle, so I knew that, sadly, it must all be down to me.

It was as I was doing bongs out of my fish tank, whilst watching *Later ... With Jools Holland*, that the end came. For some reason, as soon as The Beautiful South came on stage, I just went mad. Not in a 'Hurrah! Amazing! The Beautiful South!' way – but in a way that meant within an hour I was hysterical, holding onto the kettle, and screaming, 'This is normal! This is normal!' at myself over and over again.

It turned out that it was 'just' a panic attack – the first of a solid eighteen months of them – but however much I tried to calm myself down with a fish tank full of rabidly psycho-active cannabis, bafflingly, it just seemed to make the situation worse. Eventually, even I had to acknowledge that my stoner days were over, and I quit.

Do I regret spending four years off my face? No, not really – but only because I can't really remember any of it. I'm not being facetious. My memory's shot to bits. Apparently, we went to Montpelier once, for a week. I have absolute no recall of this.

Did I, then, learn anything, from four years of wandering through the rabbit holes of my mind, like Alice in Wonderland? To that, at least, I can say 'yes'. I learned that wasps buzz four notes lower when they're wasted. And that I am a terrible, terrible stoner.

The great thing about taking lots of drugs, of course, is that it allows you to come at the really important topics from a different, and innovative, angle.

Hello, England's Rose

Just when you think responsible adults in previous generations took care of the difficult stuff a long, long time ago, along comes a bombshell to blow your mind off its feet. This week, it was pointed out on the BBC Food website that England does not, in fact, have a national vegetable. The Welsh have the leek, Mexico has the corn-cob, France has garlic and onions, and no one is going to argue with Sweden for imprimatur over the swede. It's fine, guys. You may have it. We know that if something else was ever discovered approximating 'a disappointing potato', but this time named the 'Anglotuber', you'd throw it over to us in a shot.

However, until happy Anglotuber Day dawns, what official vegetable does England have? None. We are a country which has wholly overlooked choosing a vegetable which best defines our style, and outlook on life. Given that we have a national meat (beef), sport (football), drink (tea), and weather (a promising dawn, slowly fading into medium-to-heavy drizzle by lunchtime, 12°C), it's clear that this is an error that must be corrected immediately.

Without wishing to be venal, I would suggest our course of action should be simply to work out which is the 'best' vegetable – then bag it for ourselves. Anyone saying, 'But it should be an inimically *British* vegetable' is in for a sad awakening, should they start researching Britain's vegetable history. Basically, we don't have any inimically British vegetables. Peas are from Syria, Brussels sprouts have been comprehensively bagged by the Belgians, and everything else – even the ones no one wants, like turnips, and chard – 'originate from the Mediterranean area'. What England has left is basically acorns, dandelions, the more chewable twigs of the oak tree, and any animals so stupid they technically register as plant-life. Prawns, maybe. Or cats.

So what is the best vegetable? Well, we all know that: it's the potato. The vegetable you can't screw up. You can throw a potato *into a bonfire*, run away from it – and, an hour later, it's turned into a meal. Try doing that with broccoli, or a trifle, and it will laugh in your face. Chips, mash, roast, crisps: the potato is the vegetable for a cold country, where most of the year must be spent indoors, under a blanket, watching reality television. The potato knows that England loves it more than any other country. We need the potato in a way that, say, the Spaniards – sitting outside in their warm weather, nibbling on a fresh olive, circulation healthy in both hands and feet – will never understand. Potatoes know they will never meet another nation that would fetishise it to the point of inventing the 'Fish & Chip' flavour crisp: a crisp (made of potato) that tastes of chips (made of potato).

But of course, we can't have the potato, because they – along with tobacco, and saying the word 'Girlfriend' in an excitingly aggressive manner – are the most famous exports of the New World. As the proud country that made The Beatles, it does not behove us to go, cap in hand, to America, and ask for their potato. I think we all know it would make us look internationally weakened. We would look like their lap-tray-supper dogs. Until the happy day that UK horticulturists manage to genetically engineer a potato that is 100 per cent of Anglo-Saxon origin – named, perhaps, the 'Britato' – we must harden our hearts, and forget the spud.

So where does that leave us, national veg-wise? Not in a strong position, I'm afraid. There's not much left in the salad drawer. Asparagus? We grow the best in the world; but its mad, diva-ish aspects – only in season two months of the year, makes your urine smell peculiar – seem suited to a far more exotic and impetuous country, such as Portugal. Broccoli?

Our children won't thank us for that. Cauliflower? Personally, I'm fond – EVOLUTION GREW A VEGETABLE THAT LOOKS LIKE A BRAIN! AND TASTES DELICIOUS IN CHEESE SAUCE! RESPECT! – but I can't help noticing we're not exactly fighting off Russia and Chile for dibs on it. I think we should feel a certain amount of ... jealousy from other countries, when we announce our national veg.

I reckon, when all is said and done, the national vegetable of England must be the cabbage. The cabbage is a beautiful thing. A regal thing. Splayed fatly in a border, it looks like the most majestic ball ever lobbed over a fence. It looks like a crown. A planet. A green and lilac-veined rose. It is only the English language that has let the cabbage down – giving it, quite frankly, the ugliest name in all of veg-dom. Who would not be put off by saying a word that makes you sound like Albert Steptoe, without his teeth in? We simply need to rename it – in order to, finally, proudly claim it as our national veg. I would suggest: 'England's Rose.' Hello, England's Rose.

Oh, hang on.

If there's one thing my magazine columns do – aside from pay my mortgage and keep the kids in socks – it's give me the time and space to offer up gratitude for all the wonderful things in life. Such as not dying painfully in a ditch, with a massively scrofulous head, at the age of twenty-one.

It's Not a Heritage Centre – It's a 'Misery Centre'

We are in a farming heritage centre on the Gower Peninsula, Wales, on the last day of our holiday. The children are displaying their cosmopolitan London upbringing, by screaming every time a chicken goes near them. They don't actually know it's a chicken, though.

'The eagle is coming!' Nancy weeps, violently. 'THE EAGLE!'

Although I am aware country people would sigh that my children are gutless townies, I personally believe that the children have a point. The rooster, in particular, is very large. It comes up to their chests. Scale-wise, it's as if Ronnie Corbett were coming up to me, clucking aggressively – eyes beady, and feet all covered in poo. I too would, on balance, flee.

I love a heritage centre. The smaller and more Craggy Island they are, the better. The best one I ever visited was the 'Oceanarium' in St David's, Pembrokeshire, devoted to the 'Heritage of the Sea'. Who knows what manner of blinging update it may have had in the intervening years, but, back in 1995, it consisted of a very large paddling pool – the type you can buy at Argos, for £49.99 – which had a single, rather melancholy-looking flounder in it. A sign at the side informed you that you could, if you wished, 'stroke the flounder'. This seemed to be something that neither we, nor the flounder, desired in the remotest.

My love of heritage centres stems from a belief that I know their true, secret purpose. They're not *really* 'heritage centres'. OF COURSE THEY'RE NOT. They're actually 'misery remembrance' centres, set up by a secret post-war Labour government committee, to remind the proletariat just how benighted and godawful existence was until the intro- duction of the Welfare State, tumble dryers and The Beatles.

And man, they are effective. Walking through the area devoted to agri- cultural machinery, it seemed increasingly barking that anyone ever refers to 'the good old days'. No 'days' could be 'good' that REGULARLY involved root cutters, bean crushers and scalding pans. These are imple- ments that would have been dragged around by people waist-high in mud, still trying to shake off the plague, whilst being punched repeatedly in the face by the Sheriff of Nottingham.

Additionally, if, during their working life, any of the machines on display here killed less than three children, I would be absolutely aston- ished. The thresher, in particular, seems designed with the sole purpose of cutting children in half, then neatly stacking them up in separate ricks of legs and heads. Whilst there may have been more songbirds in the hedge- rows back in 1865, there would also have been more peasant children stuck to the rims of cartwheels, shouting out 'Get ower Dad, QUICKLY!' as their faces hurtled towards the track for the final time.

Pausing by the pig-pen, for the always-satisfying pleasure of watching a pig sleep, I consider, once again, what my own life would have been like 'in the olden days', when pig-staring was considered a satisfactory – and was, indeed, the sole – substitute for wi-fi. Considering what my life would have been like in 'the olden days' is a common event for me. It is why my greatest fear is – after baldness –accidentally falling through a magnetic anomaly in space-time, and landing in AD 1676; possibly on this pig.

With my working-class parents and unique skill-set, my employment options would have been limited to either a) village prostitute or b) mud farmer. Not that I would have made it as far as being a productive member of society, of course, as I suspect my recurrent nemesis – acute cystitis – would have seen me off at least a decade earlier. In my more dolorous hours, the thought of all the pre-antibiotic cystitis that has happened in the world can haunt me. It is an unfathomable, and unacknowledged, reservoir of pain – unrelieved by even the relatively ineffective use of cranberry juice, until Raleigh returned from America, cranberries in hand, in 1584.

As I stare at the heritage centre's primitive, nineteenth-century, outdoor dunny, I reflect on how novelist Jilly Cooper once helped fund a monument, on Park Lane, to all the animals that had been recruited, and killed, during warfare.

Should I ever coin it in with a series of bonkbusters, I reflect, looking at the draughty – doubtless rat-infested – cludge, I should like to erect a similar statue, to all the nameless women throughout time who died on the toilet of cystitis.

Of course, for some people, any kind of reminder about the past is unnecessary. Whilst we were all wandering around the heritage centre, being assaulted by eagles, and becoming morose about toilets, my dad has been sitting stubbornly in the car, in the car park, reading *Exchange and Mart*.

He was brought up in a Shropshire village in the 1950s – widely regarded as the Golden Age of childhoods.

'And I'm not going to pay a fiver to do it all again,' he'd said, briskly, an hour earlier, as we all got out the car. 'It was sodding miserable. There were lice, it was cold, and everyone was racist. I once invited a black friend back to my house when I was a teenager, and they made him sit on the roof. The only good things about the old days were 1) the bacon was better, and 2) you could smoke in the post office. And that's IT.'

And he sat in the car, downloading his emails on his mobile, while we stared at a set of village stocks, rubbing anti-bac into our hands.

One of the great things about 'progress' has been having the first ever black socialist President of the United States of America. Whichever way you slice it, this makes Earth look cool. When Obama was still on the campaign trail, I wrote this column of Obama-love – pathetically convinced he might read it, laugh his generous, open, inspiring laugh, and invite me to the White House to sit on his desk in a pencil skirt, telling him jokes, to help momentarily relieve the pressure of being the President of America. I'd be like his Monica Lewinsky, but with gags, instead of no gag-reflex.

Four years later, and he's still not got in touch. Sometimes, I tweet him. He never tweets back. I'm still metaphorically here in my beret, yearning.

Get on Down – and That's an ORDER!

As we speak (well, as I type on a laptop under an awning in the garden in the pouring rain and you read), history appears to be grinding towards an inexorable conclusion: in November, Barack Obama will become President of the United States of America. Should this occur he will be – as you are, unquestionably, aware – the first ever non-white US President. This is no mean feat for a country whose two big psychosocio-cultural turning points were a) Victoria Principal's hair in *Dallas*, and b) economic independence from Britain being funded by industrial-scale African-American slavery.

Clearly, it would do the country some good to have a non-white President for a spell. It would subtly rebalance international power structures. It would allow America – an empire that now looks close to cultural exhaustion, after just sixty years of dominance – to reinvent itself. Perhaps most importantly of all, it would act as a springboard for a frankly poor, straight-to-DVD Eddie Murphy movie, in which he plays a jive-talkin', pimp-rollin' playa-President, in a project entitled, perhaps, 'The Black House'. There is a dim part of our minds, raised by Hollywood, which craves the sight of a newly elected black President celebrating his inauguration by ordering in soul food, cranking up The Commodores' 'Brick House' and shouting 'Get on down. And that's an order!' at an uptight, white chief-of-staff.

But let's face it – we're not going to see Obama doing that. He'll spend his first night in the White House knocking up an authentic Vietnamese stir-fry and listening to Alicia Keys, quietly, while his wife opens a bottle of Tokay and writes thank-you notes.

But then again – maybe he won't. Maybe Obama won't make it to the White House, after all. For while there's many a slip twixt cup and lip, there's also much hocus-pocus between 'candidate' and 'POTUS'. Obama could, still, fail in his quest. He could default on his manifest destiny, after all. For while Obamamania rages all around us – 200,000-strong crowds in Berlin, the front pages of newspapers around the world – this enthusiasm is based, let us be truthful, on us not knowing much about him at all. More than 90 per cent of the people who support him would, if push came to shove and they had to explain why, say: 'He's just this noble, black guy, who looks a little bit like he's wearing eyeliner.' The danger is, then, that between now and November, we suddenly learn a bad, rogue fact about Obama. Something that means we stop being able to project all this delirious, over-hopeful JFK stuff on to his seductively blank canvas and start actually getting to know the man, instead. Something like:

1. Obama releases a viral 'getting-to-know-me' video on YouTube, showing his unique idea of 'down-time', and entitled 'Obamming Around'. In it, he wears a stained pair of trackie bottoms, plays Grand Theft Auto for sixteen hours a day and takes us through the construction methods of the infamous 'Barack Stack Sandwich', a snack notable for being a)

more than six inches high, even after the Pringles have been mercilessly crushed down into pulp, and b) the peanut butter being spread not with a knife, but with Obama's finger. 'You'll see I'm not all "constitutional reform" this and "standard-bearer for a generation of despairing liberals" that,' Obama promises, putting on his beer-can hat and riding around a deserted car lot on a tiny tricycle.

2. A sex scandal. It's the classic way to derail a presidential campaign – think Gary Hart, Grover Cleveland, Brock Adams, Gary Condit. The only problem with an Obama sex scandal would be that, if the world is to be honest with itself, it fancies Obama. While a sex scandal would initially put his campaign into difficulty, it would also – as details came out – work as some manner of titillating Obama-porn, which everybody would, secretly, enjoy. And, indeed, use to fuel their Obama-love even more. Unless the affair was truly sordid. Something as distasteful as Obama logging on to Real World – then having cyber-sex with the Dragon Princess on top of Thunderfist Mountain. With little speech bubbles that read: 'Let's do it CENTAUR-STYLE!'

3. One notable component of the Right's anti-Obama campaigning has been constant, disingenuous commenting on Obama's 'mixed cultural heritage'. With a Kenyan Muslim father, a white American mother – and, most exotically of all, a stepgrandmother in Bracknell, Berkshire – dimmer commentators have been 'confused' as to 'what Obama really is'. In a moment of peevish vexation, Obama decides to do a PowerPoint presentation on his exact ethnicity – using a pie chart to demonstrate precise percentage points. 'My suits are white – but I never have a break-fast that's less than 80 per cent ghetto,' Obama says, making a point of ill-advised subtlety, confusing the electorate, and subsequently chalking up the biggest defeat in presidential history.

4. In a rare moment of non-nobleness, Obama deals a low blow to his Republican opponent John McCain – referring to how squeaky his

voice is, compared with Obama's own. 'I hear he's big in New Squawk, Shrilladelphia and Tennesqueak,' Obama says – going on to hum Lee Marvin's 'Wand'rin Star' in a deep baritone.

5. Obama breaks the unwritten rule of US politics and calls time on America's ingrained obesity denial. 'You just didn't fall over some fatness and get it all over you,' he says, to a crowd of huge-bottomed policemen in Chicago. 'You all went to Walmart, and spent all of George W. Bush's tax-cuts on Squirt Cheese, Laffy Taffy and Cracker Jack. Well, I'm going to step in and tax your asses back down to 120lb.' He subsequently chalks up the biggest defeat in presidential, etc.

6. A photograph emerges of Obama wearing Crocs. Not even the white Crocs that you could pretend you bought 'to clean the pool', but a bright green pair. Which, as the incriminating telephoto images reveal, Obama has subsequently customised with Jibbitz of cocker spaniels, four-leaf clovers and a mooning Garfield.

7. Trying to diffuse the 'controversial' nature of being a black presidential candidate, he tries to put it 'all into perspective'. 'It's not like I'm gay, though, is it? Or Mexican,' he says, pulling a 'you know what I'm saying, guys' face.

In 2009, I interviewed the then-Prime Minister, Gordon Brown. It would be wrong to say it was as a long-game tactic to get in contact with Obama. Very wrong. For not only did Gordon – who was lovely – singularly fail to hook me up with Obama, but I nearly never got to Downing Street in the first place. It was a VERY vexatious day.

I am Late to Interview the Prime Minister

Of course I'm not going to be late to interview Gordon Brown. Don't be ridiculous. He's the Prime Minister of Great Britain, for goodness' sake. I'm going to leave the house at 11.30am.

'11.30?' my husband says. He looks alarmed. He is, in general, an anxious man – he keeps sachets of Heinz Tomato Ketchup in his wallet; unable to bear the possibility of being boxed into a situation where Daddies' Tomato Ketchup might be the only option. 'The interview's 12.30pm! Order the cab for 10.15am!'

I am not going to take a cab to Downing Street. In the event of Gordon Brown asking me how I arrived, I want to say, 'I travelled on the Underground transportation system of London, England, like *the people* do.' I'm not quite sure what point I would be making by saying this, but it feels like it might be an important one. Something I could score highly for.

At 11.15am, I go up to my office to print out my sixty-two, carefully planned questions. I approach the printer with great serenity. In the past, the printer and I have had an enmity that has stretched back over generations. I ended its grandmother when the cartridge jammed halfway through printing a map out. Its mother was abandoned to Freecycle, after every functionality save b&w photocopying failed. But this HP Photosmart C480 will not let me down. It's like Britain and France. We have finally come to an understanding. There will be antagonism and murder between us no more.

Nineteen minutes later, I am pulling every wire out of the back of the motherf***ing Goddamn betraying piece of shit, and screaming.

'What do you MEAN, the "cartridge alignment sheet has not been detected"? What does that MEAN? I'm supposed to be interviewing THE PRIME MINISTER!'

I've missed my train. I've ordered a cab. Already it's very, very clear that when the controller said, 'Yes – we have cars free!', what he meant was 'Yes – we have cars free! Free – to do *whatever they like*! Play in the sun; drive round and round the park really slowly. Sit and enjoy the sheer joy of North London.'

I go and stand out in the street. It is now forty minutes until I start talking to Gordon Brown. I am in a totally deserted residential area. When a learner driver crawls down the road, in her silver AA Driving School vehicle, I think, 'I am interviewing the Prime Minister. That probably means I'm legally entitled to flag down that car, and get her to drive me to Archway Tube.'

When the cab finally pulls up, it is an old, battered minivan. I realise with horror that it very closely resembles the van the Iranian terrorists shoot Doc from in *Back to the Future*. It has curtains inside, which are drawn. It looks like an Acme suicide bomb. It does *not* look like the kind of thing the policemen on the gates at Downing Street will feel relaxed about.

As we screech off towards town, the cab driver and I quickly come to an understanding with each other. I am the delusional, sweaty woman who keeps saying, 'I have to interview the Prime Minister in thirty-eight minutes!' He is the man who will cause my death when he says, 'I don't know where Downing Street is.'

This is, I admit, difficult information for me to process. On the one hand, I am alarmed that the cab driver doesn't know where 10, Downing

Street – one of the most famous addresses in the world – is. On the other hand, I don't either, really. Is it quite near the Strand?

I have terrible, anxious cottonmouth. There is a litre of water in my handbag. I drink it. Emotionally, the template I am relating to in this situation is the 1986 film *Clockwise* starring John Cleese, who plays a man battling to reach an appointment on time, despite a series of strokes of ill fortune.

This alternates from being 'useful' to 'not useful'. On the one hand, Cleese did, eventually, make that appointment on time. On the other, he arrived cut and bruised, in a monk's habit, with only one shoe, having had his speech eaten by a goat. It's not really a possibility I want to consider.

I abandon the cab at Euston, and run onto the Victoria line, onto the Jubilee line, then down Whitehall. It's 12.28pm. By now, the litre of water I drank in the cab is having its unfortunate yet inevitable consequence. I have to ask myself – is the Pulitzer enough recompense for having turned up at Downing Street having wet myself? It is not. I downgrade my running to a fraught trot.

Of course, when I finally get there, Gordon Brown is running twenty minutes late. My cardigan is, I realise, soaked with sweat. I am still stuffing it into my handbag when finally he comes into the room.

'Prime Minister!' I say, standing up. 'Good afternoon! Thank you for agreeing to this interview!'

That evening, I hand-wash the cardigan. As I pull it out of the bag, I notice it smells odd. Intense.

'This is the smell of fear,' I think to myself, holding it up to my nose. 'This is the smell humans emit when they are at the limits of their terror.'

Then I look into my handbag, and realise that it is not the smell of fear – it is actually the smell of a burst free sample of Fructis hair serum. I still don't really know what the smell of fear is.

You can see how badly I travel. Downing Street is but seven miles from my house – yet getting there nearly induced a conniptive fit. It is why all my holidays are to places as nearby as possible: Brighton. Aberystwyth. Sometimes, Bath. You'll notice, as you go through this book, that there aren't many exotic journeys to far-distant places. That's because I don't really hold with 'abroad'. I believe it to be a 'faff'. I think the only time I venture out of the country this entire book is to go to Berlin to interview Lady Gaga – something my subconscious is clearly so disgruntled about that I passive-aggressively miss my flight, and make her wait three hours for me. Yes, Gaga – I punished you for not being in Leicester. How DARE you be in another country?

I'm not a natural passport-profferer.

What I Learnt up a Mountain This Summer

A wise man once said that on a journey, it is not where you go, but who you *become* that really matters. Aside from the fact that this reveals that he clearly left his wife – or, possibly, mum – in charge of small, 'non-mattering' journey issues like tickets, accommodation, packing, researching which restaurants will accept a 6.30pm booking for a party with three children and an egg allergy, and where and when it would be expedient to stop and go to the toilet, it is obvious what journeys he *really* meant: holidays. In the absence of partition and mass migration, they're the only big journeys we ever undertake these days. The premise is that when we go on holiday, it should – if it's a good holiday – change us a little. It should improve us. We should acquire both the reddened, sun-damaged complexion of a bumpkin *and* some knowledge. In short, we should return from our holidays *cleverer*.

Well, I'm afraid that this is not a sentiment I can hold by. I don't want to get cleverer on my holidays. I want to get stupider. Once I'm off the clock, I don't want to have to think at all. If I have to have more than one thought a day – preferably the thought 'Yes, I think I *would* like to eat a cheese sandwich in the bath, whilst reading *Grazia*' – then I have, clearly, failed to book the right holiday. On the right holiday, nice things would just happen at me for six days, and on the seventh, I would be put into a coma, and posted back to London, first class.

By the time I come home, I want my brain to have totally calcified through extreme lack of use. I want to be as dumb as a bag of hair, covered in sand I'm too listless and witless to brush off, and so relaxed I stand in the middle of the front room, staring at my own feet and going 'Wha?' for an hour and a half.

So you can imagine, then, my disappointment when I realised that, over the course of my summer holidays, I actually *had* learned a few things. Thankfully, nearly all of them were stupid.

1. You can make a child climb a mountain, if it thinks there's a Disney Store at the top. Obviously you can't stand at the bottom of Stac Pollaidh and outright *say*, 'There is a Disney Store at the top of that mountain. Those are not clouds up there – that is Disney Magic!' No – the trick is simply *not* say that there *isn't* one up there. *Imply* that one would normally *expect* there to be one on top of a Highland mountain – but that the only way of really *knowing* is to spray that midge repellent all over your face, get your Cag-in-a-Bag on, and ship up 600m. Of course, when you get to the top, and the kids wail, 'But there is no Disney Store here!', then you must bring in the second half of the Mountain Climbing for Recalcitrant Children Plan. You must say: 'JESUS! It has CLOSED DOWN! This recession has hit the retail sector HARD!' Then re-motivate the children for the climb back down by not *saying*, but certainly kind of *implying*, that there might be a Disney Store fire sale going on in the car park below, with *High School Musical* figurines going half price. But only if they hurry.

2. When it comes to sleeper-trains, there are two types of people in this world. The first delight in the dollshouse-like neatness of the cabins. They adore the blankety bunk-beds, and are soothed into sleep by the night-long rattle of the locomotive's trundle. The second pull a cat's bum mouth as soon as they step inside, spend all night sighing, and ruin the morning croissant-in-a-bag breakfast by wailing, 'That was like spending all night in the video to The Cure's "Close to Me"! I am glad I am not going in one of those again – oh I am, in seven days. Maybe I will mention how fatally dispirited about this I am EVERY TEN MINUTES FOR THE REST OF THE HOLIDAY.'

3. These days, everyone gets in trouble for smoking. The last time I got caught having a sneaky fag by one of my kids, I was able to reply – with James Bond-like, ninja-swiftness – 'This isn't mine, darling! I'm just holding it for Uncle Nathan!' Unfortunately, when I repeated the manoeuvre this summer, I didn't know that 'Uncle Nathan' was supposed to have given up six months ago, and that I'd just ratted him up in front of his kids. Who immediately started crying about him getting cancer, and wailing that they didn't want to be half-orphans, and had to be placated with having virtually all of that day's gin-fund spent on ice cream, and bubble-swords. It looks like I'm going to have to revert to the excuse of their earlier years: 'It's not a cigarette, darlings – it's Sooty's wand! A naughty boy set fire to it, and mummy was trying to put it out.'

4. Scottish people do actually notice if you're Scottish or not. If you're ludicrously impressionable/borderline human clay/me, after a couple of hours in a region with a strong accent, it can be easy to find yourself 'catching' 'being local'. You can convince yourself it's both a friendly, and a beautiful, thing, to start throwing in a 'lassie' here, and a 'pet' there, and that the locals will presume that you talk like this *all the* *time* at home. The reality is, of course, that they are thinking, 'Why is this idiot moon-faced London woman talking like the Russ Abbot character C U Jimmy, the noo?' This August, I triumphantly smashed all my previous accent-slip records. Usually, it takes a couple of hours, and a couple of whiskies, for the idiomatic 'monkey see, monkey do' reflex to kick in. This year, I got off the London-Edinburgh train at 8am, and walked over to the taxi rank. 'Taxi?' the driver said. 'Aye,' I replied. My husband turned and walked away, mortified.

5, Foxes eschew board games. If a 2am, al-fresco game of Scrabble should end up being abandoned, due to excessive 'wobbly tiredness', do bring it back indoors again. Leaving it on the lawn is apparently some manner of provocation to urban foxes, who will snittishly do a plop on it – as if saying 'Here is my disdain for your dandy self-satisfied middle-class Viognier-fuelled word-games. And it's on a double word score.'

At The Times, *they love making me do stupid stuff. It's why I love working for them. Who would not wish to be rung up at 9am and asked if they want to dress up as Kate Middleton/meet Keith Richards on International Talk Like a Pirate Day/learn to do the 'Single Ladies' by Beyoncé dance?*

In this instance, the 9am phone call from the office was asking me if I'd like to be an imaginary dwarf, playing on the gaming phenomenon that is World of Warcraft. Obviously, I said 'Yes' – once I'd looked up what the Dwarven is for 'Yes' ('Ai', apparently).

A week later – because of this feature – I was invited on the Richard & Judy *show to talk about World of Warcraft, as some manner of 'expert'. As I'm sure this feature insinuates, I really was not that. Still, in order to illustrate what we were discussing, they suggested that I play the game, live on air, so that the viewers could get a flavour of life in an online fantasy world. Panicking, the second we got on air, I pressed the wrong button, and steered my dwarf off a platform and under the Deeprun Tram to Stormwind City, where he died instantly.*

'Well,' Richard Madeley said, after a second. 'The life of a dwarf really is nasty, brutish and short, isn't it?'

I am a Dwarf Called Scottbaio

When Keith at the office gives me World of Warcraft, bidding me to 'spend a bit of time with it – it's really addictive,' I do that special thing that women can do where you roll your eyes inside your head, secretly, to show that you know more than the men. Yeah *right*, I'm going to get addicted to World of Warcraft. Yeah right, I'm going to join a worldwide, online community of over eight million people, running around a gigantic and complex fantasy world, engaged on a series of quests.

I'll tell you right now, in my head, Keith: it's all highly unlikely. I'm not into all this pixie cobblers. I like real life. I like Waitrose, and *Gardeners' Question Time*. If I *had* to marry one of the cast of *Lord of the Rings*, it would be Sam Gamgee – the only completely prosaic, normal, non-magic one, who comes across like the owner of a garage in Cricklewood having a particularly bad day, what with this vexatious epic quest, and all.

In a nutshell: dragons embarrass me.

The box containing the game software didn't quite fit into my handbag, and I was slightly self-conscious about people spotting it as I caught the Tube. The last time I felt so embarrassed about the visible contents of my handbag was last spring, when I was carrying around a gigantic book on the history of the Ku Klux Klan. For two long months, that book made me want to shout 'I'm reading this because I know they were bad – not to get tips!' to any halfway-full carriage. Similarly, a visible copy of World of Warcraft makes me want to shout 'I don't seek to nullify my rampant sexual dysfunctions by pretending to be a Paladin called Thrusthammer Orcbash! IT'S FOR WORK!'

Of course, the person I want to shout this to the most is myself. I am the judgemental one here. By and large, my theory runs, people into goblins and wizards are people for whom the utopian sexual and racial equality offered by, say, sci-fi, is alarming. All those black chicks, in Lycra jumpsuits, philosophising about the fallible nature of humanity, and able to vote? Brrrr!

In short, the entire fantasy genre is the domain of the sweaty, white, non-intellectual Herbert, and has very little to offer me – a sassy, metropolitan, militant feminist with an aversion to a) items of clothing made of skinned Gnoll hide, and b) swinging at someone with a two-headed axe.

Imagine my surprise, then, on being able to write the following sentence: on the first day I had World of Warcraft, I stayed up and played it until 2am. I got into bed at 10pm, switched the electric blanket on, and opened my laptop, with the simple objective of 'getting my bearings' for twenty minutes. Three hours later, I was trying to retrieve the stolen journals of Grelin Whitebeard from a cave full of Rockjaw Troggs, whilst running a very lucrative trade in killing and skinning boars on the side. Then I accidentally got on the Deeprun Tram to Stormwind City, and had to bale out when I realised I was far too poor to be in a city where 'Heavy Mithril Pants' are twenty-seven pieces of silver. 2am! I was so engrossed, I forgot to take my contact lenses out, and fell asleep with them glued to my eyes.

Although I am pathologically, fatally prone to exaggeration, it would be a simple statement of fact to say that World of Warcraft is approximately as addictive as methadone. Indeed, when Robbie Williams recently went into rehab with the ostensibly risible addictions of Red Bull and espresso, I thought, 'It's just as well you have never been on Coldridge Pass trying to deliver a package of Kobold reports to Senir Whitebeard. Then, my friend, you would know true craving.'

As with all good drugs, World of Warcraft has turned my perceptions of the world upside-down. Take, for instance, the very beginning of the game, when you decide on the character you will play. Personally, I've never created a character to play a game with before – hey, I have to do that in front of the wardrobe every morning for real, and I think all the ladies will know what I'm saying here. But when it's for an inconsequential internet diversion, and you have almost infinite choice of what you will become – good, evil, male, female, human, weird minotaur thing with problem hair – it brings to the fore several profound self-realisations. My inner self, it turns out, is a beefy ginger dwarf – one with a huge beard. He is who I want to be. He is secret Caitlin. Discovering this is the kind of thing troubled celebrities pay therapist Beechy Colclough thousands of pounds to discover. I had done it in seven minutes, and with a choice of beard stylings to boot.

I named him 'Scottbaio' – you remember: Chachi in *Happy Days*. The obvious ginger dwarf name – and launched him out into the world. Still, at this point, deeply sceptical about the game, I had pre-formulated a plan to make the whole experience tolerable. Whereas the ultimate purpose of most participants is to overcome the evil Horde through a series of pitched battles and strategic quests, I had come up with something a little more subtle. I thought the best way to quell the Horde would be to gradually gentrify the Killing Fields, starting by opening a deli, and selling speciality cheese. After all, the lure of endless, sensual evil is as nothing compared to a good, spoonable Vacherin. Those demons would be capitulating, buying a Victorian terrace and coming over to the Alliance in no time.

However, as a new émigré to the realm of Sha'tar, I knew the deli was something I'd have to work up to slowly. I spent an hour tootling around a very pretty snowy mountain running a few errands – delivering parcels, relaying messages, buying nicer boots, earning a bob or two. Already, the addictive part of WoW was becoming apparent – through a cunning combination of small, quick tasks and longer, more complex ones that can be chipped away at over time, there's always something you could 'pop in' and do, or just spend 'ten minutes more' 'knocking off'. And – contrary to all perceptions of online gaming being a lonely, solitary pursuit for, ahem, 'bachelors' – I found WoW to be an excellent and rewarding family pastime. My two daughters – six and three – were thrilled to sit next to me, watching Mummy kill the pigs, and jump over fences.

Indeed, I was just marvelling at how female-friendly and 'untestoster-oney' it was, compared to what I expected, when a member of the Horde called 'Hellfist' started stoving my head in from behind. Having no idea what to do, I fall back on my old playground technique – I try to talk my way out of it.

'Please don't smite me – I'm having an asthma attack!' I type. 'I've come on a quest by accident, and if you hit me, it'll be murder!'

Hellfist makes a clucking chicken sound, to highlight my cowardice, and hits me until I die. When I resurrect in a nearby graveyard, a dwarf warrior called Cadisfael is sitting next to me.

'I ownz you, n00b,' he says.

'I'm afraid I'm thirty-one, and don't have a clue what you're on about,' I say, as primly as a ginger dwarf named after the over-emotional one from *Happy Days* can.

'That means that you are a newbie, and I own you. You are my bitch,' Cadisfael explains, patiently.

'Do one, you Herbert,' I say, trying to jump over a fence.

'Cait it's me, Joe,' Cadisfael says, jumping over the fence with ease, and then executing an impressive Russian dance. It's my fourteen-year-old mathematics genius brother, Joe! He's tracked me down online! Jesus!

'I've had to regenerate with a new character here,' he explains, rather crossly, as we walk up a mountain. 'I don't usually come to this realm. Sha'tar is for newbie losers. I'm usually in Hellscream, with the hardcore. Over there, I'm a Level 66 mage, with an epix mount.'

'I'm in a much higher tax bracket than you,' I counter, trying to smash him with my giant dwarven hammer. He easily dodges the blow.

I'd like to pretend that Joe and I then spent the next week or so bonding in our fantastical realm – going on a series of daring raids on the goblin mines together, before drinking a flagon of hot Rhapsody Malt back at the Scarlet Raven tavern. In actual fact, Joe is so repulsed by the easiness of my realm that he logs off after an hour, with a cheery farewell of 'I ownz you, n00b! Pwnz!', which he then has to log back on to explain means a kind of 'zapping sound that you make when you hit someone'.

Still, he's given me some good tips: find a trainer who will teach me new smiting spells, earn money skinning boars, spend the money on armour, and don't try and chat to people too much – they find it weird.

I flagrantly disregard this last rule ten minutes later, in a bar at Anvilmar, where I try to start a conversation with a room of saturnine-looking dwarven warriors.

'They need a jukebox in here,' I suggest, to kick-start the debate. 'Some Queen, bit of classic Bowie. Guns N' Roses. And maybe one of those frozen margarita machines. Razz the place up a bit.'

A couple of implacable pugilists issue a polite 'LOL' – 'Laugh out loud' – but then go back to buying huge and fatal swords from the weapons vendor. One small gnome girl called Flopsey, however, sidles over.

'Yeah – maybe a pub quiz, or a meat raffle?' she suggests. We sit down at the table, and spend the next twenty minutes discussing what we'd like to see in WoW to cater for the female palate. We'd like the option to work as prostitutes, we decide – it would be a very quick way of earning money. We'd like to be able to conceive and raise children – seeing if they look like the father, teaching them our spells. We'd like a bigger range of wardrobe and hairstyles, and the ability to gain points simply by being amusing, or wise. Or pulling off a good outfit.

Indeed, it's turning out to be a thoroughly enjoyable conversation, when Flopsey's character suddenly issues the message 'flirting', and comes over to my side of the table. Of course! She thinks I'm a buff ginger warrior-priest – called Scottbaio! All this conversation about virtual prostitution has an entirely different spin from her side of the table! She wants my hot dwarf ass!

So here I am, a thirty-one-year-old mother of two, at 2am, sitting in bed in my Bliss Spa Socks – and having some polymorphous cybersexual frisson with a fifteen-year-old gnome called Flopsey, who lives in Antwerp.

Really, the modern age is a marvel.

My job isn't just about twatting around, though. Sometimes it's about really serious things, like mental illness – which I treat here with all due seriousness, by equating it to having a load of uninvited monkeys in your head.

In this piece, you can see me refer again to having gone mad after smoking a massive bong in front of Later … With Jools Holland. *I like having this fact twice in the book, because 1) by mentioning it consistently, it proves that I'm not making this stuff up, and 2) it's obviously unendingly amusing that I lost my mind whilst watching Jools Holland play boogie-woogie piano with The Beautiful South on BBC2. If there's anything that proves I have managed to ascend the class ladder from 'working class' to 'middle class' it is, surely, this. Well done me.*

The Screaming Monkeys in My Head

Hello. Today, I don't want to talk to you about anxiety. This is because I had my first panic attack three hours after my sister described *her* first panic attack to me – and so, obviously, I don't want you to have *your* first panic attack three hours after you read this. I am worried that, if I talk about it, you might 'catch' anxiety off me – like the measles. That thought makes me anxious. It's making me think I should call this whole column off. I wish I hadn't had that coffee for breakfast. Is it quite stuffy in here? I'm just going to walk around for a bit.

Of course, there's quite a few things you can do to prevent yourself having *your* first panic attack three hours after reading this. The first one – and possibly key to the whole thing – is to not smoke a gigantic skunkweed bong, all on your own, whilst watching *Later … With Jools Holland*.

Later ... With Jools Holland is a programme that makes me quite tense at the best of times – I find Jools Holland's interview style uniquely agitating ('So, your album. A bona fide delight! Remind me of its name again, dear heart?') but on this particular day in 1997, a set by The Beautiful South, plus enough marijuana to make all The Beatles fall over, finally tipped me over the edge.

What started as a common amount of anxiety started to grow larger and larger – first disrupting my heartbeat, then filling my lungs, until, eventually, it blew out the sides of my head. Then, through the broken skull, the monkeys came – six million chattering monkeys of evil, screeching out each worry ever invented. Wow. I wasn't expecting the monkeys. It was like Pandora's Box, in reverse. I tried, desperately, to handle it for twenty minutes – but was simply outnumbered by malignant primates. I gave up, and passed out.

And, when I came round, it wasn't all a dream at all – I was still panicking, and I continued to panic, *even in my sleep,* for the next five weeks, pretty much non-stop.

Of course, something bad that happened in 1997 is, by 2010, not bad any more: just funny. That's physics. Then, I didn't know this was 'just' panic – panic is running for a train whilst trying to get your ticket out of your bum-bag. This, by way of contrast, felt like a combination of heart attack and insanity. I thought I was both losing my mind and dying and, so, obviously, I a) gave up all drugs immediately and b) bought a bicycle, on which I spent four hours a day cycling up and down every hill in North London, trying to 'sweat it out'. As it turns out, the cure for anxiety disorders is actually *not* 'getting sweaty in Archway'. The medical profession would have prescribed a massive whack of benzodiazepine, but I was worried that a GP would tell me off for smoking skunk whilst watching BBC2 ('It's an obviously risky behaviour, Ms Moran!') and so I never went. One friend recommended taking acid – 'It'll BURN the panic out!' – but he was the man who'd also claimed that he could 'live in a hedge, on a handful of rice', so I politely ignored him.

Do you know what worked, in the end? Telling myself to shut up. Setting up a series of huge, foot-thick, iron doors in my head, and learning to clang them shut as soon as the monkeys started talking. It took a while – I'd never tried to curb my imagination before. As a child, I'd been able to lie in bed and imagine faces coming out of the ceiling so vividly, I'd end up having to climb inside my duvet for protection. And, at first, there was almost a perverse temptation to leave the doors open a little – test myself with a little monkey chatter, to see if I could cope with it; in the same way you test a mouth-ulcer with the tip of your tongue.

But the result was always the same – escalation, pain, panic, weeping, wearily going 'Why have I *done* this?' at 3am, after hours and hours of unhappiness.

And so, eventually, I learned not to go near monkey-friendly corridors – thoughts about mortality or insanity – until, finally, the door handles became dusty with lack of use, and whole decades passed, and I forgot what the monkeys sounded like. The spell that kills them is, simply, 'SHUT UP'.

Of course, it's not totally over. Sometimes – when I'm hungover, or very tired, or go a bit too bongo mondo with the coffee-pot – the monkeys will mount a sudden surge, breach the walls, and swarm. Christmas Eve was bad. I find it very difficult in hotels away from my kids. And looking at Jools Holland makes me nervous. But: shut up. It's the best thing I ever learned.

I do a lot for charity, but I don't like to talk about it, apart from in this column, first published in 2009, and then obviously in this book, where I re-print it, desperate not to go on about how much I do for charity. PLEASE don't use the phrase 'She cares too much' about me. It would EMBARRASS mememememe.

I Do a Lot for Charity, But I Would Never Mention It

Walking a marathon is eeeeeasy, compared to running it. That's just obvious. That's why I agreed to walk a marathon – the Moonwalk, in May.

Apparently, it's all in aid of a charity – but I wasn't really listening to the details, to be honest. All I heard was my friends Dent, Hughes and Kennedy saying how, once they'd finished the Moonwalk, they were going for 'a massive champagne breakfast at Claridge's!'

In my head, what I could see was a giant sausage – about twenty-six miles long – and a very short stroll – around five and a half inches, and on a plate, next to some hash browns. A twenty-six-mile walk seemed like a fairly minor consideration, really, in order to have a breakfast like that. Walking? Toddlers do it! Old people! Hens! How hard can it be?

'Sign me up for the bacon – I mean the walk!' I said, cheerfully. 'What are we all wearing? Does one dress up for breakfast? 8am seems a little early for heels and a dress – but then, it *is* Claridge's.'

'You won't care what you're wearing,' Kennedy said, with an abrupt grimness. Kennedy has done marathons before. She refused to say any more. I felt my sausage get a little smaller.

The next week, Kennedy sent through an email with our training schedule on it. The email was entitled 'THE TALK OF DOOM'. Reading through, it was hard to argue with the declaration. It involved phrases like 'You're going to lose some toenails – get used to it', and, 'If you don't train, I can guarantee you the marathon is going to be one of the most miserable experiences of your life. Fact.'

As my previous high-water mark of 'miserable experiences' was attending a rave in Warrington where CS gas was released by an angry bouncer, and I ended up having it washed out of my eyes, with milk, by a man off his face on Ecstasy, who kept calling my teeth his 'pearls', I was keen not to add to the pantheon. I went on a training walk the next day.

Fifteen miles seemed like a reasonable target. Three miles in, I realised that, worn with trainers, lacy tights act as a midway point between 'exfoliating linen facecloth' and 'cilice belt'.

Four miles in, I realised that my iPhone pedometer app – although free, and, also, pretty – wouldn't let me listen to music or make phone calls. This meant that, at a pace of 4mph, I was going to spend the next three hours doing nothing but walking in total silence.

There is something deeply meditative about simply putting one foot in front of the other. The Aborigines walked the Songlines across Australia. Pilgrimages to Mecca, Knock, Lourdes or the Ganges trigger powerful connections between an ostensibly idling brain, and a constantly perambulating body. I, too, felt this deep, primal connection between body and landscape, from the top of Camden Road to the bottom of it. Then I felt so bored I could have punched a bird off a tree.

To try and pass the time – of which I had plenty – I tried to work out the last time I'd faced so many hours of unavoidable tedium. I concluded that it would have been in 1988, when I was thirteen, with no cable, internet or iPod, and hadn't yet learned how to masturbate. In those days – which I remember as a solid year of Sundays – I would pass the hours by lying on my bed, and seeing how long I could stare at the telegraph pole outside my window without blinking.

My mother would regularly come in and find me lying on the bed, tears pouring down my face.

'What's the matter?' she would ask.

'Two minutes fifty-one seconds!' I would say – high on how much my eyes hurt.

It started to rain, hard. I trudged over Waterloo Bridge as buses neatly transferred whole puddles across my right-hand side. On the South Bank, I went into Eat to get a coffee. The barista looked scared. When I saw myself in the mirror, I could see why. My fake leopardskin coat was soaked. My hair ran with water. My trainers didn't just squelch when I walked – they glugged. The barista had looked at all the evidence, and concluded that I must have just failed to commit suicide by jumping in the Thames – and that now I was having a coffee, whilst I waited for the tide to rise a little higher.

When I went to pay for the coffee, he gave me a free brownie. I translated this brownie as the message, 'Don't jump again.' It was 486 calories of humanity.

When I finally got home, it was dark. I'd been walking for five hours. I was wet, bloodied and almost sub-human with boredom. I'd seen so many dull, half-empty, rain-ruined streets that I'd started to believe they might actually affect my personality, and make me permanently dolorous. I lay down on the sofa, barely conscious. My brother was over, for a visit.

'I'm training for the marathon,' I said, by way of explanation.

'The marathon?' he said, impressed. 'Blimey. Well done, Paula Radcliffe.'

'It's not the running marathon,' I said. 'It's the Moonwalk. A walking marathon.'

'Ha!' he said. 'That's not really a marathon, then, is it? That's just a walk. You're not exactly Eddie Izzard.'

It was then that I realised the truth: walking a marathon is much, much, *much* harder than running one. Because everyone thinks it's easy.

Another one of my noble campaigns to make humanity a better place: this time, arguing for international recognition of the supremacy of Ghostbusters *above all other films. I have a longstanding pact with my sister that, if we ever get nominated for an Oscar, we will eschew ball-gowns, diamonds and £20,000 makeovers to go up the red carpet dressed as Venkman and Spengler from* Ghostbusters *– each with a REAL unlicensed nuclear accelerator on our backs. For us, there is no more glamorous look. These are our sex-clothes.*

Ghostbusters is the Greatest Film of All Time. Please Do Not Argue With Me

Last week, iTunes announced that they were celebrating the twenty-fifth anniversary of the release of *Ghostbusters*. This they did by renting it out at 99p, as their 'Film of the Week'.

I had two, quite intense and simultaneous, responses to this news.

The first was sombre. It was, if I may be frank, bordering on maudlin.

'Twenty-five years? *Twenty-five years*? My God, this is worse than when I realised it was ten years since "Vogue" by Madonna was Number One. I never *used* to be able to remember things from twenty-five years ago. I am beginning to have the memory-span – the reminiscing capabilities – of an old woman.'

The second response was, thankfully, much brisker. It was: '99p! For the best film ever made? That's an INSULT! It's like iTunes saying you can have sex with the Queen for a pound! It won't stand, by God! IT WON'T STAND!'

But – on reflection – in many ways, the two responses kind of merged together in the middle. For the simple truth of the matter is that *Ghostbusters is* the greatest film ever made – and yet, currently, the world is too scared to admit this. In 2009, if you stood up at a party and spoke factually – '*Ghostbusters* should still be nominated for an Oscar every year, even now – that's how good it is' – you would probably experience great feelings of squirminess and embarrassment.

And that is because the generation before us have done an excellent propaganda job on installing *Star Wars* as the best film ever made, and we – their younger brothers and sisters – never realised how late in the day it was getting. If we'd realised that twenty-five bleeding years had passed a little sooner, we would have got a hustle on with shooting George Lucas's overrated, po-faced bundle of space-tat out of the water. As it is, I think we all still thought it was, like, 1992 or something, and there was plenty of time to make the case for *Ghostbusters*, after we'd got over how good this new Blur album was.

So with the startling jolt of the quarter-century anniversary, the urgency of the task is now revealed. The Great *Ghostbusters* Campaign must start today. Here. Starting with this inarguable, scientific fact: *Ghostbusters* is still the most successful comedy film of all time, with a 1984 box office of $229.2m. But this, of course, in turn, makes it the most successful film OF ALL TIME, FULL STOP – given that comedy is the supreme genre, and rules over every other format, such as 'serious', 'foreign' or 'black and white'.

Of course, there are those who will argue that comedy *isn't* the greatest genre. 'What art should be about,' they will say, 'is revealing exquisite and resonant truths about the human condition.'

Well, to be honest – no, it shouldn't. I mean, it can *occasionally*, if it wants to; but really, how many penetrating insights into human nature do you need in one lifetime? Two? Three? Once you've realised that no one else has a clue what they're doing, either, and that love can be totally pointless, any further insights into human nature just start getting depressing, really.

On the other hand, what humans *do* need is 'things to say'. They need a huge supply of them. Amusing, essentially inconsequential things, which will make as many people in the room feel relaxed and cordial as possible. In this respect, *Ghostbusters* reveals itself, once again, as the greatest film ever made. When I mentioned this column on Twitter, I had over fifty suggestions as to what the best line in the film is – nearly all of them useful in everyday life.

'Back off, man – I'm a scientist' is the one I find myself using the most often; most recently when the logic in opening a bottle of warm rosé at 3am was brought into question. 'Listen – do you smell something?' is equally handy. 'I think he can hear you, Ray,' can be utilised whenever you think an indiscreet conversation has been overheard; but, also, when a large animal suddenly looks up, as if it might run towards you and attack you. Whenever you buy a takeaway, it is traditional to nix all conversation about future plans with the line, 'This magnificent feast represents the *last* of the petty cash.' And there is no more succinct way of explaining why certain table placements would be ill advised than, 'Don't cross the streams.' There's literally twenty more great lines; but one of them involves a piano, and another needs someone to mention sponges before you can use it.

By comparison, what has *Star Wars* got? 'Luke – I am your father.' I tell you what – you *never* get to wedge that into conversation.

Because if this is the start of the campaign to rightfully install *Ghostbusters* as the best film of all time, *Star Wars* is the one that has to be beaten. It is Connors to *Ghostbusters'* Borg.

To those who still deludedly think they prefer *Star Wars* over *Ghostbusters*, all I need to ask you is this: you don't *really* want to be a Jedi, do you? In a greige cowl, getting off with your sister, without a single gag across *three* films? I think if you thought about it a little while longer, you'd realise that you'd far rather be a Ghostbuster: a nerd in New York with an unlicensed nuclear accelerator on your back, and a one-in-four chance of being Bill Murray.

I urge the world to greatly accelerate their acknowledgement of *Ghostbusters'* true canonical placing – for, in this period of uncertainty, terrible things are happening. Last week, the twenty-fifth anniversary of the film was marked by a celebrity party, attended by, in descending order of fame: Dizzee Rascal, Nikki Grahame from Big Brother 7, DJ Ironic, Dave Berry and Rick Edwards. I know. I'm not trying to be rude but, really, if you're at that level of fame and someone invites you to a party in honour of something you love, the most effective way to show you care is to stay away.

For the rest of us – the ones who have realised the Great Truth about the Greatest Movie Ever Made – the serious campaigning must start *now*. Let's go show this prehistoric bitch how we do things downtown.

And then, a couple of months later, I interviewed Keith Richards. At the time I was going insane writing How To Be A Woman, *and working seven-day weeks for months on end – but couldn't let pass the opportunity to meet the man who, more than any other on Earth, could claim to be rock'n'roll on two, very thin, legs. I mean, really thin legs. It's like two bits of string covered in denim.*

This was another time I was attempting to give up smoking, but was derailed by someone legendary offering a fag. The next time I tried to give up, it was when Benedict Cumberbatch, dressed as Sherlock, offered me a Marlie outside 221b Baker Street. WHO WOULD EVER SAY NO TO THESE CIGARETTES?

'Keith – Noddy Holder Says You Wear a Wig'

I meet Keith Richards on International Talk Like a Pirate Day. It feels only right to inform him of this.

'International Talk Like a Pirate Day?' Keith says, with his wolfy grin, wholly amused. 'ARRRGHH! ARRRHHH! Oh, I can't do it without the eye patch,' he sighs, mock-petulantly. 'I can't speak like a pirate without an eye patch. Or being pissed – HARGH! HARGH!'

But of course, he can: to be frank, everything Keith Richards says is in the cadence of Pirate. With his black eyes, bandana and earring, even at sixty-seven, he has the air of a rakish gentleman forced to steal a frigate and abscond from polite society – due to some regrettable misunderstanding about a virgin daughter, a treasure map and a now-smouldering Admiralty building. You can see why he was the inspiration for Johnny

Depp's Captain Jack Sparrow in *Pirates of the Caribbean*. Richards apparently taught Depp how to walk around a corner, drunk: 'You keep your back to the wall at all times.'

Today, Richards is a pirate in on-shore mode. The mood is tavernish. Even though we are in the Royal Suite of Claridge's, which has a grand piano ('Shall I have a go? You can bootleg it – HARGH HARGH HARGH'), and so many rooms we never even go in half of them, Richards still brings an air of a man who's left his parrot, cutlass and Smee in the hallway – lest he need to make a quick getaway. On walking into the room he spots me, and does a double-take.

'I had no idea I was going to talk to a *lady,*' he says, ordering a vodka and orange. 'I need a drink when I do that.'

Spotting a packet of Marlboro on the table, he eschews them, and brings out his own supplies.

'*Those* are the ones that say they'll kill you,' he says, pointing at the pack on the table, with their large 'SMOKING KILLS' label. 'They are English, and they *would* kill you; they're bloody awful.'

'Are they different to American ones?' I ask.

'Oh yes. You take them apart, if you're going to roll a hash joint, and there's bits of stalk and crap in there. It's *unacceptable* to a smoker.'

He takes one of his own out of his pocket, and lights it. The smell of the smoke mingles with his cologne.

'What have you got on?' I inquire.

'I've got a hard-on – I didn't know you could smell it,' he says – and then starts laughing again, in a fug of smoke. 'That's a rock'n'roll joke – one of Jerry Lee Lewis's,' he explains, almost apologetically. 'We're at the Rock'n'Roll Hall of Fame, and Jerry's got his rig on – frilly shirt and tuxedo – and he's coming down the steps and this chick rushed out and was like, "You smell great – what have you got on?" And Jerry says, "I've got a hard-on – I didn't know you could smell it." Pure rock'n'roll.'

Keith takes another drag on his fag, beaming.

''Ere,' he says, suddenly concerned, looking at the cigarette smoke. 'I hope you're not … allergic.'

Apologising for a hard-on joke, and worrying that a journalist might develop a tickly cough from passive smoking is a long way from Richards' interviews in his outlaw hey-day – he once spent forty sleepless hours with the *NME* journalist Nick Kent, 'pinballing' around London in a Ferrari, and consuming ferocious quantities of cocaine and heroin – a cocktail quaintly referred to, by Richards, as 'the breakfast of champions'.

But then, Richards has mellowed considerably, over the years – possibly out of necessity, if one considers how difficult it would be to parallel-park in modern-day London on a 1.5mg speedball. Giving up heroin in 1978, after his fifth bust, Richards reveals today that he's finally given up cocaine, too – in 2006, after he fell from a tree in Fiji, and had to have brain surgery.

'Yeah – that was cocaine I had to give up for that,' he says, with an equanimous sigh. 'You're like – "I've got the message, oh Lord." He raps on the metal plate in his head. It makes a dull, thonking sound.

'I've given up everything now – which is a trip in itself,' he says, with the kind of Robert Newton-esque eye-roll that indicates how interesting merely getting out of bed, sober, can be after forty years of caning it. Not that Richards is disapproving of getting high, of course:

'I'm just waiting for them to invent something more interesting, hahaha,' he says. 'I'm all ready to road-test it when they do.'

Richards' image is of the last man standing at the long party that was the sixties – and the man who'd invited everyone over in the first place, anyway. During his junkie years, Richards spent over a decade on the 'People Most Likely to Die' list – 'I used to read it, check I was still on there. I was on it longer than anyone else. Badge of honour, hur hur.'

But having spent from 1968–1978 with everyone expecting him to keel over in a hotel (the classic Richards quote: 'Which I never did: it's the height of impoliteness to turn blue in someone else's bathroom'), Richards has now, ironically, gone on to be one of those people we now think will just … live forever. His tough, leathery, indestructible air gives the suggestion that heroin, whisky and cocaine, when taken in large enough quantities, have a kind of … *preservative* quality. Richards has been cured in a marinade of pharmaceuticals. He both gives off the aura of, and bears an undeniable physical resemblance to, the air-dried Inca mummies of Chachapoya.

'Well, I'm not putting death on the agenda,' he says, with another grin. 'I don't want to see my old friend Lucifer just yet, hurgh hurgh. He's the guy I'm gonna see, isn't it – I'm not going to The Other Place, let's face it, HARGH!'

We're here today because having – resolutely, persistently and, in many ways, unfeasibly – not died, Richards has finally published his autobiography, *Life*. When Richards announced the project, he was subject to a massive bidding war that ended with Richards getting a £4.8m advance – acknowledgement of the fact that, barring Bowie or McCartney deciding to write their stories, Richards' was the motherlode, in terms of understanding that most incredible of decades – the sixties – from the inside; recounted by one of the very people pinballing the psychedelic charabanc off the bounds of 'decent' society.

'Have you read it?' he asks – trying to look casual, but unable to suppress an incongruous note of eagerness.

'Oh God, yes,' I say. 'Oh man, it's a total hoot. Really, really amazing.'

'Oh good,' he says, relaxing. 'You know, you start off thinking you can spin a few yarns – and by the time you get to the end of it, it's turned into something much more. One memory triggers another, and before you know it, there's 600 rounds per second coming out.'

'Did you want to write your version because other books on you, and the Stones, had got it wrong?' I ask.

'I read Bill Wyman's book, but after three or four chapters – where he's going [assumes dull, priggish Wyman monotone] "And by that point, I only had £600 left in Barclays Bank" – I was like, "Oh, Bill." You know what I mean? You're far more interesting than that; do me a favour. And Mick attempted it once, and ended up giving the money back. It was ten, fifteen years ago, and he'd keep ringing up and going [does Mick impression], "'Ere, what were we doing on August 15th nineteen-sixty-somefink?" I'd be like, "Mick, *you're* writing it. I can't remember." And knowing Mick, there would have been a *morass* of blank chapters because there would have been a lot of stuff he would have wanted to put to one side, hur hur.'

Richards is dismissive of Stones books written by non-Stones – claiming the authors would have been 'too scared' to write the truth: 'Who's really going to put Mick Jagger, or Keith Richards, up against a wall and say "I demand you answer this?"' he says, eyes suddenly flashing black.

'Because, you know...' He takes a drag on his fag. 'You end up dead like that.'

The reason *Life* attracted such a bidding war is because the life of Keith Richards and the Stones is one that – even in today's modern, anything-goes pop-cultural climate – takes in a still-astonishing amount of, for want of a better word, scandal. 'Would You Let Your Daughter Marry a Rolling Stone?', the Redlands bust, Marianne Faithfull in her fur rug, 'Who Breaks a Butterfly on a Wheel?', the still-controversial death of Brian Jones, the Hell's Angels running amok at Altamont, the Marianne Faithfull/Mick Jagger/Anita Pallenberg/Richards four-way love-rectangle, numerous arrests, heroin, cocaine, acid, whisky, infidelity, groupies, Margaret Trudeau, riots, billions of dollars, and four decades of sweaty fans, screaming without end.

And, at the centre of it all, arguably the greatest rock'n'roll band that ever existed. 'Gimme Shelter', 'Jumpin' Jack Flash', 'You Can't Always Get What You Want', 'Wild Horses', 'Brown Sugar', 'Start Me Up', 'Sympathy for the Devil', 'Satisfaction' – each one with the ability to alone answer the question, 'Mummy – what is rock'n'roll?', and, when taken *en masse,* the reason why Keith Richards is referred to, almost factually, as 'The Living Riff'.

For those expecting an explosive story, *Life* certainly doesn't disappoint: it opens in 1975, with Richards in a diner in Fordyce, Arkansas, about to be busted for the fourth time. Written like a *Fear and Loathing in Las Vegas* with infinitely more resources for getting wasted – Richards is driving to the next gig because he's 'bored' of the Stones' private jet – it joins Richards at the high point of his caner years.

As Richards describes it, he is the sole long-haired man in a room full of rednecks, and is basically wearing a hat made of drugs ('There was a flap at the side in which I'd stowed hash, Tuinals and coke'), and driving a car made of drugs ('I'd spent hours packing the side-panel with coke, grass, peyote and mescaline').

High on cocaine ('Merck cocaine – the fluffy, pharmaceutical blow' as he describes it, lovingly), Richards is arrested, dragged to the courthouse, and becomes the centre of an international news incident ('There were 5,000 Stones fans outside the courthouse') – until Mick Jagger sweet-talks the local governor, and bails him out.

'Mick was always good with the locals,' Richards writes, half-admiringly, half-condescendingly – like a pirate captain commending a handsome cabin-boy who has the ability to 'talk posh' to the gentry.

The following 620 pages scarcely let up from there. Although things tail off in the mid-eighties – as they invariably do in the stories of sixties icons. By then, they are retired from the heart of the storm to their mansions, and are merely watching Madonna from the sidelines, puzzled – the first half of *Life,* up until 1984, is in a league of its own. As rock memoirs go, only Bob Dylan's imperial, awe-inspiring *Chronicles* can beat it.

Sitting in Richards' agent's office, reading it – the secrecy around it is immense; I have to sign confidentiality agreements before I can even see the manuscript – was like getting into a TARDIS, and being witness to events only ever previously recounted by hearsay.

One of the first stories is one of the most amazing – Richards quoting from a letter he sent his aunt in 1961: 'This morning on Dartford Station a guy I knew at primary school came up to me. He's got every record Chuck Berry ever made. He is called Mick Jagger.'

It's like discovering Cleopatra's page-a-day diary, and the entry: 'Tuesday, 4.30pm: meeting with Mark Antony.'

And so it goes on from here – recruiting all the Stones one by one, Bill Wyman sighingly tolerated because he has a better amp than anyone else. They work hard, but it comes ridiculously easy: the first song they ever write together – locked in the kitchen by their manager, until they come up with something – is 'As Tears Go By', which both goes to number one, and bags Jagger the beautiful Marianne Faithfull as a girlfriend. They buy houses. They buy drugs. Here's the Redlands bust, recounted by the man who owned the house: casually mentioning another guest – David Schneidermann, the acid dealer. As the inventor of both the Strawberry Fields acid and the Purple Haze acid, Schneidermann dosed the charts with two of the greatest psychedelic singles ever made.

Keith can tell us the Marianne Faithfull/Mars Bar story is a myth – but adds, casually, that he was the man who left a Mars Bar on the coffee table, as a snack, for when he was stoned.

Here's John Lennon – 'Johnny. A silly sod, in many ways' – coming round with Yoko, and keeling over in the bathroom.

'I don't think John ever left my house, except horizontally,' Richards sighs, having found Lennon – godhead for a generation – lying by the toilet, murmuring, 'Don't move me – these tiles are beautiful.'

On another night with Lennon, Richards tries to explain to him where The Beatles – the fucking Beatles! – have been going wrong all these years: 'You wear your guitar too high. It's not a violin. No wonder you don't swing. No wonder you can rock, but not roll.'

Redlands burns to the ground, and Richards – high – escapes with only 'a cutlass, and a box of goodies, hur hur. Fuck the passports'.

Allen Ginsberg – the high priest of beatnik – is regarded as a bit of a twat: coming over to Keith's house, he 'plays a concertina and makes "ommmmmm" sounds', as Richards relates, still sounding beleaguered by an unwelcome house guest, thirty years later. Brian Jones is dismissed as little more than 'a wife-beater'.

In this rollercoaster blur, Altamont – where the Hell's Angels, high on LSD and speed, stab Meredith Hunter to death – is merely an incidental point. For generations of lazy documentary makers, it's been seen as the point that the sixties turned sour: the moment that Flower Power idealism dies; the undeniable beginning of the darkness.

To the man on stage at the time, however, playing 'Under My Thumb' as Meredith dies, it's a story that merits little more than two paragraphs. The first Stones fan to die had been back in 1965 – plunging from the balcony of an early gig. By 1969, Keith Richards had seen it all. He couldn't be surprised by anything.

But for all the drugs, car chases, jets, stadiums, Presidents, fist-fights and deaths, the core of *Life* is a small, human, timeless story. The story of Keith Richards' life revolves around two things: the friend he never quite understands, and the girl who got away: bandmate Mick Jagger, and former wife, and mother of three of his children, Anita Pallenberg.

Reading *Life*, I was shocked by how candid Richards is about his relationship with both Jagger and Pallenberg. Indeed, I gasped at two of the stories. My thought was, as I read them, 'Keith Richards – you're going to be in trouble.'

'In trouble?' Richards says, laughing. 'Hur hur. Why?'

Well, let's take Mick Jagger. You reveal that your secret nickname for him is 'Your Majesty', or 'Brenda' – and that you openly had conversations with the other Stones, in front of Mick, referring to 'that bitch Brenda'. Your review of Mick's solo album, *Goddess in the Doorway* – which you refer to as *Dogshit on the Doorstep* – is 'It's like *Mein Kampf* – everyone had it, but no one read it'. You describe an annoying pet mynah bird as 'like living with Mick'. There's a chapter that starts, 'It was the beginning of the eighties when Mick started to become unbearable.' There's quotes like, 'Mick plays harmonica from the heart – but he doesn't sing like that.' 'Mick Jagger is aspiring to be Mick Jagger.' 'I think Mick thinks I belong to him.' 'I used to love Mick, but I haven't been to his dressing room in twenty years. Sometimes I think, "I miss my friend." I wonder, "Where did he go?"'

Has Mick read the book?

Keith seems resolutely unfazed.

'Yeah!' he says, equanimously. 'I think it opened his eyes a bit, actually.'

'Were there any bits he asked you to leave out?' I ask.

Keith starts laughing again. 'WURGH WURGH WURGH.' It sounds like a crow stuck in a chimney.

'Yeah! Funnily enough, it was the weirdest thing he wanted taken out. I mean, look. You know, I love the man. I've known him since I was four years old, right. But the bit he wanted taken out was how he used a voice coach.'

'Really?'

'Yeah! And everyone knew it anyway. It's been in a million interviews, but for some reason, he was like, "You know – could we leave that out?" And I went, "No! I'm trying to say the truth here."'

I pause for a minute. I clear my throat.

'So he didn't ask you to take out the bit about how small his cock is, then?' I ask, in a rather prim voice.

'Hey – I was only told that by others,' Keith says, with a wolfish smile and a shrug.

This is the height of disingenuousness, because the 'other' Richards is referring to is Marianne Faithfull – Jagger's girlfriend at the time – and a story that is one of the key 'OH MY GOD!' moments of the book.

Rumours have long circled about just what was going on in 1969 – the year the world's two most glamorous couples were Keith Richards and Anita Pallenberg, and Mick Jagger and Marianne Faithfull.

As Pallenberg and Jagger started work on *Performance,* in the roles of lovers, Richards was convinced that director Nicolas Roeg – whom he hates – is trying to get Mick and Anita together for real, so that he can have 'hardcore pornography' in his film.

In one of the most evocatively written passages in the book, Richards describes how the jealousy and fear that he's losing Anita to Jagger, coupled with his escalating heroin abuse, results in him writing 'Gimme Shelter' on a filthy, stormy day – staring out of the window of his house, waiting for the sound of Anita's car. It never arrives. She doesn't come home that night. He presumes she lies in his bandmate's bed.

Partly in retaliation, Richards then goes about bedding Marianne Faithfull. Despite the undeniable dark, fratricidal overtones of screwing Jagger's girlfriend, Richards' account of it in *Life* is recounted in Pirate Tavern mode, concluding with his joy at having 'my head nestled between those two beautiful jugs'.

When Faithfull and Richards hear Jagger returning home, Richards jumps out of the window, like Robin Askwith in *Confessions of a Window Cleaner*, leaving his socks, and his cuckolded bandmate's girlfriend, behind him. As a final stab, forty years later, Richards adds:

'[Marianne] had no fun with [Mick's] tiny todger. I know he's got an enormous pair of balls – but it doesn't quite fill the gap.'

For a Stones fan, it's a real double-or-quits moment. On the one hand, as a description of what it's like to be inside a legendary song as it makes landfall, Keith Richards' recollections of writing 'Gimme Shelter' are without parallel. On the other hand, there is the massive risk that – after reading the chapter – every subsequent listening of the song will be haunted by the image of Mick Jagger's allegedly tiny todger, nestled on a pair of gigantic testicles.

It's one of those side-effects of rock'n'roll that no one ever warns you about.

'Well, I *did* say he had enormous balls,' Richards says now, generously. 'I'm sure he's had worse thrown at him by women. I mean, Jerry Hall pretty much decimated him anyway.'

'It does seem like you're trying to … wind him up,' I say.

'We've had our beefs but hey, who doesn't. *You* try and keep something together for fifty years,' Richards says, palpably not caring.

There is similar, breathtaking candour in his recounting of his relationship with Anita Pallenberg. In a physically abusive relationship with fellow Stone Brian Jones, Pallenberg has the hots for Richards, and Richards has the hots for Pallenberg. When Jones gets hospitalised with asthma, Richards and Pallenberg end up together in a car, being driven from Barcelona to Valencia. Without a word ever being exchanged, Pallenberg kicks off their relationship by silently unzipping Richards' jeans, and giving him a blowjob.

'I remember the smell of the orange trees in Valencia,' Richards writes, still sounding post-coital, forty years later. 'When you get laid by Anita Pallenberg for the first time, you remember things.'

'Oh – the great blowjob in the car?' Keith says today, when I bring it up – again, quite primly.

'What was your chauffeur doing all this time?' I ask, incredulously.

'He's got to keep his eyes on the road,' Keith shrugs. 'I should imagine he was going "about time", to be honest. It had been in the air for ages.'

Although it was Richards who eventually called time on the marriage, when Pallenberg's subsequent heroin addiction got out of hand, Pallenberg still comes across as 'unfinished business' in *Life* – with Richards repeatedly addressing Pallenberg directly from the pages; calling on her to think of what would have happened if they'd managed to stay together; in rocking chairs together, 'watching the grandkids'. Although Richards is now married to, and has two children with, Patti Hansen, Pallenberg recurs throughout the book like perfume; melody; a ghost. While Richards rails at Jagger, he sighs over Pallenberg. The girl that gave herself away.

Perhaps you keep coming back to Anita and Mick, I suggest to Richards, because as an artist, there's nothing to say about the people you love and understand. It's the ones who mystify you that you need to write songs and books about. That's how you try and figure them out.

'Yeah.' Richards nods. 'You've got nothing to say when it's all understood.'

It's the best inference to make – because any other suggests Richards is still a little in love with the woman whose clothes he's wearing on the cover of *Their Satanic Majesties Request*.

At sixty-seven, having come into life-transforming wealth and fame in one of the most controversial bands of the counter-cultural era, one could easily assume that Keith Richards became a pirate *because* of rock'n'roll – around the time the Stones went out on the road, and never really came back: 'A pirate nation, moving under our own flag, with lawyers, clowns and attendants.'

But the other revelation of *Life* is that this was how Richards was raised: Richards has always been a pirate. He describes post-war Dartford as somewhere where 'everyone's a thief'. Dartford – where the highway-men would hold up the stage to London, explosions from the fireworks factory 'would take out the windows for miles around' and patients from the lunatic asylum would regularly abscond.

'In the morning, you'd find a loony on the heath, in his little night-shirt,' Richards recalls, fondly.

Richards' family were not respectable, or God-fearing. They numbered musicians, actors and prostitutes: his mother would 'cross the road' to avoid the priest, and divorced his father to marry a younger lover.

Richards' mother, Doris, was a classic, working-class matriarch – her last words to Keith, as he played to her on her deathbed, were 'You're out of tune' – and as an only child of a poor, bohemian couple, the only things Richards was brought up to respect were the local library, and music. When he got his first guitar, he slept with it in his bed.

Twenty years later, guests to Redlands recall Richards' guitar collec-tion being on every sofa and chair, and being left with nowhere to sit but the floor.

So when you come and talk to Keith Richards, this is who you feel you are meeting: not a millionaire Rolling Stone, with houses in Suffolk, Connecticut and Turks and Caicos – but the guy from Dartford who would always have been out of kilter with normal society, however his life had turned out. You get the very strong feeling that this is what Keith Richards would be like even if we were down the pub, instead of Claridge's, and Keith had got here on the bus – not least because his bandana is, on closer inspection, quite grubby, and he's wearing a pair of shattered trackie bottoms, and the kind of incongruously bright-turquoise trainers you often see on meths-drinking tramps.

Ask him about his daughter – twenty-four-year-old Alexandra – doing a nude shoot for *Playboy,* and he seems truly baffled by the notion he could have been disapproving.

'You know – my girls are like me,' he says. 'They try to avoid work as much as possible, hehehe. A bit of modelling is a bit of freedom. Hey, baby – with a frame like that, flaunt it.'

The story of how he came to work with Johnny Depp on *Pirates of the Caribbean* is a case in point.

'It took me two years before I realised who he was,' Keith says, lighting another fag. 'He was just one of my son Marlon's mates, hanging around the house playing guitar. I never ask Marlon's mates who they are, because you know, "I'm a dope dealer", hahaha. Then one day he was at dinner' – Richards mimes Johnny Depp holding a knife and fork – 'and I'm like, "Whoa! Scissorhands!" Hahaha. Then I find out he's an actor, and like one of the biggest Keith Richards fans in the world – and how do I deal with that? "Get over it, Johnny." HURGH HURGH.'

Depp and Richards are currently shooting *Pirates of the Caribbean 4*, where Richards plays, for the second time, Captain Jack Sparrow's father – 'It takes two hours to put the wig and make-up on. Back into the hairy prison. "Ooooh, sorry about my sword, babe," hahaha.'

Filming a bar-room scene, Richards has roped in 'a couple of mates. Well, it's a bar-room, innit?'

In between the last film and this, Depp has been shooting a documentary on Richards: 'Kinda behind-the-scenes stuff. Johnny does interviews. Dunno when it's going to be finished.' He shrugs again. The idea of being followed around by a documentary crew, and one of the most famous actors in the world, seems resolutely normal.

Possibly because of his upbringing – 'I'm just a retarded gangster, really. Maybe that's what I should have called the book. *Retarded Gangster*' – Richards seems genuinely at ease with his fame. He lives now, as he always has since a child, 'in a world outside most others' – he doesn't watch TV (*'Lovejoy'*, he says, finally, having struggled to think for some minutes about his favourite show), exists on old-fashioned comfort food (the book includes his recipe for bangers & mash: 'Put the fuckers in the pan and let them rock'), has never voted ('I suppose democracy is the best there is to offer. But for a lot of people, it's like telling the slaves they're free. "Hey man – where's the next meal coming from?"'), and as for when he last travelled by public transport, he wrinkles his forehead and asks, mistily, 'Have they still got trams?'

This leaves him at ease in the company of other infamous people ('My favourite head of state? Václav Havel. Very impressed with the man. He had a telescope in his office, trained on his old prison cell. He used to refer to it as "my old house". I liked Clinton. He's a lousy sax player. A little indiscreet, but as a guy – I'd take him on any time. He's great.' As for Tony Blair: 'I wrote him a letter [about the Iraq war], telling him he had to stick to his guns. I got a letter back, saying "Thanks for the support".' He views the recent imprisonment of George Michael with equanimity, and not a little amusement.

'Fame has killed more very talented guys than drugs,' he says, sighing. 'Jimi Hendrix didn't die of an overdose – he died of fame. Brian [Jones], too. I lost a lot of friends to fame. There's that bit in the book, where I talk about how I cope with fame, and say "Mick chose flattery, and I chose junk". Because I kept my feet on the ground – even when they were in the gutter. You know what? I bet George Michael is loving it. I say, "Stay in jail, George." There's probably some dope, and some gays. He probably won't want to leave – it's the best place for him. He's playing around with fame. I can't remember a song of his. I don't want to knock the guy, but I'm an immortal legend, according to some,' he shrugs.

The implication is that, however wasted Richards got, he wouldn't have crashed into a branch of Snappy Snaps on something as lightweight as a joint.

Keith Richards is a man without regret. When I ask him if – given the chance to do it all over again – he'd start taking heroin, he doesn't pause. 'Oh yes. Yes. There was a lot of experience in there – you meet a lot of weird people, different takes on life that you're not going to find if you don't go there. I loved a good high. And if you stay up, you get the songs that everyone else misses, because they're asleep. There's songs zooming around everywhere. There's songs zooming through here right now, in the air.'

He looks up, as if he can see them, hovering over the grand piano.

'You've just got to put your hand out, and catch them.'

During our whole chat, the only time he seems roused to genuine annoyance is when I ask him what I think might be the most amazing question of my entire journalistic career. Thanks to a meeting at a party last year, I am able to say to Keith Richards – one of our greatest living rock stars – 'Keith, I met Noddy Holder last year, and he's convinced you wear a wig.'

'Not yet!' he says, looking genuinely indignant. 'Hey man, what's his problem with wigs?'

'He thinks both you *and* Mick wear them,' I say, with mock-disapproval.

'Get out of here!' Richards roars. He pulls down his bandana and shows me his hair – grey, a little wispy, but looking undeniably real. 'Hey Noddy, you know, there are more important things in life than hair. Mick definitely doesn't wear a wig. I KNOW! I'VE PULLED IT! What's Noddy's problem?'

'I think Noddy's just very proud he's still got a gigantic afro,' I offer.

'Well, that's about all he's got,' Keith says, sniffily. 'Well done, Nod.'

Our hour is up. Keith is off to get ready for another day of shooting on *Pirates* – possibly the most high-profile busman's holiday in showbusiness.

'Any plans for the future?' I ask, as he picks up his cigarettes – still eschewing the British ones on the table.

'Well, you know, we'll be on the road again in the future,' Keith says, pocketing his lighter. 'Yeah. On the road. I think it's going to happen. I've had a chat with … Her Majesty. Brenda.'

And Richards leaves the room, laughing. He's at it again. Winding up Mick; doing what he wants; being Keith Richards, for the sixty-seventh year in a row.

'I had to invent the job, you know,' he said, earlier. 'There wasn't a sign in the shop window, saying, "Wanted: Keith Richards".'

And he's done a bloody good job of it.

I don't think I can hold out any longer: I think it might be Sherlock *time.* Sherlock *blew my mind like I wanted it blown – hard, fast, properly, and while I was too busy laughing to notice that it was quietly, and at the same time, breaking my heart.*

I loved the way it entered – kicking the door open shouting 'BANG! And I'm in!' in such a confident manner that, twenty minutes into the first episode, people on Twitter were saying 'This really might be one of the greatest TV shows of all time'. After twenty minutes! That is one hell of a mesmeric aura for a show to be throwing off.

When people said, smugly, 'Oh, it's just because you fancy Benedict Cumberbatch as Sherlock,' it was as if they were saying to a plant, 'Oh, you only photosynthesise because of the sun.' Well, YES. DUH. That's what the sun/Cumberbatch does to me/a plant. Why are you arguing against the miracle of Nature? You might as well punch a tree. Just buy the box set.

Anyway. Here's my review of the first episode, written with a spinning head and a bursting heart, and a bid going on eBay for a deerstalker hat.

Sherlock Review 1: Like a Jaguar in a Cello

Oh dear. That was bad timing.

In the week where Culture Secretary Jeremy Hunt questioned if the BBC licence fee gives 'value for money', the advent of *Sherlock* donked his theory quite badly. It's a bit embarrassing to be standing on a soap-box, slagging a corporation off as essentially wasteful and moribund, right at the point where they're landing a bright, brilliant dragon of a show on the rooftops, for 39p per household. And with the rest of the BBC's output that day – theoretically – thrown in for free.

I don't want to be racist against ITV1, but you know what a bag of bollocks they would have made of a Sherlock Holmes reboot in 2010: Robson Green as Holmes, Christine Bleakley as Watson, Pixie Lott as 'dead prostitute'. And the Go Compare advert every thirteen minutes – as unwelcome as finding flyers for a local double-glazing firm wedged into your copy of *Animal Farm*.

The BBC, on the other hand, went in and did it magnificently: like craftsmen retro-fitting a vintage Rolls-Royce Phantom with the engine from Virgin's SpaceShipOne.

The casting was perfect. Benedict Cumberbatch – the first actor in history to play Sherlock Holmes who has a name more ridiculous than 'Sherlock Holmes' – was both perfect and astonishing: an actor pulling on an iconic character and finding he had infinite energy to drive the thing. He is so good that – ten minutes in – I just started laughing out loud with what a delight it was to watch him.

He looks amazing – as odd as you'd expect the Cleverest Man in the World to look. Eyes white, skin like china clay, and a voice like someone smoking a cigar inside a grand piano, this Holmes has, as Cumberbatch described it in interviews, 'an achievable super-power'. He might not have actual X-ray vision, but his superlative illative chops mean that London is like a Duplo train set to him: an easily analysable system, populated by small, simple, plastic people.

At one point, a suspect speeds away from him in a taxi. Holmes can call up the A-Z, and the taxi's only possible route, in his mind: 'Right turn, traffic lights, pedestrian crossing, road works, traffic lights.'

By climbing over the right rooftop, ducking down the right alleyway, and running very, very fast whilst looking hot, Holmes can beat the taxi to its destination: as easily as if he were the size of the Telecom Tower, or Big Ben, stepping over the city laid out on the rug at 221b Baker Street.

Of course, this view of humanity's masses makes him a high-function-ing Asperger's/borderline sociopath. Questioning why someone would still be upset about their baby dying fourteen years ago – 'That was ages ago!' he shouts with the frustration of a child. 'Why would she still be upset?' – Holmes notes that the room has gone quiet.

'Not good?' he hisses to Watson.

'*Bit* not good, yeah,' Watson replies.

So this is why Holmes needs Watson – their advent into each other's lives managed with three perfect flicks of the script. Yes, Watson is impressed by Holmes: 'That's amazing!' he gasps, as Holmes deduces he has an alcoholic sibling, merely from scratch-marks on his mobile.

'People don't usually say that,' Holmes blinks, pleased. 'They usually say, "Piss off."'

But this Watson isn't the usual, buff, conservative sidekick. In a role rivalling his turn as Tim in *The Office,* Martin Freeman's Watson is altogether more complex and satisfying. Yes, he's here as dragon-trainer – to whack Holmes with a stick when he starts monstering around, and climbing up on the furniture – but he's also as quietly addicted to 'the game' as Holmes. It's Watson with the nervous tremors because he misses active service, in Afghanistan; Watson with the gun.

Sherlock is so packed with joy and treats, to list them means bordering on gabbling: Una Stubbs as secret dope-fiend landlady Mrs Hudson ('It was just a herbal remedy – for my hip!'), Mycroft Holmes' mysterious, posh, texting, superlatively composed assistant, 'Anthea'. The little nods to the possibility that Holmes might be gay. The insanely generous casting of Rupert Graves as DI Lestrade. The line 'I love a serial killer – there's always something to look forward to!' And the perfect placing of what is, presumably, the series arc: 'Holmes is a great man. And I hope, one day, a good one, too.'

'Value for money' isn't even the start of it. Every detail of this *Sherlock* thrills. Given that it was written by Steven Moffat in the same year he knocked off the astonishing, elegant and high-powered re-booting of *Doctor Who,* at £142.50, Moffat's scripts alone are value for money.

If the funding is ever called into question, I'll pay it myself. In cash. Delivered to his front doorstep. With a beaming, hopefully non-stalkerish, 'Thank you.'

Then, two weeks later, it was all over: there were only three episodes in the first series. And I'd lost the bid on the deerstalker to someone in Leicester. I was gutted. The rest of that week's review was about Simon Amstell's new sitcom, which I include here to explain why I continue not to be married to Simon Amstell, for those who were curious about the situation.

Sherlock Review 2: The Frumious Cumberbatch

'But why are there only three episodes?' Britain asked, scrabbling around in the schedules, in case there was a *Sherlock* left they'd overlooked, at the bottom, or underneath some *Coast* or something. 'Only three? Why would you make only three *Sherlocks*? Telly comes in SIX. SIX is the number of telly. Or TWELVE. Or, in America, TWENTY-SIX – because it is a bigger country. But you never have three of telly. Three of telly is NOT HOLY. WHY have they done this? IS THIS A GIGANTIC PUZZLE WE MUST DEDUCE – LIKE SHERLOCK HIMSELF?'

But yes. On Sunday, *Sherlock* came to an end after a fleet, flashing run. Like some kind of Usain Bolt of TV, perhaps it finished so early simply because it was faster than everyone else. Either way, it had left scorch-marks on the track: in three weeks, it flipped everything around. Sunday nights became the best night of the week. Martin Freeman went from being 'Martin Freeman – you know, Tim from *The Office*' to 'Martin Freeman – you know, Watson from *Sherlock*'. Steven Moffat had – extraordinar-ily – constructed a serious rival to his own *Doctor Who* as the most-loved and geekily revered show in Britain. And Benedict Cumberbatch had, of course, gone from well-respected, BAFTA-nominated actor to pin-up, by-word, totty, avatar and fame: the frumious Cumberbatch.

'The Great Game' opened with Holmes – slumped in a chair, legs as long as the TV was wide – bored, shooting at the wall without even looking. Popping holes in that lovely 1970s wallpaper at 221b Baker Street; lead-like with torpor.

'What you need is a *nice murder*,' Una Stubbs' Mrs Hudson clucked, sympathetically, in the hallway. 'Cheer you up.'

So when Moriarty came out to play, Holmes' glee at the oncoming chaos was inglorious, but heartfelt. He received phone calls from weeping innocents, parcelled up with TNT. Moriarty told them what to say: they give Holmes a single, cryptic clue about an unsolved crime, and tell him he has twelve, ten, eight hours to solve it, or they will die.

With increasing dazzle, Holmes busts each case. On the foreshore by Southwark Bridge, with London frosty and grey behind him, Holmes looks at the washed-up corpse in front of him, and in less than a minute concludes that because this man is dead, a newly discovered Vermeer – going on exhibition tomorrow – must be a fake. His torrent of illation is extraordinary – his mind has anti-gravity boots; he bounces from realisation to realisation until he's as high as the sun.

Ten minutes later, and he's in the gallery, staring at the Vermeer. He knows it's fake but doesn't know how to prove it. Then Moriarty's latest, TNT-garlanded victim calls him. The voice is tiny.

'It's a child!' Lestrade, Watson and the audience horror. 'A child!' The child starts counting backwards from ten – Holmes has ten seconds to prove the Vermeer is a fake. The tension is insane – I was biting my wrists with distress – but when the answer bursts on Holmes, he almost doesn't shout out the answer in time: the pleasure he's had from smashing the case has him high as a kite. He is wired.

But the whole series has been building up to Holmes meeting Moriarty and, finally, in a deserted swimming pool, here he is: Jim Moriarty. Young, fast, Irish – looks like Ant McPartlin, sounds like Graham Norton. An amalgam of Saturday-night light-entertainment hosts. How *fiendish*.

Sherlock seems oddly *relieved* at finally meeting Moriarty. Yeah, he's completely evil – but he's also the only person in the world who doesn't, ultimately, bore Holmes. He's made the last week thrilling. Moriarty makes Holmes come alive – even when he's trying to kill him. And Moriarty knows this.

'Is that a Browning in your pocket – or are you just pleased to see me?' he asks.

'Both,' Holmes says, during a scene that had an undeniable undercurrent of hotness.

But things suddenly turn. Moriarty knows that Holmes is bad for business. And – oh yeah – Dr Watson's still standing in the corner, covered in TNT. Moriarty's threatening to explode him. I'd forgotten about that, during the hotness.

'The flirting's over, my dear,' Moriarty says, warning Holmes off.

Holmes is in accord. 'People have died.'

And suddenly, the awfulness of Moriarty comes roaring out. 'THAT'S. What people DO,' he screams – eyes dilating so huge and black, I wondered if it might have been done with CGI. 'I will BURN the HEART out of you,' he continues, warning Holmes off his patch, boilingly insane. It was like when Christopher Lloyd shows his evil Toon eyes in *Who Framed Roger Rabbit?* – truly startling. Andrew Scott has some serious chops.

And there, five minutes later, we left them, on a cliff-hanger. Moriarty's snipers shining their laser-sights on Holmes' and Watson's hearts; Holmes pointing his gun at a pile of TNT, telling Moriarty he's happy to blow them all sky-high; 'The Great Game' ended in checkmate. Not quite as amazing as the first episode , but a different league from Episode Two; and still the best thing on all week by several, palpable, indexable leagues.

Sherlock ends its run as a reekingly charismatic show, flashing its cerise silk suit-lining in a thousand underplayed touches: Holmes watching *The Jeremy Kyle Show* – 'Of course he's not the father! Look at the turn-up on his jeans!' The neat one-two of, 'Meretricious!', 'And a happy New Year!' A myriad of amazing moments from Cumberbatch, who will surely – surely – with his voice like a jaguar in a cello, and his face like sloth made of pearl – get a BAFTA for such a passionate, whole-hearted, star-bright re-booting of an icon.

No one can be in any doubt that the BBC will re-commission *Sherlock*, and that – so long as Steven Moffat and Mark Gatiss are in charge of the scripts, as they were for the first and last episode – it will continue to totally delight anyone who watches it.

But next time, in sixes, or twelves, or twenty-fours, please. Not threes. Threes are over far, far too quickly. Now Sunday is just … normal again.

Even though he's teetotal, gay and on the one occasion I met him, at a party, seemed to kind of hate me quite a lot, I had always thought that, at some point, I would marry Simon Amstell. As a bitchy Jew with a movingly beautiful range of haircuts and cardigans, he ticked nearly every 'Want' box on my Imaginary Husband List: his reign as chair on *Never Mind the Buzzcocks* was one of the most consistently brilliant comedy turns on television ('It's Jordan's third-favourite tit and second-favourite twat – Peter Andre!').

But now, Amstell has given up TV presenting entirely, to concentrate on stand-up and, latterly, script-writing. And why has he given up presenting?

'Because I was just being unkind to people,' the character 'Simon Amstell' says in *Grandma's House,* co-written by Amstell, which started this week.

Before its broadcast, *Grandma's House* had poor word of mouth.

'It's not very good,' people kept saying, forebodingly – like punters leaving a disappointing B&B, and warning the new customers, waiting on the doorstep.

But when I finally got to watch it for myself, I actually quite liked it. It's essentially an Essex version of *Curb Your Enthusiasm* – TV presenter 'Simon Amstell' has just quit his job, as a pop quiz-show host, in order to do something 'more meaningful'. He goes to his grandma's house to break the news to his family – *Thick of It* twosome Rebecca Front and James Smith (as Amstell's mother and mother's new boyfriend, both pin-sharp), his grandmother and father, eleven-year-old cousin and schlumpy aunt. The whole family are brilliantly cast – particularly the aunt (Samantha Spiro), who is the family's whipping boy (her hair is dry, her moustache is visible – she's given a reel of Sellotape and made to wear a hat) and does torrents of panicky outrage when things go wrong. She's ace.

The only real problem with the show is Amstell himself. To say he can't act would be totally inadequate to the gravity of the situation. The scale on which Amstell can't act is – and I say this as sombre fact – unprecedented. I think it may be the worst acting ever done, for cash, on British television. They might just as well have cast a giant ball-bearing. The fact is that Amstell is playing 'Simon Amstell' in a show he's written himself – therefore, we presume, tailoring the role to showcase his best abilities.

Simon Amstell being Simon Amstell on television is one of the funniest things possible. Simon Amstell being 'Simon Amstell' on television is just shocking.

And of course, now I've said that, I will never be Caitlin Amstell. That's my chance gone. I have sacrificed all my future happiness for the truth. I'm just a bit of a hero like that.

I still haven't got round to doing what I propose in this next piece. I really must. I am still haunted by the boy in the playground. I wonder what he did next? I hope he continued to escalate his look commensurately with each passing year, and now walks around Solihull dressed like fucking Batman.

Hello. You Look Wonderful.

When I was fourteen, and bored, I used to walk the five miles into town, sit on the patch of grass outside St Peter's Church, and look at people. Obviously, at that age, it was mainly boys I was looking at. And obviously, given that I was sitting in the drizzle, staring at them, and wearing – it's a long story – a red tartan dressing gown instead of a coat, they would cross the street, and go into Argos, to avoid me. But still, I would look. I would look and look and look. They literally could not stop me.

Anyone who'd seen Desmond Morris's *The Human Zoo* would suggest I was studying humans like animals, but I know that I was not. It was far more formless, and thoughtless, than that. I was definitely just staring – like a mono-browed lollygagger, creating a patch of unease by the village well.

I think that, at the time, I thought that if I looked at people – particularly boys – long enough, I would somehow work 'it' out. That I had no idea what 'it' was is, of course, one of the hallmarks of adolescence. If I'd been forced to put money on what 'it' might be, it sadly would not have been, 'Whether my life would be immeasurably improved if I stopped wearing a dressing gown, tried to be normal, and bought a coat, instead.' I was, as you can see, quite hopeless.

We *all* look at people, of course. We cannot help it. Mankind has hot-air balloons, and crampons, and mine shafts, and submersibles. Mankind has been on the Moon. Anywhere we look, people get in the way – hanging off ladders, falling from windows, putting their face a little too close to yours to ask you if you're all right. Everywhere we look, we are looking at people. They are like Nature's little screensavers.

But one of the things I most love about this country is that we do not, *will* not, stare at each other. The British will not spend all day gawping at each other in the drizzle; however odd we may look. The entire cast of *Priscilla, Queen of the Desert* could roll into Starbucks, with candy-coloured cockatiels flying out of their hair, and after a brief glance upwards – everyone would studiously go back to reading their papers; as if the door had merely been blown open by the wind. In a cramped, crowded nation, we know the essence of politeness is ignoring pretty much everyone around us.

And yet – and yet, this saddens me, also. For whilst it means we do not cause anguish in the hearts of the sweaty, the harried or the deformed, it means that, with the Olympic Committee of our gaze, we also fail to hand out Gold medals to those who actually *should* be looked at.

Yes. I'm talking about people who look hot. People who look really, really hot. Not necessarily classically staggering, like a Moss, or a Best. But those who've put together a smoking outfit, done something foxy with their hair, artfully clashed their shoes with their bangles, or just gone the whole hog and backcombed their fringe until it looks like a hat. Straight boys in pink nu-rave hoodies. OAPs in scarlet ballet pumps. Waitresses with 1940s up-dos. Ghanaian girls in pigtails and jodhpurs, trotting round Topshop like it's a gymkhana. These are the people who *want* to be looked at. They are abiding by Quentin Crisp's maxim – to live their lives as if they were in a movie. But their tragedy is that, by living in Britain, it's a movie that will be furtively glanced at, for a mere second, and then pointedly ignored.

For those who believe, as I do, that the next stage in human evolution will be neither a giant leap in intelligence, nor partial DNA-merge with robots, but all of us looking consistently better dressed, it is a crime against Nature itself.

Instance: I was in Solihull last week, in a park. It was starting to look – as all parks must, in the middle of a wet September – a bit like a plate of boiled cabbage, with some swings stuck in it. Sitting on the edge of the skate-park was a boy of about fifteen, who had clearly recently seen *The Dark Knight* in the last few months, and was now desirous to be the Joker. On this day, he was doing so by dressing all in black – skater trousers, knee-length pea-coat, beanie-hat. When he took the coat off, it revealed a cropped black waistcoat over a white shirt – a shirt that bordered, thrillingly, on blouse.

While the other kids skated – in nondescript trousers, and greige tops – he leaned against the monkey bars, smoking a fag, and photographed them with an impressively old-fashioned Nikon. Now, I'm not entirely deluded. I know that the photos were probably awful, the cigarettes had a one-in-three chance of giving him cancer, and he was, in all probability, a bit of a dick. But I loved him. I loved him for treating his outfit like an atmosphere-controlled space-suit, which shielded him from the world he was actually in. I loved that his clothes were a signal to vaguely like-minded people – the opening line of a conversation, which you could hear from the other side of the park.

But as I looked at him, I felt a melancholy steal upon me. I feared that, without the support of a watching world – a couple of thumbs-up here, a 'nice one' there, maybe some winks from a bus driver – he would eventually find that the leaden lure of jogging bottoms and an Aston Villa top too great to resist, and just give up on being beautiful. There is a paradox in being cool, as I have learned over the years from interviewing pop stars, actors and sundry cultural beacons. They have all noted that one of the little sorrows of being cool is that similarly cool people are too cool to ever come over and tell you you're cool – because that's just not cool. And so, gradually, the entire point of being cool is being eroded.

What the cool people need, then, is some gawping, moon-faced, resolutely non-cool person to come and tell them that they're cool, instead.

To this end, I am about to order up 1,000 old-fashioned calling cards – string-coloured, Verdana typeface, one side only. They will read 'I just want you to know, I really appreciate your look'. And I'm going to walk around London, handing them out as and where truly necessary.

part**two**

Homosexuals, Transsexuals, Ladies and the Internet

In which we explore pioneering nineteenth-century lesbians, demand employment quotas for women whilst using a lengthy analogy about a pelican, nerd out with the gayest sci-fi series ever – Doctor Who – and point out that the internet was invented by humans, and not dystopian robots, or Satan.

But first: back to me and Pete in bed again.

You might think there are too many of these conversations. On that basis, you would immediately be able to strike up a cordial and mutually agreeable conversation with Pete.

First Time Ever I Saw Your Face

It's 11.38pm. The children have finally gone to sleep. The foxes have not yet begun their nightly panoply of bin-upping, bag-shredding and mad fox-love. It's the Golden Hour. It is peaceful. It is time for sleep.

'Pete?'

'No.'

'Pete?'

'No.'

'Pete?'

'I am asleep. No.'

'Pete – what's the first thing you think of when you think of me?'

'What?'

'When someone says my name, or you think of me – what's the picture that comes into your head?'

'Please remember that I just said "I'm asleep". Please.'

'For instance,' I say, turning over into my 'Interesting Chat' position. I have intrigued me with this question. This is a good question. 'For instance, when I think of *you*, straightaway – quick as a flash – I see you standing at the kitchen table, wearing a cardigan, and looking down at a pile of new records that you've just bought. You've put one on, and you're kind of bopping to it a bit, and you're eating a slice of bread and butter, while you wait for the tea to cook. You might be humming a bit. That's my go-to image for you. That's your essence. That's what I think of, when I think of you. In the kitchen, with your records, all happy.'

There is a big pause. Pete appears to need a prompt.

'That's what I think of, when I think of you,' I repeat. 'So what about me? What do you see in your head when someone says my name? "Cate." What's in your head? "Cate." "Cate." What do you see? "Cate." "Cate." "Cate." "Cate." What you getting? "Cate."'

There's another pause.

'"Cate",' I say, helpfully. Third pause.

'Your face?' Pete replies, eventually.

'My face?'

I am hugely disappointed.

'My face?' I repeat. 'I see a whole scene with you in – I can even see what record you're holding: it's *The Best of Atlantic Psychedelic Funk*. It's a gatefold – and you've just got … *my face*?'

I am determined to make Pete see that he actually sees more than that. There's no *way* all he sees is my face. We've been together seventeen years. I have blazed a cornucopia of images into his head. I've given him a visual love pantechnicon. The material is endless. Instance: he's seen me dressed as a 'sexy Santa', falling off a castored pouffe. He's got loads in there.

'OK,' I say, patiently. 'Look *down* from my face. What am I wearing?'

I think this is all key questioning. I want to know what, in Pete's mind, is my 'classic era' – my imperial phase. Does he remember me most vividly from the early years of our relationship, when I was a slightly troubled teenager with a winning line in bong-construction – but also the dewy appeal of innocence, and youth? Or does his subconscious prefer me now – a far more rational mother-of-two whose knees are going, and who says 'Oooof!' every time she sits down; but who will also never again wake him up crying because the central heating has come on in the night, and she thinks her legs have melted and got stuck to the radiator?

There is another pause.

'You're wearing your blue and white striped pyjamas,' he says, finally; confidently.

This time, I pause.

'Blue and white striped pyjamas?' I am wounded. 'I've never had blue and white striped pyjamas.'

'You did!' Pete sounds a little panicked. 'Once! Blue and white striped pyjamas.'

'Pete,' I say, quite coldly, 'I am a woman. I know every item of clothing I have ever owned. And I can tell you now – I have never had a pair of blue and white striped pyjamas. Are you sure you're not getting me confused with the boy from *The Snowman*?'

'It's far too late at night for me to deal with you accusing me of imaginary paedophilia with a cartoon,' Pete says, despairingly. 'Again. And anyway – you *did* have blue and white striped pyjamas.'

'I once had blue and white *Paisley* pyjamas,' I say, grudgingly.

'There you go!' he says, triumphantly. 'That's near enough!'

'No!' I say, outraged. 'That's not a *memory*. That's not a *real memory*. You've made those pyjamas up. You've just got this … fantasy version of me in your head, instead.'

'Fantasy version of you! I've hardly gone into my brain, cut out a picture of your face and stuck it onto a picture of … Carol Chell from *Playschool*,' Pete says, agitatedly.

'Carol Chell from *Playschool*?' I ask.

'She's a very pretty and lovely lady,' Pete says, in a firm and non-negotiable manner.

'Carol Chell. Well,' I say, staring up at the ceiling. 'Well. Carol Chell. We've learned a lot tonight, haven't we? We really have learned a lot.'

I let a vexed air fill the room. Let's see if you remember *this*, I think, angrily.

'Talking to you is like being on *The Crystal Maze*,' Pete says, mournfully. 'I have literally no idea what to do. I'm just about to get locked in the Aztec Zone. Richard O'Brien looks really sorry for me.'

The Gay Moon Landings

Last week I was compiling a quick-cut YouTube montage of humanity's greatest moments – what can I say? The kids are seven and nine now; weekend activities have moved on from cupcakes and colouring-in – and came across an awkward fact: there is no Gay Moon Landing.

There are single, iconic images for every other blockbuster moment in humanity's progress. The Civil Rights Movement has Martin Luther King, giving his speech. The Suffragette movement has Emily Wilding Davison, trampled by the king's horse. The triumphs of medical science: the mouse with the ear on its back. And the Space Race has, of course, the Moon Landing – Neil Armstrong making the most expensive footprint in history.

But there is no single, iconic news image for gay rights. There's no five-second clip you can put in that marks a moment where things started getting better for the LGBT guys. The Stonewall Riots in '69 are an obvious turning point, of course – but footage of it needs captions to explain what's going on. Otherwise, it just looks like a lot of late-sixties men of above-average grooming experiencing a very unwelcome fire evacuation from a disco, whilst a load of policemen hit them. Anyone who went clubbing in the rougher parts of the Midlands, or Essex, at the time will have seen scenes almost identical. It's not particularly gay.

Perturbed by this lack of relevant news footage, I went on Twitter and asked what people would regard as a putative 'Gay Moon Landing'. There were dozens and dozens of replies: David Bowie and Mick Ronson's homoerotic sparring on *Top of the Pops,* John Hurt as Quentin Crisp in *The Naked Civil Servant* – dumb with lipstick, blind with mascara and brave as a lion. Seminal teenage fumbling/nascent emancipation in *My Beautiful Laundrette* and *Oranges Are Not the Only Fruit.* Cindy Crawford – straight – acting all geisha, and slathering a beaming kd lang in shaving foam on the cover of *Rolling Stone.*

All of these instances crashed into people's front rooms and started things: conversations; realisations about sexuality; imagining, for the first time, a possible future. In that way – millions of lights, sparking up in millions of minds – they *were* news events; albeit ones that never actually made it onto the news.

Because what was notable was that nearly every single instance of a Gay Moon Landing suggested was from pop, TV, magazines or film. The history of gay rights, and gay progress, has included keynote speeches, legislation, protest and rioting – but the majority of its big, watershed moments have taken place in the art world. It was good to be gay on *Top of the Pops* years before it was good to be gay in Parliament, or gay in church, or gay on the rugby pitch. And it's not just gay progress that happens in this way: *24* had a black President before America did. Jane Eyre was a feminist before Germaine Greer was born. *A Trip to the Moon* put humans on the Moon in 1902.

This is why recent debates about the importance of the arts contain, at core, an unhappy error of judgement. In both the arts cuts – 29 per cent of the Arts Council's funding has now gone – and the presumption that the new, 'slimmed down' National Curriculum will 'squeeze out' art, drama and music, there lies a subconscious belief that the arts are some kind of ... social luxury: the national equivalent of buying some spendy scatter cushions and big candle from John Lewis. Policing and defence, of course, remain very much 'essentials' – the fridge and duvets in our country's putative semi.

But art – painting, poetry, film, TV, music, books, magazines – is a world that runs constant and parallel to ours, where we imagine different futures – millions of them – and try them out for size. Fantasy characters – Beth and Margaret in *Brookside*, say – can kiss, and we, as a nation, can all work out how we feel about it, without having to involve real shy teenage lesbians in awful jumpers, to the benefit of everyone's notion of civility.

Two of the Gay Moon Landings Twitter suggested were C4's *Queer as Folk* from 1999, and Captain Jack kissing the Doctor in *Doctor Who* in 2008 – both, coincidentally, written by Russell T Davies. *Queer as Folk* was cited as a Gay Moon Landing because, when it aired, it was the first ever gay drama, and caused absolute, gleeful outrage. Conversely, the

Doctor Who gay kiss was a Gay Moon Landing because it caused absolutely no outrage at all. The two were separated by just nine years. I would definitely call that another big step for mankind.

But then perhaps I'm barking up the wrong tree here. Maybe I don't need to look for a Gay Moon Landing, after all. As someone on Twitter pointed out, 'The Moon Landing itself is pretty gay. A close-knit group of guys land in a silver rocket, make a really dramatic speech, and then spend half an hour jumping up and down? Please.'

Let's put the Gay Moon Landings piece next to my piece on transsexuals
– making a little LGBT ghetto within the book. These pages will have mark-
edly better delis and bars than the delis and bars in the rest of the book, and
feature a mini-cab company run by a drag queen whose Grease *tribute act*
goes under the name 'Sandra Wee'. You can find me on these pages most
Friday nights – wearing only one shoe and singing 'Womanizer' by Britney
Spears with a male nurse wearing a sombrero, and waving poppers.

We Only Had Two Transsexuals in Wolverhampton

In Wolverhampton in 1991, we had two male-to-female transsexuals, who would unfailingly be in the chip shop at the end of Victoria Street at 2am, sobering up on curry sauce and chips after a night out clubbing.

As I went past them on the 512 bus, I would feel a kinship with them – a kinship that I would try to project through the glass.

'I feel as if I were born in the wrong body, too!' I would think, loudly, at them. 'You were trapped, unhappily, in the bodies of men. I too am unhappily trapped – in the body of a fat virgin with a bad fringe. I wish *I* could have an operation to sort things out, like you guys – I mean ladies.'

I was reminded of what a div I was this September, when a ten-year-old boy returned to school after the summer holidays as a girl. As the media coverage made clear, some parents at the school claimed to be 'outraged'.

'We should have been consulted,' one said – presumably imagining a scenario where parents regularly throw open the raising of their children to a school-wide committee of other parents; possibly via a Facebook page called 'Penis Or Vagina: YOU Choose Which One You Think Suits My Weeping Child Best'.

Then, last week, the Department of Education announced that it was considering schoolchildren should be taught about transgender equality – which was greeted, again, with a predictable series of complaints.

Margaret Morrissey, founder of campaigning group Parents Outloud, said: 'We are overloading our children with issues they shouldn't have to consider.'

This is an interesting stance to take on an issue – mainly because of its unappealing and extreme impoliteness. We have to remember that the descriptor 'our children' includes both transgender kids (0.1 per cent of the population), and kids who live in a world with transgender kids (the other 99.9 per cent – thus making 100 per cent of all the world's children).

With those kind of stats, it seems to be a good idea to enable children in learning about it nice and early on – before they start getting the kind of weird ideas adults have. We constantly underestimate children in these situations. I recall, when I was a teenager, the suggestion of 'lessons' in homosexuality being decried for similar reasons of 'complexity'. A generation later, and I watch kids in the playground, arguing over who should play the bisexual Captain Jack Harkness from *Doctor Who* – who fancied both Rose *and* the Doctor. Not only do they seem to have got their heads around it quite easily – but they're incorporating it into games involving time travel, wormholes and paradox, too.

And, anyway, as a general rule of thumb, I don't think we need worry much about overloading kids with interesting philosophical subjects which help them develop both understanding, and tolerance of, other human beings. That's like worrying that The Beatles might have made *Sgt Pepper* 'too good'. That's what's supposed to happen. Carry on! Everything's fine!

One of humanity's less loveable tropes is an ability to get hurt, self-righteous and huffy about someone else's problem. It's amazing that 'normal' people would turn on some transgender kid and go, 'But what about meeeeee? What about myyyyyyy kids?' It's a bit like those dads in the labour wards who complain of being knackered.

And as a strident feminist, I'm always saddened by other feminists who rail against male-to-female transgenders – claiming you can only be born a woman, and not 'become' one.

Holy moly, ladies – what exactly do you think is going wrong here? Having your male genitals remodelled as female, then committing to a lifetime of hormone therapy, sounds like a bit more of a commitment to being a woman than just accidentally being born one. And, besides, it's an incredibly inhospitable stance to take. Personally, anyone who wants to join the Lady Party is welcome as far as I'm concerned. The more the merrier! Anyone who's been rejected by The Man is a friend of mine!

Anyway. Since I was a badly fringed sixteen-year-old on the bus, I've found out that the word isn't 'normal' – it's 'cis'. In Latin, the opposite of 'trans' is 'cis' – and so most of humanity is 'cisgender'. This opens language up to a subsequent possibility: finally finding the 'otherness' in transgender fascinating, and useful. We'll hurl satellites out into space in order to find new and enthralling wonders – but we could simply turn to someone next to us, and ask a question about their life, instead. We endlessly debate what it is to be a man, or what it is to be a woman – when there are people who walk the Earth who've been both. If transgender people didn't exist, we'd probably be spending billions of pounds trying to invent them. Instead, we won't even tell kids they exist.

One of the more inspiring stories ever told in a BBC drama – the true story of Miss Anne Lister, noted nineteenth-century businesswoman and lesbian. Me and my brother started watching it together for wildly differing reasons, but I like to think that the narrative won him over in the end. Or the tits. Either/or.

You've Got to Love a Nineteenth-century Lesbian

'The thing about lesbians,' my brother Eddie says, eating his pizza over the opening credits to *The Secret Diaries of Miss Anne Lister*, 'is that pornography has totally sorted it out for them. Previously, men may have been homophobic, and been all like, "Lesbians – no! Stop being a lesbian! Put that other lesbian down!" But now pornography has shown us all the good stuff they're up to, we're like, "Go ahead, ladies. Be a lesbian. That is perfectly fine with me."'

Although there's obviously a long, stern lecture to be given about the history of lesbian emancipation – starting with 'inverts', Gertrude Stein and the Ladies of Llangollen, and ending with the Stonewall riots – in the most reductionist and populist manner possible, Eddie is kind of right.

After all, *The Secret Diaries of Miss Anne Lister* is based on, yeah, the secret diaries of Yorkshirewoman Anne Lister – written in the nineteenth century, at a time when public opinion was split between not having a clue what lesbianism was ('Is it the latest invention of Mr Kingdom Brunel? Is it a rival to the daguerreotype, or the moustache holder? Will it transport us to Cornwall?'), and total revulsion. In the streets of Halifax, Lister's nickname of 'Gentleman Jack' is enough to have her pushed, jeered at and threatened. Polite society hustles its young women away from her, lest they accidentally go gay, and ruin everyone's carefully laid patriarchal plans for inheritance and succession.

But here in the twenty-first century, a TV adaptation of her story advents in a flurry of prurient interest: the advance frisson has it as Jane Austen with muff diving; *Wuthering Heights* with, instead of Heathcliff, Miss Cliff. Whilst there's still a million miles to go in terms of full social equality and acceptance, at least lesbians in corsets are *hot* now. 'Hot' is an important stepping stone on the path to liberation.

Anne Lister certainly thought so, anyway: her diary recorded every seduction, orgasm and moment of self-discovery, in a self-devised code rigged up from algebra and ancient Greek. And there was a lot to record, because she was, essentially, a total filth-bag: charming the birds – 'Your hair is so becoming, done in this way!' – one by one into her feather-filled tester-bed; stirring the local dizzy blonde into a swoon of unrequited love, simply by dispensing a gracious bow outside the church.

'My manners are ... not at all masculine, but, rather, softly gentleman-like,' she noted. 'I know how to please this maiden of mine.'

And so, periodically, as the source and, indeed, sauce material demanded, *The Secret Diaries* would erupt in shivering, illicit woodland kissing; or two sets of petticoats churning by candlelight. Necks, finger-tips, hair brushed out like gold – you know the drill.

But in the main, *The Secret Diaries of Miss Anne Lister* was notable for just how brilliantly right-on and rad it was, in a world otherwise filled with predictable, patriarchal soft-porn toss. For starters, it was an almost entirely female cast. Yeah, there was a kindly, loaded uncle, and a sexist baddie who obviously spent his evenings staring into the fire, sighing, 'I wish they'd hurry up and invent *Top Gear*, Norris. I miss The Stig,' to his butler – but that was about it.

For everyone else was female, in their thirties or forties or fifties, without a scrap of make-up, clothed from neck to ground, and often having conversations about coal mining, or the importance of studying Latin.

And, in the middle of it all, was the amazing Miss Lister –300 years ahead of her time, a little outpost of early rock'n'roll amongst the calico, carpets and coal of Halifax. As Lister, Maxine Peake jumped right in, buttoned ankle boots first, and immersed right up to Lister's rakish, black riding hat – which often, as she paced around, gave her the air of Slash from Guns N' Roses about to play 'Paradise City' on a lute.

So here's Miss Lister striding across the moors, equipped with a small, gold pocket telescope – for perving tha honeyz as they picnic on a hillside. Bonnets at twelve o'clock, and she's in like Flynn – wooing any blushing, fresh-faced chick, and bantering with her buddy, Tibb: a fabulous, guy-ish, lush-lipped invert, who 'struts', and drinks 'hard liquor', and sees hours of languorous, Sapphic sex as no more or less consequential than a game of croquet.

In the end, Lister triumphs. She might have had a decade-long runaround from the capricious Marianna – 'ONLY IN BED were you excellent!' – but she ends up 'marrying' a rich heiress, sinking her own coal mines, climbing mountains across Europe, and generally being well regarded within society. She has essentially devised how to be a lesbian, with little more by way of resources than the works of Byron, immense intelligence and a ferocious horn-on. Throughout, Peake depicts her as what she was – in her own way, as much of an explorer as Livingstone, as much of a revolutionary as Guevara.

'I love and only love the fairer sex – and, thus beloved by them in turn, my heart revolts from any love but theirs,' she wrote, alone, but still sure enough to tell the truth: sending a message in a bottle into the twenty-first century.

Is it time for my Lady Gaga interview? Let's do my Lady Gaga interview –
given that this is the gay ghetto of the book, and Gaga is the most gay-friendly
pop star ever.

Interviewing Gaga was one of the more extraordinary moments of my
life – not just the night out with her itself, which is all in the feature, but the
reaction to it afterwards as well. I posted it on Twitter on the day of publica-
tion with the message, 'I'm not being funny, but you really won't ever read
a better interview with Lady Gaga than mine.' This is mainly because I was
drunk when I tweeted it – but also because it's got the lupus exclusive, and
a sex club, and her having a wee, and an empowering talk about feminism,
and us getting hammered, and me exclusively finding out she didn't have a
penis, and me ruining a couture cloak. Everything you want, really.

In the three days following my tweet, and the link to the piece, it got
re-tweeted over 20,000 times. It went around the world. I lost count of the
people who read it and told me they liked it – mainly because I have very poor
both long- and short-term memory. My favourite person who told me they
liked it was some orange, handsome dude I met at the Glamour Awards in
2010. We were in the smoking area having a puff and, when I told him my
name, he went 'Oh, you! You went to the sex club with Gaga!' and we had a
lovely chat. Throughout our conversation I was aware of an odd atmosphere
around us – a semi-circle of women had gathered, and were watching us
with expressions of what can only be described as 'hunger'.

When we finally finished our fags and bid each other adieu, the moment Mr
Orangeio walked away, a woman, who looked on the verge of fainting, went,
'What's he LIKE? I CAN'T BELIEVE YOU WERE TALKING TO HIM!'

Turned out he was some bloke from Sex and the City *who all the birds*
fancy. I didn't have a danny. I hate that show like bum-plague. I thought he

was the PR for Vaseline Intensive Care, who were sponsoring the awards. No wonder he looked confused when I asked him if he took his work home with him, and used it to keep his elbows moist.

Mind you, that was the same party where I talked to an old dear in a tiara for ten minutes, thinking it was the editor of Glamour*'s mum – and it turned out to be Home Secretary Theresa May. I'm not so good with the faces.*

Come Party with Gaga

There's nothing quite like watching a plane take off without you to really focus your mind on how much you want to be on it. As flight BA987 knifes off the runway, and begins its journey to Berlin, I'm watching it through a window in the Departures Lounge – still holding the ticket for seat 12A in my hand.

Due to a frankly unlikely series of events, I got to Heathrow three minutes after the flight was closed. Although no missed flight ever comes as a joy, this one is a particular mellow-harsher because, in five hours, I'm supposed to be interviewing arguably the most famous woman in the world – Lady Gaga – in an exclusive that has taken months of phone calls, jockeying and wrangling to set up.

It's not so much that I am now almost certainly going to be fired. Since I found out how much the model Sophie Anderton earned as a high-class call-girl, my commitment to continuing as a writer at *The Times* has been touch and go anyway, to be honest.

It's more that I am genuinely devastated to have blown it so spectacularly. Since I saw Gaga play 'Poker Face' at Glastonbury Festival last year, I have been a properly, hawkishly devoted admirer.

Halfway through a forty-five-minute set that had five costume changes, Gaga came on stage in a dress made entirely of see-thru plastic bubbles, accompanied by her matching, see-through plastic bubble piano. You have to respect a woman who can match her outfit to her instrument. Although the single 'Poker Face' is a punching, spasmodic,

Euro-house stormer, Gaga took to her piano and started to play it as cat-house blues – all inverted chords and rolling fifths, with falling, heartbroken semitones on the left hand; wailing out like Bessie Smith sitting on the doorstep at 4am.

It was already incredible *before* she did the second half of the song standing on her piano stool, on one leg – like a tiny, transvestite ballerina.

Twenty minutes later, she ended her set literally bending over backwards to please – fireworks shooting from the nipples of her pointy bra, screaming, 'I fancy you, Glastonbury – do you fancy me?' The audience went wholly, totally, dementedly nuts for her.

It caused me to have this – unprecedented – thought: 'She's making Madonna look a bit slack and unimaginative here. After all, when Madonna was twenty-three, she was still working at Dunkin' Donuts in New York. She weren't playing no rolling fifths.'

Since then, I have followed her career like boys follow sports teams. As a cultural icon, she does an incredible service for woman: after all, it will be hard to oppress a generation who've been brought up on pop stars with fire coming out of their tits.

She's clearly smart and clearly hilarious – she pitched up at the Royal Variety Performance on a 16ft-high piano, modelled on Dali's spider-legged elephants – but has never ruined the fun by going, 'Actually, I'm smart and hilarious,' like, say, Bono would.

And, most importantly of all, she clearly couldn't give a f*** what anyone says about her. When she appeared on *The X Factor*, it was the week after Simon Cowell had said that he was 'looking for the new Lady Gaga'. She performed 'Bad Romance' in an 18ft-long bathtub with six dancers – then played a piano solo on a keyboard hidden in a pretend sink, whilst sitting on a pretend toilet. Clearly, Simon Cowell would never sign up anything like that in a million, billion years. It was very much in his face.

So yes. I am a Gaga supporter. I'm Team Gaga. She's my girl. My pop Arsenal; my dance Red Sox; my fashion England.

*

At Heathrow, as I go through the rigmarole of booking the next available flight – which will get me to Berlin two hours after my appointed slot – I know what awaits me at the other end. Angry Americans. Very angry Americans from her management team.

Because in the year since Glastonbury, Gaga has taken on a semi-mythic air, like Prince, or Madonna. Since she sold fifteen million albums and forty million singles, and become a tabloid staple, she now rarely does interviews. The last one she did in the UK – with *Q Magazine* – ended with her leaving halfway through, in tears. Pap pictures of her looking spindly – covered in scratches and bruises – have carried with them the inference of those most female of traits under stress: eating disorders, self-harm. There have been collapses: last-minute cancellation of concerts in Indiana, West Lafayette and Connecticut after irregular heartbeat and exhaustion; near-collapse onstage in Auckland.

When you've just been named one of *Time* magazine's '100 Most Influential People in the World', this is, traditionally, where you are expected to start going a bit … Jackson.

It's incredible I was ever granted access at all – and now I've, unbelievably, stood her up.

I will be genuinely, tearfully grateful if I get even a ten-minute Q&A from a piqued megastar pulling a gigantic huff, and answering all my questions with monosyllabic 'yes/no' binary tetchiness.

This is the worst day of my life that hasn't involved an episiotomy.

'Hi!'

Gaga's dressing room, backstage at the O2 World Arena in Berlin. With the walls and ceiling draped in black, it resembles a pop-gothic seraglio. But whilst scented candles burn churchishly, a gorgeous vintage record player on the floor – surrounded by piles of vinyl – and works of art hung on the wall give it a cheerful air. There is a table, laid with beautiful china. There are flowers, growing in the dark. And at the head of the tea-table, amongst the flowers: Gaga.

Two things strike you about her immediately. Firstly, that she *really* isn't dressed casually. In a breast-length, silver-grey wig, she has a black lace veil wound around her face, and sits, framed, in an immense, custom-made, one-off Alexander McQueen cloak. The effect is having been ushered into the presence of a very powerful fairytale queen: possibly one who has recently killed Aslan, on the Stone Table.

The second thing you notice is that she is being lovely. Absolutely lovely. Both literally and figuratively, what's under the veil and the cloak is a diminutive, well-brought-up, New York Catholic girl from a wealthy middle-class family, with twinkly brown eyes, and a minxy sense of humour.

'So glad you finally made it!' she says, giving a huge, warm hug. 'What a terrible day you're having! Thank you so much for coming!'

Holding her for a moment, she feels – through the taffeta atmosphere of billowing McQueen – borderline Kylie-tiny, but warm, and robust. Like a slender, teenage cheerleader. This is some surprise, give the afore-mentioned presumption that she's cracking up.

So when Gaga says, with warm good manners, 'This tea is for you,' gesturing to a bone china cup hand-painted with violets, I can't help myself from replying, uncouthly: 'I know you're tiny and must get knack-ered – but why do you keep collapsing?'

'My schedule is such that I don't get very much time to eat,' Gaga says, holding her tea cup daintily. I don't think the tea cup is her infa-mous 'pet tea cup' that she took everywhere with her earlier in the year – including nightclubs. Perhaps it's too famous to be merely drunk from now. Maybe it has its own dressing room.

'But I certainly don't have an eating problem,' she continues. 'A little MDMA once in a while never killed anybody, but I really don't do drugs. I don't touch cocaine any more. I don't smoke. Well, maybe a single ciga-rette – with whisky – while I'm working, because it just frees my mind a little bit. But I care about my voice. The thrill of my voice being healthy on stage is really special. I take care of myself.'

Later on in the interview, Gaga takes off the McQueen cloak – perhaps pointedly, for the nosey journalist – and reveals that, underneath, she's only wearing fishnets, knickers and a bra. As someone who is practically seeing her naked, from two feet away, her body seems non-scarred, healthy: sturdy. She is wiry, but not remotely bony. It's a dancer's body – not a victim's.

I hand Gaga a page torn from that day's paper, which I read on the plane. It's a story about her performance at the Met Ball in New York – one of the big events of the global celebrity calendar. In the report, it is claimed that Gaga 'angered' organisers by 'refusing' to walk the red carpet, and then suffered an attack of stage fright so severe she locked herself in her dressing room, and had to be 'persuaded out' by 'her close friend Oprah Winfrey. It's merely the latest of the 'Gaga cracking up' stories in the press.

'Is this true?' I ask her.

She reads through the story – frowning slightly at first, eyes wide open by the end.

'I wasn't *nervous*!' she says, witheringly. 'To be honest with you? I don't give a fuck about red carpets, and I never do them. I don't like them. First of all – how could any of these outfits possibly look good with an ugly red carpet under them?'

For a moment, I recall some of Gaga's more incredible rig-outs: the silver lobster fascinator. The red PVC Elizabethan farthingale. The tunic made of Kermit heads. The red lace outfit that covered her entire face, peaking in a 2ft-high crown. She has a point.

'It's just visually horrid,' Gaga continues, in a merrily outraged way. Her manner is of your mate in the pub, slagging off the neon tabard she's been forced to wear working at Boots. 'Hollywood is not what it used to be. I don't want to be perceived as … one of the other bitches in a gown. I wasn't *nervous*,' says the woman who appeared in her 'Telephone' video dressed in nothing more than 'POLICE: INCIDENT' tape, strategically placed across her nipples and crotch. 'Don't be SILLY!'

But still these rumours persist – of collapses, and neuroses. You are, after all, a twenty-three-year-old woman coping with enormous fame, and media pressure, on your own. You are currently the one, crucial, irreplaceable element of a 161-date world tour. How do you keep depressive, or panicked, thoughts at bay?

'Prescription medicine,' she says, cheerfully. 'I can't control my thoughts at all. I'm tortured. But I like that,' she laughs. 'Lorca says it's good to be tortured. The thoughts are unstoppable – but so is the music.

It comes to me constantly. That's why I got this tattoo,' she says, proffering a white arm through the black cloak-folds.

It is a quote from the poet and art critic Rainer Maria Rilke: 'In the deepest hour of the night, confess to yourself that you would die if you were forbidden to write. And look deep into your heart where it spreads its roots, the answer, and ask yourself: "Must I write?"'

'I think tattoos have power. I did it as a way to kind of … inject myself with a steadfastness about music. People say I should take a break, but I'm like, "Why should I take a break? What do you want me to do – go on vacation?"'

On stage, later that night – dripping in sweat, just after playing a version of 'Bad Romance' where the chorus sounds even more tearfully euphoric and amazing than usual – Gaga shouts to the crowd, 'I'd rather not die on a vacation, under a palm tree. I'd rather die on stage, with all my props, in front of my fans.'

Given that one of her props is a 6ft-high hybrid of a cello, keyboard and drum machine, with a golden skull nailed to the side of it – something that makes the 'keytar' look like a mere castanet – you can see her point.

But it has to be said, for a twenty-three-year-old, death is a recurrent theme in her performances. The thematic arc for the Fame Monster tour was 'The Apocalypse'. In the current Monster Ball tour, Gaga is eventually eaten by a gigantic angler fish – a creature she was terrified of as a child – only to be reborn as an angel. Her MTV Awards performance of 'Paparazzi', back in September, had her being crushed by a falling chandelier – amazing – before bleeding to death whilst singing.

'What's the nearest you've ever come to death?' I ask her. 'Do you have any recurring illnesses?'

She goes oddly still for a moment, and then says, 'I have heart palpitations, and … things.'

'Recently?'

'Yes, but it's OK. It's just from fatigue and … other things,' she shrugs, before saying, very carefully, 'I'm very connected to my aunt, Joanne, who died of lupus. It's a very personal thing. I don't want … my fans to be worried about me.'

Her eyes are very wide.

'Lupus. That's genetic, isn't it?' I ask.

'Yes.'

'And have you been tested?'

Again, the eyes are very wide and steady. 'Yes.' Pause. 'But I don't want anyone to be worried.'

'When was the last time you called the emergency services?' I ask.

'The other day,' Gaga says, still talking very carefully. 'In Tokyo. I was having trouble breathing. I had a little oxygen, then I went on stage. I was OK. But like I say – I don't want anyone to worry.'

It's a very odd moment. Gaga is staring at me calmly, but intently. Lupus is a connective tissue disease, where the immune system attacks the body. It can be fatal – although, as medicine advances, fatalities are becoming rarer. What it more commonly does is cause heart palpitations, shortness of breath, joint pain and anaemia, before spasmodically but recurrently driving a truck through your energy levels, so that you are often too fatigued to accomplish even the simplest of tasks.

Suddenly, all the 'Gaga cracking up' stories revolve round 180 degrees, and turn into something completely different. After all, the woman before me seems about as far removed from someone on the verge of a fame-induced nervous breakdown as possible to imagine. She's being warm, candid, smart, amusing and supremely confident in her talent. She's basically like some hot, giggly pop-nerd.

But if she were regularly running into physical difficulties because she had lupus – being delayed on stage, cancelling gigs, having to call the emergency services –- you can see how a world press, desperate for stories about her, ignorant of any other possibility, would add these things up into a wholly different picture.

Gaga is certainly very affected by her aunt's death: the date of her death, in 1976, is interwoven into her Rilke tattoo on her arm. When I ask her if she ever 'dresses down', she says the only thing remotely 'dress down-y' she has is a pair of pink, cotton shorts – embroidered with flowers – that once belonged to her aunt.

'They're nearly forty years old,' she says. 'But I wear them when I want her to … protect me.'

The story that I thought I would find when I met Gaga – dark, other-worldly, borderline autistic diva-genius failing under the pressure of fame – just dissolves, like newsprint in the rain.

All that's left is a mardy pop sex threat – the woman who put out three, Abba-level classic singles in one year, at the age of twenty-three, whilst wearing a lobster on her head. As I'm sure Mark Lawson says at times like this, Booyakasha.

'What's the best thing you've spent your money on so far?' I ask, in a far more cheerful mood.

'I bought my parents a car,' Gaga replies. She has often spoken of how close she is to her parents – particularly her father, who she appears to borderline worship. Presumably, she sees herself in him – a self-made man, he started as a rock'n'roll bar musician, before making his fortune as an internet entrepreneur. By the time Gaga was thirteen, the family were rich enough to send her to the same school as heiress Paris Hilton.

Gaga is not faking her current outsiderness – even then, when she was still just 'Stefani Germanotta', she was the goth girl with dyed black hair, obsessed with Judy Garland, Led Zeppelin and David Bowie, and wearing her skirts really high.

'It's a Rolls-Royce,' she continues, sipping on her tea, daintily. She has lifted the veil now: she looks as casual as it is possible to in a wig and couture. 'It's black. My dad's very Italian, so I wanted to get him a real *Godfather* car. I had it delivered on their anniversary.'

When Gaga rang her father, and told him to 'Go outside!', he refused.

'He thought I'd got him a dancing gorillagram,' she giggled.

The car had a huge bow on it, and the message 'A car to last like a love like yours'. At first, Gaga's parents just thought they had it for the day, to drive round in. When she told them it was theirs to keep, her father shouted 'You're crazy!' and burst into tears.

'You see, I don't really spend money, and I don't really like fame,' Gaga says. 'I spend my money on my shows – but I don't like buying *things*. I don't buy diamonds, because I don't know where they came from. I'll spend it on fashion.' She hugs the McQueen cloak close.

'I miss Lee every time I get dressed,' she says, sadly. 'But you know what I spend most of my money on? Disappearing. I hate the paparazzi. Because the truth is – no matter what people tell you – you can control it. If you put as much money into your security as you put into your cars or your diamonds or your jewellery, you can just … disappear. People who say they can't get away are lying. They must just like the … big flashes.'

The conversation turns to the music industry. Gaga has an endearingly schoolmarmish belief that most acts are 'lazy'.

'I hate big acts that just throw an album out against the wall, like "BUY IT! FUCK YOU!" It's mean to fans. You should go out and tour it to your fans in India, Japan, the UK. I don't believe in how the music industry is today. I believe in how it was in 1982.'

She explains she doesn't mind about people downloading her music for free, 'because you know how much you can earn off touring, right? Big artists can make anywhere from $40m for one cycle of two years touring. Giant artists make upwards of $100m. Make music – then tour. It's just the way it is today.'

Whilst on this huge, technically complex, sell-out world tour, Gaga has written and recorded the majority of her next album: 'I don't understand bands who say they'll tour for one year – then record the next!' she exclaims at one point, going Thatcher again. 'I make music every DAY!'

Although she 'can't talk about it yet', she is clearly excited about the next album. She keeps trying to tell me things about it, then claps her hands over her mouth, going, 'I can't!'

'But everyone's going to fucking know about it when it comes out,' she says, excitedly. 'You know when people say, "If you could say one sentence about who you are, what your life is?" It's that. *For the whole album*. Because I recently had this … miracle-like experience, where I feel much more connected to God.'

You were raised a Catholic – so when you say 'God', do you mean the Catholic God, or a more spiritual sense of God?

'More spiritual,' Gaga says, looking like she's biting her tongue. 'I don't want to say much, because I want it to stay hidden until it comes out – but I will say that religion is very confusing for everyone, and particularly me, because there's really no religion that doesn't hate or condemn a certain kind of people, and I totally believe in all love and forgiveness, and excluding no one.'

'Would you play for the Pope, if he asked you?'

'Yeah,' Gaga says. There's a pause. Perhaps she considers her current stage show, and the section where her male dancers grab their gigantic, fake white penises, and bounce them off their palms to 'Boys Boys Boys'.

'Well. I'd do an acoustic show for the Pope,' she amends.

Astonishingly, given how late I was, Gaga has given me a full hour of interview time. I later find out that she turned down doing a video acceptance speech for the World Music Awards in order to fit me in. I feel I've done amazingly well, considering how badly the day started. Then Gaga puts her cup down, and turns to me.

'You should come out with us tonight,' she says, warmly. 'Actually, I've never had a journalist come out with me, so you'd be the first. It's going to be fun. It's like an old sex club, in Berlin. Come party with Gaga!'

It is midnight. Gaga came off stage half an hour ago. Dressed, once again, in knickers, bra, fishnets and her black taffeta McQueen, she has been standing in freezing, driving rain outside the O2 World Arena, signing autographs for fans.

Her fans are infamously, incredibly devoted – as she is to them. She calls them her 'Little Monsters'. They draw pictures of her, get tattoos like hers, weep when she touches them. Her den-mother championing of 'all the freaks' – fat girls, gay boys, lesbian girls, goths, nerds. Everyone who gets picked on at school – allied to her global pop juggernaut, makes her relationship with her fans intense. When you watch her with them, you see that culturally, what she's doing is … providing a space for them. Giving them somewhere to meet.

Then, her security guy gives the signal, and we are all bundled into people carriers with blacked-out windows, and whizzed across Berlin.

Paps in cars try to follow us, but it seems what Gaga said earlier was true: if you spend enough money on security, they can't follow you. She simply has two burly men stand in front of their cars, impeding them, until we have vanished.

'It's, like, a sex party,' Gaga explains. 'You know – like in *Eyes Wide Shut*? All I can say is, I am not responsible for what happens next. And wear a condom.'

As we take the alleyway to the sex club, security men appear and close off the alleyway with giant, blacked-out gates.

The club – The Laboratory – is an industrial, maze-like building. To get to the dancefloor, you have to pass a series of tiny, cell-like booths, decked out with a selection of beds, bath-tubs, hoists and chains.

'For fucking,' a German member of our entourage explains – both helpfully, and somewhat unnecessarily.

Despite the undoubted and extreme novelty of such a venue, Adrian – Gaga's British press officer – and I give away our nationalities instantly when we comment, excitedly, 'Oh my God! You can SMOKE in here!' It seems a far more thrilling prospect than … some bumming.

It's a small entourage – Gaga, me, Adrian, her make-up artist, her security guy, and maybe two others. We walk onto the small dancefloor, in a club filled with drag queens, lesbians dressed as sailors, boys in tight T-shirts, girls in black leather. The music is pounding. There is a gigantic harness hanging over the bar.

'For fucking,' the same German says again, helpfully.

Gaga is heading up our group. Even, like, Keane would slope off to a VIP booth at this point, and wait for people to bring them drinks.

Instead – cloak billowing, and very much looking like one of the Skeksis in *The Dark Crystal* – Gaga marches up to the bar, leans on it in a practised bar-fly manner. With a bellowed, 'What does everyone want to drink?', she gets the round in.

It reminds me of what was possibly the best moment of this year in Gaga world: the tabloids running a shot of Gaga – dressed only in fish-nets, a bra and leather cap – sitting in a pub in Blackpool, with a pint of Stella and a plate of chips.

'I really love a dingy, pissy bar,' Gaga says. 'I'm really old-school that way.'

We go into an alcove with a wipe-clean banquette – 'For the fucking!' the German says, again – and set up camp. Gaga takes off her McQueen cloak, and chucks into a corner. She's now just in bra, fishnets and knick-ers, with sequins around her eyes.

'Do you know what that girl at the bar said to me?' she says, sipping her Scotch, and taking a single drag of a fag before handing it back. 'She said, "You're a feminist. People think it means 'man-hating', but it doesn't." Isn't that funny?'

Earlier in the day, conversation had turned to whether Gaga would describe herself as feminist or not. As the very best conversations about feminism often will, it had segued from robust declarations of emancipa-tion and sisterhood ('I am a feminist because I believe in women's rights, and protecting who we are, down to the core') to musing on who she fancied ('In the video to "Telephone", the girl I kiss, Heather, lives as a man. And as someone who does like women, something about a more masculine woman makes me feel more … feminine. When we kissed, I got that fuzzy butterfly feeling').

We had concluded that it was odd most women 'shy away' from declar-ing themselves feminists, because 'it really doesn't mean "man-hating"'.

'And now she's just said the same thing to me! AND she's hot!' Gaga beams. She points to the girl – who looks like an androgynous, cupid-mouthed, Jean Paul Gaultier cabin-boy. 'Gorgeous,' Gaga sighs.

This is Gaga off-duty. Although the booth becomes by way of a shrine to her – between now and 4am, fully two-thirds of the club come over to pay obeisance to her: drag queens and tom-girls and superfreaks, all acknowledging the current definitive pop-cultural salon keeper – Gaga alternates being wholly gracious and welcoming to them, and getting absolutely off her cake. With the thrill of like recognising like, I realise she's a total lightweight – giggly after two Scotches, dancing in the booth after three, and wholly on the prowl after four.

'Are you straight?' she asks some hot, American boy we've been talk-ing to at one point, in the manner of someone who needs to make plans for the rest of the evening based on the reply. When he says, regretfully, 'No,' her attention seems to, amusingly, wander.

But that's just for sex. Gaga's devotion to, and promotion of, every aspect of gay culture is legendary. Bisexual herself, whilst her musical education might once have been classical, her cultural education was homosexual, and comes to a head in the video to her forthcoming single, 'Alejandro'.

Sprawled across the banquette, in a mood of eager excitement, Gaga shows me stills from the video shoot on her BlackBerry. She's dressed up as Joan of Arc, with a ferocious Purdey haircut. To be honest I can't see much more than that, because she's a bit pissed, and her thumbs keep getting in the way.

The video is about the 'purity of my friendships with my gay friends', Gaga explained, earlier. 'And how I've been unable to find that with a straight man in my life. It's a celebration and an admiration of gay love – it confesses my envy of the courage and bravery they require to be together. In the video I'm pining for the love of my gay friends – but they just don't want me.'

We look at the photo on her BlackBerry again.

'I'm not sure about my hair,' Gaga says, suddenly, staring at the BlackBerry.

3am. I am pretty wasted. I am kneeling on the banquette, with Gaga lying by my knees. I have just come up with the theory that, if you have one of your heroes lying tipsily next to you, you should tell them all the pretentious pop culture theories you have come up with about them. So I slurringly tell her that the difference between her and, say, Madonna, is that you don't penetrate Gaga. Her songs and videos are – whilst sexual – about dysfunction and neuroses and alienation and self-discovery. They're not, in any sense, a come-on. Despite having worn very little clothing for most of her career, Gaga is not a prick-tease.

'Yeah! It's not what straight men masturbate over when they're at home watching pornography,' she confirms. 'It's not for them. It's for … us.' And she gestures around the club.

Earlier in the day, she had said – somewhat unexpectedly – 'I still feel very much like an outsider. And I have zero concept of how I'm assessed in the world.' As one of the most discussed women in the world, this is a surprise. Does she really not read her press? Perhaps this is how she's stayed so ... normal. Ordering drinks, chatting to everyone. She's the least pretentious multi-million-selling artist I've ever met.

A minute later, Gaga springs up, and beckons for me to follow her. Weaving her way down a series of corridors, we eventually end in – the VIP toilet.

'You're wearing a jumpsuit,' Gaga says, with feminine solidarity. 'You can't get out of one of those in the normal toilets.'

As I start to arduously unzip, Gaga sits on the toilet with a cheerful, 'I'm just going to pee through my fishnets!', and offloads some of those whiskies.

For the first year of her career, massive internet rumours claimed that Gaga was, in fact a man – a rumour so strong that Oprah had to question her about it when Gaga appeared on her show.

Perhaps uniquely amongst all the journalists in the world, I can now factually confirm that Lady Gaga does not have a penis. That rumour can, conclusively, die.

4am. Time for bed. We pull up outside the Ritz-Carlton, in a people carrier with blacked-out windows. Gaga opens the door, and totters out, looking – despite the McQueen cloak – like any tipsy twenty-three-year-old girl on a night out in Newcastle, on a Saturday night. Her grey wig looks dishevelled. Her face sequins are wonky. Her eyes are pointing in slightly different directions – although, to be fair, I can only focus on her myself if I close one eye, and rest my head against the window. Tonight, she played to 40,000 fans. Tomorrow, it's Sting's Rainforest Benefit, where she takes her place among the pantheon: Debbie Harry, Bruce Springsteen, Elton John.

She leans against the car for a moment, issues a small hiccup, and then turns, dramatically.

'I. Am. KNACKERED!' she roars. She then walks, slightly unsteadily, up the steps of the Ritz-Carlton hotel. A total, total dude.

Gaga is, of course, the perfect bridging subject between 'ranting about gays',
and 'ranting about feminism'. And so we move on, to the vexed subject of
wondering where all the clothes went on MTV.

MTV Hoes

'I wish,' my friend Jenny tweeted last week, 'there was an MTV Normal.
For people who love pop – but don't want to watch a load of girls dressed
as hoes.'

I knew exactly what she meant. Twenty-first-century pop music
presents one of the biggest vexes for the modern feminist – and by 'feminist' I mean 'all women', really; unless you have recently and decisively
campaigned to have your voting rights removed.

When I was a teenager, all my pop heroes were Britpop, and grunge
– unisex jeans and sneakers for all. I was raised with the expectation that,
if I wanted to, I could sell twenty million albums with my upper arms
covered at all times.

My daughters, on the other hand, are being raised in the Era of the
Pop Ho. This is a time where the lower slopes of Britney Spears' leotard-
clad pubis mons are more recognisable than – although oddly redolent
of – David Cameron's face, and pop videos for female artists have become
so predictable, I can run you through what will happen in 90 per cent of
them, right here:

1) 'Just checkin' my legs are still there.' Self-groping which begins
with a lascivious sweep across the collar-bone, develops into decisive

breast-rubbing, and then ends with some pretty full-on caressing of your own buttocks, belly and thighs. The ubiquity of this dance-move is baffling: however much healthy, positive self-love a woman has, she's still not going to be this mesmerised and excited by having an arse by the age of twenty-three. She knows it's there. She doesn't have to keep checking. By and large, women generally can keep their hands off themselves for the three minutes it takes to make a pop video. I know up to nine women, and none of them have ever had to excuse themselves from the table, saying, 'Sorry – just going to feel myself up in the coat cupboard. Back in a moment.'

2) Having sex with an invisible ghost. Sooner or later, every modern popstress is going to have to vibrate in a squatting position, in order to pleasure the Ghost of Christmas Horny. That's what we ladies do in 2011. We hump spooks.

3) 'Making your booty touch the ground.' Women of pop – if you want to get to Number One, you will, at some point, have to make your 'booty' (bottom) touch the ground. It is as regulation a move in twenty-first-century pop as having incredibly dry-looking hair was in the 1980s. Of course, making your booty touch the ground isn't that difficult – almost any woman can do it, given a full minute or so to get down and up again, and allowed to repeatedly say 'Ouf!' and 'Argk' whilst clutching at the mantelpiece. In the scheme of things, it's no biggie. But what may sadden the viewer, after a couple of hours, is noting how 'booty grounding' is solely the province of women. You never see the boys doing it – despite them having legs that are anatomically identical to women's, and rocking the considerable advantage of not being in six-inch heels. I have never seen Bob Dylan make his booty touch the floor. It is not something that was asked of Oasis.

4) 'Having some manner of liquid/viscose substance land on your face, then licking it off lasciviously.' In no other field of human experience does

someone busily engaged in their work – in this case, miming to their latest single – have something land on their face, and react with anything other than a cry of 'WHAT? WHAT IS GOING ON? I am gonna start effin' and jeffin' if we cannot keep the rain-machine/mud/custard off my face, Andrew. Just – stop hurling stuff at me! I'm trying to look thoughtful! I sold fifteen million singles last year!'

Do not get me wrong. It's not as if I *dislike* women acting all fruity in videos – I was raised on Madonna. Beyoncé and Gaga are my girls. Put The Divinyls' 'I Touch Myself' on, and I will terrify you on the dance-floor. Literally terrify you. You will want to leave.

It's just the … *ubiquity* of female pop stars dressing up as hoes that's disturbing. It's as weird and unnerving as if all male pop stars had decided, ten years ago, to dress up as farmers. All the time. In every single video. Imagine! Sitting down to watch your 5,000th video incorporating a hay-baler, and a man in a straw-covered gilet giving medicine to a coughing ewe. You'd think all men had gone insane. But that's what it's like with the women, and the ho-ing.

Anyway, I've finally found the best moral through-route for watching MTV with my daughters, without making them feel that, if they want to sell twenty million albums, they must dress like hoes. And it is pity. Every time we see Rihanna on her hands and knees with her coccyx hanging out of her knickers, my girls will shake their heads, sadly, and say, 'It is a great song – but we feel sorry for Rihanna. If she was really one of the biggest pop stars in the world, she'd be allowed to wear a nice cardigan once in a while. Poor Rihanna. Poor, cardigan-less Rihanna.'

Rihanna has too few clothes. Someone in a burqa, meanwhile, could be argued to have too many. Sometimes, it's hard to be a woman. Your wardrobe might as well have 'socio-sexual-political minefield' written on it.

I lifted a paragraph of this column – on burqas – from How To Be A Woman, *but have included it in full here, because the idea of a 'woman-made religion' continues to deeply intrigue me, to the point of maybe making one myself. After all, how much did L Ron Hubbard coin off inventing Scientology? And that's a* bollocks *religion. People being controlled by tiny aliens inside? You've just lifted that off 'The Numskulls', Ron. It's pathetic.*

Burqas: Are the Men Doing It?

Over the last few weeks, I've whiled away hours imagining how different the world would be if the major religions – Christianity, Islam, Sikhism, Hinduism – had been invented by women. As someone who had atheism burned into them when they were fifteen and noticed a) all the terrible, unanswered suffering in the world and b) the first growths of a desperately unwanted woman-moustache, apparently given to me by a cruel God, my subsequent interest in theology became one of sociological curiosity: looking at religions' rules, and working out why people thousands of years ago would have invented those particular guidelines in the first place.

Lots of them are obvious and laudable morality – not killing, not lying, not stealing, doing your very best not to have sex with next door's wife; or else common-sense housekeeping tips for hot countries – pork and shellfish would have been perilous in a pre-Smeg era in the Middle East, for instance. They're all fine.

Then there are the more questionable rules. For anyone who's watched *The Jeremy Kyle Show* or read *Hello!*, 'respecting your parents' doesn't make sense if your father is basically Frank from *Shameless*, or your mother some neurotic socialite who abandoned you to a host of disinterested nannies on year-long contracts.

And, finally, there are the rules – scattered across all religions – that would only have been made up in an era where women were second-class citizens, i.e., any point before the release of *Working Girl* in 1986. The value on female virginity; female sexuality being 'dangerous'; divorce being considered shameful: understandable rules from a pre-contraceptive society where women's main purpose was to keep family bloodlines undisputed, and prevent small, muddy villages exploding in a series of *EastEnders*-like plotlines.

And, so, to the burqa – currently the world's most controversial outfit. Last week, the French government brought in a law making the burqa illegal in public places – prompting complex, but often inconclusive, emotional reactions, from pub gardens to broadsheets.

On the one hand, there feels something deeply amiss about seeing a woman walking down a street, in twenty-first-century Paris, shrouded from head to toe as if she were some ghostly, flickering projection from 1,000 years ago. Some official urge to address this seems understandable.

On the other hand, the pictures that went around the world on the day the laws came into statute – French policemen grabbing a woman, on her own, and dragging her away; the inference, if not the actuality, being that they would then strip the burqa from her face, even as she protested – were also deeply disturbing. Xenophobic governments telling immigrant women what to wear – making laws about their wardrobes – *also* feels medieval. With another cultural shift, what other laws could be brought in to legislate against the clothes on women's backs: Fur? Mini-skirts? Trousers? You could find passionate advocates against all of them. But in the case of the French government against burqas, who is *really* telling who what to wear here?

Well, I have a rule for working out if the root problem of something is, in fact, sexism. And it is this: asking 'Are the boys doing it? Are the boys having to worry about this stuff? Are the boys the centre of a gigantic global debate on this subject?'

And this is the basis on which I finally decided I was against both the French legislation, *and* women wearing burqas. France was the last European country to give women the vote, the French Senate is 76.5 per cent male, and it's never passed a law on what French men can wear. Not even deck shoes; or alarming all-in-one ski-suits in bright pink nylon. So there's clearly some sexism going on there.

Secondly, meanwhile, the logic of the burqa is a paradox. Yes, the idea is that it protects your modesty, and ensures that people regard you as a human being rather than just a sexual object. Fair enough.

But who is your modesty being protected *from*? Men. And who – so long as you play by the rules, and wear the correct clothes – is going to protect you *from* the men? Men. And who is it that is regarding you as just a sexual object, instead of another human being, in the first place? Men.

And – most importantly – which half of the population has never been required to walk around, covered from head to toe, in order to feel like a normal human being? Men.

Well, then. Burqas seem like quite a man-based problem, really. I would definitely put this under the heading, '100 per cent stuff that the men need to sort out'. I don't know why women are suddenly having to put things on their heads to make it better.

Men invented burqas – men are banning burqas. And they are the only people who *would* have invented them. Because I can't believe a female-invented religion – with a female god, female prophets, and laws based on protecting women's interests – would *ever* have invented an item of religious clothing that required so much ironing.

Other times, however, fashion is a bit easier to deal with. You just have to look its insanity firmly in the eye, and say, 'No. No, fashion – stop being silly. Shoo. I am too busy for this nonsense, as well you know.'

This Cape Makes Me Look Like Wizbit

I love this time of year, when the autumn/winter trends are minutely detailed in the media, and womankind can observe the fashions which are bearing down upon it at 100mph.

As someone who is both technically and actually a woman, I would never wish to absent myself from these vital dispatches. So, as is tradition, I spent this summer holiday as I have the last five – casting an eye over the forthcoming fashion weather, and making my wardrobe calculations accordingly. I learned that the forecast for 2011 is both varied, and absorbing.

Capes, for instance, will continue to be a hot look – despite their unnerving ability to make the wearer look like Wizbit and/or someone who's had their arms chopped off in a jousting tournament, and is inexplicably coy about admitting it in front of their peers.

'No – no, there's nothing wrong. Just gonna wear this cape for a while. No reason. Could you just … put that sandwich in my mouth, please? It's for … a dare.'

Should you not favour the cape, and/or prefer to have the use of your arms, A/W11 has another option for you: the 'Mannish Coat', instead.

'It should look like it's borrowed from the man in your life,' *Vogue* explained, over shots of tweedy, boyish, single-breasted numbers.

This, of course, would be fine advice if the man in your life were Benedict Cumberbatch in *Sherlock,* who rarely has less than a grand's worth of hot and alluring tailoring hanging on the peg by the front door. Were I to wear a coat borrowed from the man in my life, however, I'd be pitching up at smart dinners in a bright yellow Radiohead Pac-A-Mac, decorated with one of Thom Yorke's trademark cartoons of a sad, abused panda.

When it comes to actual clothes, the summary for A/W11 is apparently 'sophisticated' and 'modest'. In a post-Middleton era, it's 'all about' pussy-bow blouses, tight midi-skirts, and court shoes. I cannot say I receive this news with great joy. At thirty-six, I'm a seasoned Fashion Veteran now – and in all my years of Style Combat, I have come to have particular reason to view tight midi-skirts with Feud Eyes.

Don't get me wrong – your *Mad Men*-style skirt looks great when you're lolling around in it, smoking a fag. Attempt to get down a flight of stairs in one, however, and the extreme restriction around the knees becomes apparent, causing all manner of problems in posture and gait. However many icy martinis you're holding at the time (and FYI more than two is difficult, although certainly possible; particularly if you're not shy about utilising the crook of your elbow), it's hard to maintain an air of sophisticated allure when you're having to kick your calves out sideways, in the style of a wind-up plastic bath-frog. And court shoes look Thatcher. Always have done, always will do. And they tend to fall off when you're running, like you're some union-crushing Cinderella.

So – having spent my holiday genning up on the A/W11 mood-board – I returned this week to London, and did what all women do every year; head full of the 'must haves', 'directional pieces' and 'looks' we'll be 'channelling' until spring: went to Topshop, and bought whatever made me look thinnest.

Obviously that's not the *entirety* of my A/W11 wardrobe make-over – I also popped into Mango and Zara, as well; and bought whatever made me look thinnest there, too. And I certainly wouldn't rule out, at some later point, buying something from H&M if it in any way makes me look a bit like Elizabeth Taylor drinking gin whilst sitting on Richard Burton's lap. But, frankly, that's it. When all the fashion editors were on Twitter in August fretting about which coat they were going to go for this autumn, I just looked in my coat cupboard, noticed that my duffel coat was still there, and said, 'Yes. I know which coat *I* am going for this autumn. The one that I already have.'

Because the truth about the gigantic hoopla of each new season's developments is this: there is no must-have, platinum-plated, worn-by-Anna Wintour item in the *world* any woman would wear if it does anything other than make her look thin and a bit 'likely'.

On top of this, *Vogue* can list as many 'must have' 'directional pieces' as they like – if it's not in a shop we're wandering past we're going to kind of … forget to buy it. Yes. That's right. Simply not get around to it. We might sometimes *like* the idea of getting the £600 green snakeskin belt by Dior but – like whale-watching in Peru – it's not very local, and would, financially, require cancelling Christmas in its entirety.

This is why the phrase 'I wear a mixture of high street and vintage' – the 'quirky' wardrobe descriptor claimed by Alexa Chung, Kate Moss, et al – amuses me so much. That just means 'a mixture of cheap stuff, and old stuff'. That's what we're *all* wearing, dear. That's what we'll all be wearing in A/W11.

Some discrimination isn't bad, ladies. Like positive discrimination. That's the good discrimination.

We Need Quotas, Ladies.
Or We Will Be Lonely Pelicans

In a report as interesting to read as it must have been wearying to compile, the *Guardian* recently ran statistics on the male dominance of British public life.

Over a month, they painstakingly recorded that 78 per cent of newspaper articles, 72 per cent of *Question Time* contributors and 84 per cent of the presenters and guests on Radio 4 were men. Ninety-three years after women got the vote, they still aren't saying very much. Well, obviously they *are* saying a *lot*: they're in the kitchen getting the tea ready, and shouting at Toby Young spraffing on on *Today* – his ability to be a total tit about any and all events so reliable, you could use it to power an atomic clock. But. Still. Women aren't getting paid to say things *publicly*. That – like coal-mining, and arranging illegal dog-fights – is still the domain of men.

If you do ever see women commenting on current affairs, it's usually as a vox-pop of 'just' 'a mum' outside a shopping centre on the *Six O'Clock News,* being asked what she thinks of the government's plan to open up a Hellmouth, just by the ring-road, and let all the demons of the lower realms pour forth.

'I don't know much about these things,' she will say, doubtfully; jiggling the buggy to keep the baby quiet. 'But it worked out quite badly that time when they raised all the dead, and let them traverse the streets at night, eating cats to fuel their evil quests. *And* they've closed the library. I some-times worry they might have gone too far. Not that I'm political. Sorry.'

So. Given that these are pretty embarrassing statistics for a first-world country in 2011, what are we going to do about it? Many, of course, would say that 'we' shouldn't 'do' anything – that attaining a position in public life is just something best left to Nature. Women should think of themselves as salmon, say – and just keep trying to leap up that waterfall, over and over again, until they finally get to the top and lay their eggs (appear on *Newsnight* talking about Syria).

Personally, however, I think that idea is – to use the technical term – cobblers. Society isn't Nature – it's made by people. Hopefully, polite and civilised people. And if society isn't working for 52 per cent of the people, then it would be mannerly to change it so that it does. That's why I'm totally in favour of employment quotas and positive discrimination.

'But Cate,' those who object will say, who know what my nickname is. The good nickname. Not 'Snakey Mome Rath'. 'But Cate – if you insist 50 per cent of your workforce is women, and force employers to hire them, that means you're gonna get women who are wildly ill-qualified desk-meat, smashing at the keyboards with their faces, and making a total hash of it. Women racketing around the office who don't know the differ-ence between "up" and "down", keep pressing buttons on the air-con saying "This printer isn't working", and posting confidential client infor-mation on Twitter. That can't be right!'

Well, it's not 'right'. It is, however, totally normal. After all, in an office that's 70 per cent men, at least 20 per cent of *them* are going to be wildly ill-qualified desk-meat, smashing at the keyboard with their faces, and making a total hash of it. Of course they are. That's just statistics. People who are anti positive discrimination are ignoring the fact that we've been giving jobs to MILLIONS of stupid, unqualified people for millennia: men.

Please don't misunderstand – I am not prejudiced against the stupid men. Or the stupid women, for that matter. As we all know, any office – from Budgens in Crouch End to the White House – only needs three clever people to run it. Everyone else there is essentially just a background extra, to stop the important, capable people feeling lonely. And that's another reason why we need quotas. When women are in a minority in any situation, they feel as understandably odd and stressed as two pelicans in a camel enclosure. And the camels can't help but look at the pelican beaks oddly, and go off and do 'camel things' in the corner, whilst the pelicans feel awkward and alone, and go on a weird diet, out of self-loathing.

In this situation, you just need to wang half a dozen stupider pelicans into the enclosure, to keep the best pelicans company, and even out the numbers – so that both 'being a pelican' and 'being a camel' is totally normal in London Zoo's New Pelican & Camel Experience.

Men who complain about positive discrimination look like – to use the technical phrase – girls. Let's face it – the next Bill Gates or Barack Obama isn't going to be held back because AAAAAAABBA Office Supplies in Dartford have been forced to hire three female accounts managers. Come ON! Do you really think you have something to complain about? Do you really think you're at a disadvantage? Stop whining! Rosa Parks managed to kick-start the Civil Rights movement in America, on a bus, WHILST CARRYING SOME SHOPPING. You need some perspective on just how hindered you really are.

Here I can go into a lovely segue – from the politeness of female employment quotas, to the politeness of chivalry – all as smoothly as a local radio presenter going from the sport into travel and weather. And that's plenty smooth.

As 'Downton Fever' (some people watching Downton) swept the nation in 2012, an interview with Michelle Dockery, who plays Lady Mary, and – as revealed later in the book – crunks to 'No Diggity', provoked controversy when she lamented the end of chivalry in an interview in the Radio Times.

'Those old manners – such as men standing when women arrive at the dinner table, or opening doors for you – are lovely, and it's lovely when you see a man doing that today,' she said. 'But young men wouldn't think about that for a second [now], because that's not the culture any more.'

This prompted much squabbling over the desirability of a chivalric revival, with many women and men arguing against it, as they believed all chivalry was essentially men patronising women, and implying they were weak and helpless.

I strongly disagreed – primarily on the basis that I like sitting down.

I Would Like Some Chivalry, Please, Dude

There has recently been some debate on the place chivalry has in the modern era – prompted by the massive success of *Downton Abbey*, which shows a forgotten world of gentlemen rising as a lady enters the room, using quadrille gloves when engaged in quadrilling, and making only the faintest legal protest over women gaining the vote in 1918.

Having now observed its full glory on television, modern opinion seems to be split on the desirability of now staging a full chivalric revival.

The main argument against it is that it presupposes weakness in women. The common complaint is that if a man, say, stands up to give his seat to a woman on the Tube, he is basically saying, 'Lady, I think you are having a massive period, and might faint if you remain standing. That would then delay this Tube for all of us normal, non-menstruating people. So, on behalf of everyone with a tight schedule, have my chair and sit down, lest we all suffer from your physical misfortune.'

And I can see why that might be slightly annoying – if you were, perhaps, a hale and hearty wench, who prides herself on her upper-body strength, and can climb up a rope rather than hanging at the bottom of it, uselessly, like a 5'5" lady-bauble.

However. Speaking as someone who, four days a month, really *might* faint on the Tube if someone doesn't give up their seat, I am eternally grateful for any gentleman who stands as I limp into his carriage. Sometimes, I have been suffering so badly on public transport I have inadvertently let out a low, animal-moan of 'Maaaaa' – then had to style it out by pretending to be a slightly unhinged person, singing along to 'Mamma Mia' on my iPod. I have had swooning moments so intense I had to rest my head on a Slovakian's rucksack, whilst mouthing the words 'Don't faint, Cat-Mo; don't faint' into a gigantic outside zip.

And that's before we even mention pregnancy. The first three months of gestation – when there are no visible indicators to the onlooker – are a panoply of astonishing and debilitating physical side-effects. I had one incident where my feet became so mysteriously hot, I eventually had to go into a changing room in New Look, and sluice them down with a bottle of Purdey's. All kinds of head-spinning insanity can be going on inside a woman's body. Some days, it's like we're covering up a circus that's on fire, using only an A-line skirt and a blouse. Underneath, there's clowns jumping out of windows, and crying seals everywhere.

In these circumstances, then, any man aware of what women might be enduring, and offering some manner of solidarity, is a kind, gentle, bright brother to me. He is doing something both polite, and hot. He is a man who has quietly concluded that – given how frequently women are dealing with some manner of Big Top Crisis – it's generally best for men to give us *all* both the benefit of the doubt, and their seats. I suspect this was the origin of chivalry in the first place – a simple, kind logic.

The only alternative to universal, automatic chivalry, of course – giving up seats for all women – is to make chivalry more specific. In this system, women who were physically indisposed would have to indicate their situation with some manner of 'period badge', or 'special pregnancy hat' – so that men may only offer courtesy to those who are genuinely in need of it. As you can see, that would be only slightly worse than having to walk around in public with your teenage diary entries pinned to your chest. Most women would die of mortification on their first commute to work. It would be a massacre.

Of course, there are bad men – men who abuse the concept of chivalry. Their unspoken deal is, 'Yes, I am going to open this door for you, Amelia – but I will leer at you as you walk past me, then maintain a vague air of "ownership" over you all night: as if I am a great silverback who has now inducted you into his harem of lady-gorillas. You will now bear my gorilla-babies, in my mind.'

But here, ladies, we must keep some manner of perspective. Given how much random perving the average woman will have to put up with in the course of a week – I was once perved when I was nine months pregnant, wearing a duffel coat and carrying a Vileda Supermop back from a local hardware store; I really was not the Girl from Ipanema – at least we have got something out of this particular perv-instance: in this case, being spared the indignity of having to open a door with our teeth, because our arms are laden with parcels and coat.

At least, in this instance, we're a door-opening up on the deal. For that reason alone, I'm pro-chivalry.

On top of this baffling rejection of men being nice – LADIES! In turning down acts of chivalry, we are behaving in an unchivalrous manner! The irony would kill me were I not already reeling from the impossibility of a situation where OPENING A DOOR is seen as an aggressive act. Come on, fellow breastkateers – we can be more noble than this. Why not pat these well-meaning fellows on the back, and simply say 'Thank you'? That's a) manners and b) what you would want in return.

I write a lot about the internet. There are two reasons for this. The first is because it is, quite clearly, the greatest invention of the twentieth century: the equivalent of the wheel, or fire, but for the mind.

With mass communication no longer limited to newspapers or TV companies – to which access was previously and jealously guarded by professional writers and broadcasters – the nearest thing to a meritocracy of opinion and experience has now come about, thanks to Tumblr, Facebook, YouTube and Twitter. Some teenage kid in Buttfuck, Idaho can come up with a joke, campaign or picture of a funny raccoon, and, if it catches people's imagination, it can be (ironically) making old-fashioned newspaper headlines by sun-down. Ideas and thoughts and experiences can spread like pollen in the air, blood in water. For good or bad, of course: the unsayable becomes the unstoppable just as easily as some beautiful attempt for a better world. There are people whose lives have literally been ruined by a bad picture on Facebook, or an email being sent to the wrong address – then being passed on across the world.

But the sheer, awesome, exhilarating power of the internet is absolutely captivating: it is the biggest game on Earth. The twenty-first century equivalent of the birth of rock'n'roll. For those who don't work in it – who are merely customers, rather than Mark Zuckerberg – having access to it is like standing on a rocky ledge, halfway down Victoria Falls, in the middle of an all-enveloping monsoon. The roar and the spray – the constant motion and hydrating mist – are intoxicating. Thousands of new things tumbling past you every second – swept into the river above in the flood – that you can just reach out and grab. Maps and shops and faces and friends from 1987 and that clip from that show that time, and snowflakes, and explosions, and Crosby Stills and Nash singing 'Helplessly Hoping' in three-part harmony, as many times as you want.

The idea of moving away from it – back inland, back offline – seems wholly desolate and mean. Dry. Silent. How would you know … anything, without the internet? How could you make things happen? What would be left of you? Just some jumped-up hapless monkey in a dress, trying to buy a train ticket to Nottingham by being put on hold by another jumped-up yet hapless monkey in a dress.

No, no – every time I am offline, I am half-off. I can't get anything done. I love the internet. It is where I live.

And the second reason I love it is because pissing around on Twitter is an excellent *substitute for smoking. I think I'm on 120 Twitter a day. I am* chaining *that shit.*

In the following piece, I explore – with another smoooooooth segue from the last column – the lack of chivalry on the internet.

Don't Feed the Troll

The thing I like most about the internet is that it's just humans, interacting with other humans – but in a sufficiently novel manner for new guidelines to be needed. Because there's no one in charge – no, despite the claims of thousands of teenage boys, 'King of the Internet' – online is a world where billions of people are trying to get through another day of posting amusing pictures of cats, typing in capital letters and lying slightly about how amazing they are – all whilst not getting in each other's way, or offending each other.

By and large, it works so well as to stir the heart. Observed from above, the internet must look like the Magic Roundabout gyratory system in Swindon: trillions of opinion-cars from all over the world, ploughing into what seems like certain fatality – only for everyone to, at the last moment, avoid each other, and seamlessly continue their journey to Bristol/some pornography. No international wars have *ever* been declared on the internet. It is a remarkably amiable place.

But there are exceptions. 'Trolls': anonymous posters whose kink is making deliberately inflammatory comments – then getting visibly high off others' subsequent outrage. Imagine an adolescent boy breaking wind at the breakfast table – then smirking as everyone shouts 'Jesus, that smell has irradiated my Weetos. Why? WHY would you DO that Julian, WHY?'

Typical troll-behaviour would be, say, going on a Beyoncé fan-site, observing the conversation for a few minutes, and then saying, 'Yeah – but she's got a fat arse, hasn't she?' As more inexperienced fans castigate the troll for sexism, possible racism and stupidity, older hands utter one of the internet's most used catchphrases: 'Don't feed the troll.' In other words: if some anonymous armchair cowboy pitches up and deliberately provokes a fight, don't satisfy their need for attention. Ignore them. Don't feed the troll.

Until recently, I, too, would intone, 'Don't feed the troll.' Firstly, it's a waste of time that could be spent engaging in a pleasant early-summer stroll, searching out the first buds of pussy-willow. And, secondly, there's always the undeniable feeling that, as you castigate a troll, he's rubbing his *Red Dwarf* mouse-mat against his crotch and sighing, 'Angry liberal women typing at me. Oh yah. That's how I like it.'

But then I started to notice that, as a phenomenon, trolling isn't just confined to pseudonymous IT workers hanging around Justin Bieber fan-sites, making fourteen-year-old girls furious. When, a few weeks ago, on *Top Gear*, Jeremy Clarkson made his 'amusing' remark about Katie Price having a 'pink whore's box' – 'I meant PINK HORSE BOX!' he corrected, knowingly – it occurred to me that Clarkson's entire career is essentially an exercise in trolling: gleefully vexatious comments on Mexicans, homosexuals and women, thrown out with the 'Ho ho! Our "PC" friends won't like THIS!' expression that is the carat-mark of the true troll.

Clarkson isn't the only professional troll on the block: consider his friend, the *Sunday Times* columnist A A Gill, with his liberal sprinkling of references to 'dykes', 'ferret-faced Albanians' and the 'ugly Welsh'. Both Clarkson and Gill know that these kind of comments provoke massive reactions – in their cases, literally to the point where ambassadors from other countries get involved. Essentially, they're trolling the entire concepts of diplomacy and civilisation for a reaction. This is something which some hopelessly small-town troll, flaming for kicks on the breast-feeding boards of Mumsnet, can only sighingly aspire to.

If there is one thing that defines the troll world-view, it's a sour, dissatisfied sense that the world is disappointing. Trolls never troll enthusiasm. The default troll attitude is one of inexplicably vituperative disapproval for something millions find joy in. The first time I thought that sentence, I went, 'Oh my God – you know what this means? The *Daily Mail* is the fucking LODESTONE of trolldom! It's the Magna Carta of trolldom! It's the Dead Sea Trolls!'

Because if you look at the *Mail*'s website, your presumption that *Daily Mail* readers actually like bitchy headlines about female celebrities putting on weight ('Fuller-Faced Cheryl Cole'), is blown out of the water. All the comments are actually from reasonable people baffled by the *Mail*'s tactic ('Can't celebrities put on an ounce without it being news?' Ivy, Barking) – making you realise that the *Mail* are, in practice, trolling their entire readership. Amazing.

So this is why I can't agree with the internet's first rule: 'Don't feed the trolls.' It's *fine* when it's just some spenk on a messageboard, with only five users. Ignoring provocative squits is only right and sensible. But when millionaire celebrity broadcasters, and entire publications, start trolling, ignoring them isn't really an option any more. They are gradually making trolling normative. We have to start feeding the trolls: feeding them with achingly polite emails and comments, reminding them of how billions of people prefer to communicate with each other, every day, in the most unregulated arena of all: courteously.

Controversy with the next column, in which I defended the paywall – which is the sexy, medieval-sounding phrase that we use instead of 'subscription', or 'fee' – at The Times. *You have to pay to read* The Times *online. It is one of the few newspapers in the world to attempt such a thing.*

I feel many people who hated the paywall were confusing 'the idea of paying for stuff, like we used to' with 'personal and long-standing animosity towards Rupert Murdoch', which is unhelpful in an industry in crisis, in which previously lucrative newspapers lose money hand over fist, thousands of journalists have been made unemployed, and ad revenue is tanking – all since the rush to put everything online, for free.

I feel my clarion-call of 'bitch gotta make rent' could be useful for many now-free newspapers to bear in mind, as they fire a third of their staff, and supplements disappear overnight, like sugar in tea.

In Defence of Rupert Murdoch's Paywall

All told this is a marvellous job, and certainly better than anything I hoped for aged ten, when I presumed I would grow up to be – given my class and location – either a picket, or a murdered prostitute.

Indeed, there is only one real downside to it: a certain kind of person who, on discovering which paper you are employed by, pulls what I can only describe as a *'Guardian* face' and makes some disapproving comment along the lines of 'You must have to watch what you say,' 'given who you work for'.

The presumption being that, at 9am every morning, Rupert Murdoch walks into my kitchen, points a taser-gun at one of my children, and says,

'G'day. Write "Gordon Brown is a bonk-eyed homosexual" in the middle of your "wry" column about zoos, or the kid gets voltage.'

I mention all this merely in order to forestall any tiresome comments of 'Of course, you *would* have to say that' following my next declaration, which is this: I THINK YOU SHOULD HAVE TO PAY FOR CONTENT ON THE INTERNET.

Yeah, that's right. You heard me. *The Times* is putting up a big paywall, all over the dream of free global communication, and I like it. Despite being so left-wing I cried when I interviewed Tony Benn, and so laidback and groovy that I named my second daughter after a Teardrop Explodes album, I am all for paywalls, prosecuting illegal downloaders, and generally getting all monetising on the internet's ass.

Why? Because the internet is currently split into two halves. The bit that's making all the money is the bit selling holidays, dishwashers, weekly groceries and fake Vlll1agra. It's San Francisco during the Gold Rush over there. If you're selling stuff on the internet – however tatty or unenvironmentally friendly it is – you've got it made.

Then there's the half that makes no money at all – where you can download music, films, TV shows, photography and journalism for free. Because if you're selling *creativity* on the internet, it seems – brilliant, complex or just plain entertaining visions – you're not supposed to charge. Or complain about it, either. When Lily Allen spoke up against downloading last year, the internet exploded with – mainly male, it has to be said – commentators, castigating her for wanting to get paid for her work. We're at the odd point where it now seems reactionary for artists to want to earn a living from art.

By way of contrast, the comparethemeerkat.com crew are driving around in a golden hovercraft, wiping their arses with fifties. The internet didn't make *businesses* start giving their stuff away for free, I note. Topshop aren't handing out free jumpsuits, just the arty boho groovy people. And simply because they were scared of not looking 'cool'. I don't know quite how it happened, but you have to hand it to The Man. He aced that one. I don't know how The Man does it, to be honest.

You know what? I liked the twentieth century. The twentieth century was great – the first time in history artists stopped starving in garrets, or being indentured to wealthy patrons, and got paid decent money, thanks to massive tranches of dull yet hard-assed copyright legislation. As a consequence, the twentieth century was artistically dominated by the working classes – because, for the first time, they could actually afford to be artistic.

Yes. As I suspect you may have guessed, what all this is essentially saying is that I don't think journalism should be free, because, tbh, bitch gotta make rent. I've spent twenty years clawing my way out of a council house in Wolverhampton, to reach a point where I can now afford a Nigella Lawson breadbin. If I have to start blogging everything for free, I am simply going to have to fall back on Plan B and go and get murdered in a red-light district somewhere. Meanwhile, the only journalists left will be posh people who can afford to do it as a hobby – in between skiing, or renovating a folly. This column would be written by Lady Helen 'Melons' Windsor, or George Osborne.

However, it's not writers, or musicians, that are the workers most affected by free internet content. Have you seen how much free porn there is out there? You will never need to pay to see a penis again, that much is certain. And whoever is was that decided to fill the net with trillions of hours of gratis humping, I bet it wasn't the cast. If I had spent the afternoon being bummed across a landing by a man who looks like Burt Reynolds, I would want to make sure the resultant work was exploiting every revenue stream it could; in order to buy fur coats, and antibiotics.

As a society, we now charge for essential dental work – but somehow found a way to throw in HD spit-roasts and three-way MILF-fests for free. What does that say about us?

And when someone works out what that says about us, will there be anywhere left where they're paid to explain it?

Throughout this book, a few recurring themes will make themselves appar-
ent. A fear of the sixteenth century; continuing enjoyment over the Moon
Landings; the bangingness of Sherlock; *an irresponsible love of alcohol and*
loud pop music; and a deep, beyond-primal adoration of the BBC series
Doctor Who.

In this feature, the BBC let me go around the Doctor Who *studios,*
where I found the Face of Boe in a warehouse and sat on him. For two years,
a picture of me doing so was the screensaver on my laptop. There is no doubt
in my mind that, when I'm dying, and my life flashes before my eyes, that
particular picture will get a longer slot than many other pivotal life moments,
with a caption saying 'WINNING!' flashing over it.

On the Set of *Doctor Who*

Cardiff train station, 10am. The cab driver is unsure as to where, exactly, we are going. He pulls to a halt at the end of the rank, and hails the cab opposite.

'I've got passengers for *Doctor Who*,' he says, with an expansive gesture at us in the back. 'Where do I turn off?'

'For *Doctor Who*?' the other cab driver says. 'For *Doctor Who*?'

There's a huge pause, where a more overexcited cab passenger might begin to speculate as to whether *Doctor Who* is actually shot on Earth at all. Maybe it's only accessible via a closely guarded magnetic anomaly, in a disused bronze-mine, guarded by the Sontarans!

'You go right at the BP petrol station, mate.'

*

Doctor Who and *Doctor Who*'s spin-offs – *Torchwood*, *The Sarah Jane Adventures*, *Doctor Who Confidential* and *Totally Doctor Who* – occupy Cardiff, in much the same manner an army barracks occupies a small town. With a crew of 200, 180 special FX technicians, 200 prosthetics technicians, 2,000 extras and 200 guest stars, the population of the city is divided into civilians and non-civilians; *Who* and non-*Who*. The pivotal question in Cardiffian nightlife is 'You on *Who*, then?'

'Some of them act a bit cliquey like they've seen attack ships on fire off the shoulder of Orion,' a friend who lives in Cardiff said. 'When, in actual fact, they've just spent all day waving a foam-rubber leg around.'

But much like the army, this clannishness is understandable – *Doctor Who* is both a huge, and a hugely secretive, operation. Having made the decision to try and keep the plots a surprise – extremely rare in television, where tabloid pre-publicity is key in getting ratings-spikes – phenomenal amounts of thought and energy are put into keeping details from the public. On the way to Cardiff, the show's press officer, Lesley, has a wary weather-eye out for possible leaks.

'We can't discuss the show on the train,' she says, firmly, as soon as we sit down. 'People have done it before, and had passengers who've overheard ring the tabloids. Everyone knows what you're talking about as soon as you say "the Doctor", you see.'

So an hour later, when I am standing in a dark, otherwise deserted warehouse, with the TARDIS looming over me like the monolith in *2001*, I feel genuine frissons of both privilege, and slight fear. Privilege, because I am in a place where thousands of fans of the show would love to be. After all, a mere twenty feet away, there's a top-secret spaceship being referred to as 'the James Bond set', which will titivate the spod-glands of any Western adult between the ages of seventeen and fifty.

And fear, because the TARDIS – despite sitting on top of a pallet – looks unexpectedly legendary. It has the aura of something that has bounced off comets, arced over nebulae and oscillated through the furthest reaches of space-time. Even though, when I knock on its door, it's clearly made of wood.

The *Doctor Who* warehouse is a surreal place. Despite our last sighting of the Cybermen being during Series Two, when an impassively muscular army of millions tried to take over the Earth, there are, in fact, only ten Cybermen in existence. Well, four now, due to breakages. I can see three of their legs poking out of a large cardboard box, at right angles. The Daleks, meanwhile, are – contrary to all lores of celebrity – actually *bigger* than they seem on TV.

Being quite common, my first instinct is to steal something cool. I cannot be alone in this impulse. These warehouses are, presumably, an open invitation for cast and crew to take 'mementoes'. Everyone wants a Cyberman codpiece on their mantelpiece, surely?

'To be honest, no,' says our tour guide, Edward Russell, Brand Executive of *Doctor Who*. 'It's like a family. It just wouldn't be worth their while to steal anything, because, if they got caught, they'd never work again. Everyone on this show is very protective.'

He makes it sound as if, in the event of any possible transgression of trust, a hit squad of Daleks would be seen trundling into a local pub, and emerging again, minutes later, with smoking plungers.

Of course, an operation this big and, indeed, a universe this vast would all be pretty pointless were we to venture into it without a char-ismatic galactic chaperone. As we all know by now, the resurrection of *Doctor Who* is down to one man – the joyous, expansive and prodigiously talented Russell T Davies, the man who traded all his success with *Queer as Folk, Bob & Rose* and *Casanova* in order to do what the BBC had thought impossible for sixteen years – regenerate the abandoned *Who* into the BBC's flagship. It is he, above all others, who is responsible for the best programme in Britain in the twenty-first century being, against all the laws of probability, a children's show, made on a minuscule budget, in Wales, by gays.

But it is, perhaps, in Davies' choice of the Doctor that he made his most crucial decision. For whilst, in the first series, Christopher Ecclestone's leather-jacketed, slightly demented hard-nut Doctor was the right person to make a full break from the show's heritage of frock-coats, frilly cuffs and hammery, it is in David Tennant, the tenth and current Doctor, that the show has found its most appealing emissary. Whilst Ecclestone approached the role prosaically, as a difficult job to be done well, Tennant has taken on the role with, well, love. A fan of the show since childhood, he has been voted 'The Best Doctor Ever' in acknowledgement that it is his performance, above all others, that has best embodied the show's values: anarchy, vigour, moral rigour, silliness, and a reverential awe at how big, scary, complex, beautiful and full of bipedal aliens made of foam-rubber the universe is.

Meeting with him – in the tea-rooms of the Landmark Hotel in Marylebone – it's clear to see why Davies cast him in the role. He has quick wit, excess energy, and self-deprecates at every available opportunity ('Look at my mobile! It's really boring! It's about as intergalactic as a brick!'). He is, also, let's be frank, the First Hot Doctor. He is the primary Timephwoard. He has been voted 'Hottest Man in the Universe' by the *Pink Paper*, whilst *New Woman* placed him at Number 13 in their poll of 10,000 women's crushes – just below Brad Pitt.

Tennant, however, disputes his assignation as the First Hot Doctor.

'Tom Baker!' he says, with a Bakerish roar. 'Come on! He was a huge hit with the ladies.'

He was more of a specialist taste, I offer, primly. Something WHSmith would keep behind the counter, and you'd have to ask for.

'I'm sure Peter Davison was in polls at the time,' he continues, gallantly. Perhaps aware that he is seconds away from attempting to mount a defence of the sexual allure of Sylvester McCoy, Tennant changes the conversation with a confidence that just, to be honest, proves how hot he is.

'This is a terrible anecdote, so I must tell it,' he says, settling into a chair with a coffee. 'Last year, Billie [Piper] and I kept getting invited to guest at award ceremonies but we could never go – we were either filming in Cardiff, or because we would be presenting Best Wig or something, and what's the point of that? But when the Brit Awards rolled around, we let it be known, through our "people", that we'd love to present a Brit for Best Drunkard, or something. But – pleasingly for the laws of hubris –

they said, "No, we'll be fine, thank you." They turned down the Doctor and Rose! Famous across the universe!'

Tennant does a self-deprecating boggle.

Talking to him is an experience of mild surreality. On the one hand – it's the Doctor! You're talking to the Doctor! On the other hand, he's as obsessive and passionate about the show as any fan. This is a man who can talk about the Gravitic Anomalyser without any protective layer of irony.

Dismissing the possibility that, paradoxically, becoming the Doctor could ultimately ruin the show for him – 'I know what you mean, because all the surprises are gone, but I'd have gone mad if I'd turned it down and watched someone else do it' – Tennant, instead, spends the next hour discussing the show with all the enthusiasm and mild geekery of a fan, albeit a very privileged one. Discussing certain titillating morsels that Russell T Davies has thrown into previous episodes and then not returned to – such as the intriguing news that the Doctor has, at some point, been a father – Tennant yelps, and then says, 'I know! I'll be reading these things going, "When are you coming back to that?" Often he does. But sometimes,' he says, leaning forward, 'he just drops them in for wicked-ness. There's something he's done in the next series, and I said "What's that all about?" and he replied, "Oh, I've just put it in because it's funny." The internet forums will go into meltdown.'

He beams. 'But you know – he knows what he wants as a fan. You want to be discussing it all the next week. You want to float your different theories on what will happen next. That's part of the pleasure.'

Together with Russell T Davies, he comes across like a steam enthusi-ast who's taken over an old rail-line. Every detail of the show thrills him – even the clothes. Indeed, perhaps the most surprising moment comes when he explains how the image of his Doctor was, fairly unguessably, based on the saviour of our fat school children, Jamie Oliver.

'I'd always wanted a long coat, because you've kind of got to. You've got to *swish*. Then when Billie was on *Parkie*, she was on the same week as Jamie Oliver, who was looking rather cool in a funky suit with trainers. And I rang Russell T Davies and said, "Are you watching this? Could we do this for the Doctor?" They had wanted me to wear a stompy pair of posh boots, but the trainers were the one thing I did go to the wall on.' Tennant bashes his hand down on the table, and then laughs. 'Although,' he adds, 'I have to say, I do regret it when I'm doing a night-shoot in a quarry of stinking mud, and they're putting plastic bags on my feet.'

The big news for the forthcoming series, of course, is that Billie Piper, who played the Doctor's assistant, Rose, has left. As well as being phenomenally popular in the role – she was credited with bringing a young, female audience to a show that had previously lacked one – she and Tennant formed a famously matey duo. They always emanated the vibe of having spent their downtime in Cardiff Nando's, eating huge amounts of fried chicken with their hands and laughing with their mouths open. When discussing her departure, Tennant becomes quite tender.

'The last scene we shot was for [the episode called] "The Satan Pit". Our very last line was someone saying "Who are you two?", and we reply "The stuff of legend", and then zap off in the TARDIS. We just could not get a take where we weren't crying. If you look very carefully, you can still see us starting to go "Wah!".'

Tennant, however, is stalwart in his enthusiasm for the new assistant, Freema Agyeman.

'It's a totally different energy – she comes from a totally different starting place. She's very upfront about fancying [the Doctor], and so he has to be very upfront about not being into it. It's a completely new dynamic. She's a completely new girl.'

It's *Who – 2.1*, perhaps, I suggest.

'Yes!' Tennant beams. '*Who 2.1*!'

Breaking for lunch, the whole crew travel down the hill to the 'base station' – a line of location buses and Portakabins. When David Tennant turns up, dandy and wire-thin in his new, electric-blue suit and precipitous quiff, the effect is roughly equivalent to the advent of The Fonz in Al's Diner. He is clearly lord of this domain – he manages to simultaneously hail, chat to and tease three crew members at once.

By contrast, John Simm's entrance onto the set is intense and low-key. As the pivotally evil Mr Saxon, Simm is in a black suit, wearing an ominous-looking ring, and eschewing the buffet in favour of a quiet lunch in his trailer.

'I can't tell you anything,' he says, sighing. 'I don't think I'm even officially here, am I?' He shrugs.

Later on, in a waterfront bar back in Cardiff, Simm starts an admirably brisk line of whisky ordering, and explains exactly why he left a three-week-old baby to spend a month in Wales, on the side of a windy hill.

'It's *Doctor Who*, innit?' he says, with admirable succinctness. 'You've got to do it. And Christ, the energy they all put into it. Julie Gardner [producer] and Russell T Davies were getting on midnight trains up to Manchester, to the set of *Life on Mars*, to ask me to do it.'

The deciding vote, though, was cast by Simm's five-year-old son, Ryan. 'He's *Doctor Who* mad. He's got the lunchbox, the dolls, the screwdriver. As a dad of a small boy, you kind of have a moral duty to be a baddie on *Doctor Who* if you can, don't you?'

Simm is keen to illustrate just what he and Tennant have gone through to thrill this new generation of *Who* fans – just how far their dedication extends.

'We were shooting one scene, just me and David, on this deserted mountain-top. We're giving it our all when, from fuck knows where, you can hear the faint sounds of an ice-cream van. David carries on, so I thought, well, I'm not going to stop if you're not going to stop. So we carried on right to the end – despite the fact that this must be the only ice-cream van in existence that does the theme tune to *The Benny Hill Show*. The least intergalactic sound imaginable!'

He shakes his head.

'We were, looking back, very professional that day.'

For Series Three, the BBC have taken the publicity for *Doctor Who* out of their own, often ramshackle, house, and placed it in the hands of Taylor Herring – PRs to Robbie Williams, *Big Brother* and Al Gore.

The new PRs, seemingly more aware of just how much interest there is in the show, have accordingly ramped up the screenings of the first two episodes. Whilst screenings normally consist of a small room, forty scruffy journalists and a table of coffee and buns, the *Who* screenings are treated like a movie premiere. Outside the Mayfair Hotel, fans scream as a phalanx of paparazzi snap at the guests. Whilst the celebrities do, by-and-large, look like someone took a van down to the BBC canteen and shouted, 'Anyone want to come and watch *Doctor 'oo*?' – Ian Beale, Michelle Collins, Reggie Yates – there is also Jonathan Ross, Catherine Tate and Dawn French.

Freema Agyeman is wearing a pair of £4,000 earrings, and both David Tennant and Russell T Davies are resplendent in sharp suits, and working the line of TV crews like pros.

At the beginning of the screening there is, momentarily, no sound. The TARDIS, iconic as ever, spins through electric-blue space-time to complete silence. Then the audience, as one, begin to sing the theme tune themselves: 'Oooo WEEE oooooo/OOOO ooo.' There is even an impressive counter-accompaniment of 'De duddle le dum/De duddle le dum'. It's a moment of happy, communal rejoicing.

Russell T Davies floats around, looking as joyous and serene as someone recently voted 'The Third Most Powerful Man in British Show Business' should, on pulling off another considerable success.

'The show is simply one of the best ideas ever, really, isn't it?' he says, dragging on a ciggie and beaming. 'So simple, yet so complex. How can you not love a sexy anarchist, roaming through time and space?'

When asked if – given that *Doctor Who* has now, to all intents and purposes, overtaken *EastEnders* as the BBC's flagship show – a larger budget would be more useful, he says a series of vaguely blustery and on-message things before roaring, dramatically, 'Yes! Yes! Yes, I want more money, goddamnit!'

And it's hardly surprising that he does, considering that *Who* is still not being shot in HD – surely a foolish short-term economy, given the show's inevitable longevity in repeats and DVD sales.

But in all, 'I am a happy man,' Davies sighs, exhaling, and staring across the room at the Doctor, his assistant, and a circle of a dozen grown adults, all squealing with excitement about being able to touch the TARDIS. 'A very happy man.'

And he should, perhaps, feel a quiet satisfaction. After all, in a world where very little is a surprise, and everything is viewed with cynicism, *Doctor Who* is a genuine rarity. It represents one of the very few areas where adults become as unashamedly enthusiastic as children. It's where children first experience the thrills and fears of adults, and where we never know the exact ending in advance. With its ballsy women, bisexual captains, working-class loquaciousness, scientific passion and unremittingly pacifist dictum, it offers a release from the dispiritingly limited vision of most storytelling.

It is, despite being about a 900-year-old man with two hearts and a space-time taxi made of wood, still one of our very best projections of how to be human.

More geekery, vicar? My second Doctor Who *feature. I know. It's like I'm obsessed. This time, I ended up getting absolutely hammered with David Tennant and Kylie. During our booze-fest, I did literally the worst thing I've ever done: bringing a tray of drinks over to my new celebrity chums, I noticed the metal tray it was on was still warm, from the dishwasher.*

'Feel how warm this is!' I said, joyfully. 'Feel how warm!'

Taking the drinks off it, I pressed the tray to David Tennant's handsome face.

'So warm! Like a mother's loving hand!' I said.

Lovely Tennant suddenly went quiet. I remembered – with kaleidoscopic horror – that his mother had actually died five days ago, and this was his first night out since. He subsequently dropped out of the conversation completely, and went to bed ten minutes later. I spent fully an hour in my hotel room, shouting 'WHY? WHY WAS THAT THE WARMNESS ANALOGY YOU GAVE ME???' at my cowering subconscious.

Note how I gloss over it, like a pro, in the feature.

Me, Kylie and the Doctor

The first tone meeting. March 2007

This is what tone meetings are: everyone is gathered together in an almost wholly airless room at the BBC in Cardiff. We have the heads of make-up, costume, photography, lighting, practical effects, publicity, prosthetics, personnel, and representatives from independent special effects company, The Mill. Everyone is gathered around a gigantic conference table. Here, tea is drunk, and a box of sad-looking doughnuts are attacked with vigour. Everyone has gossip to catch up with, and industry chit-chat to make.

Then everyone sits down, the meeting begins and, one by one, every head of department explains, very cheerfully, why the show can't actually be made.

It all starts well. Russell T Davies, writer and executive producer, arrives with Julie Gardner, executive producer with BBC Wales, and Phil Collinson, the producer.

'Welcome to the Christmas Special!' Russell says, opening the meeting. There is a big pause. Everyone considers the fat script on the table in front of them.

'There's a lot of shots, aren't there?' Russell says, finally. This is greeted with stoic, wartime laughter. 'A lot of shots' is the least of it. As a TV production, *Doctor Who* is unprecedented. There is an almost wholly new cast and new set every week, and many episodes have as many special effects and prosthetics as a Hollywood movie. The scale, ambition and logistics are the stuff of small coronary failures. And yet it is still a children's TV show, shot in Wales, by the BBC.

'Well, every episode has a key word we all refer to if we ever feel like we're getting lost,' Davies says, when the laughter dies down. 'And the word for this one is ... DISASTER MOVIE! I want you all to think of fat old Shelley Winters swimming down the tunnel, God bless her, Steve McQueen looking incredibly handsome in *The Towering Inferno*. That's the heart of it. Hopefully, we've got Kylie Minogue as the sexy alien waitress, Astrid Peth—' The room cheers '—but we've also got Claire Goose on speed-dial, in case Kylie can't do it.'

The tone meeting is adjourned by 4pm. Outside, there is provision made for smokers in the shape of a small, bus-stop-like Perspex shelter by the side of the car park. Russell – a man who smokes cigarettes in much the same blithe, joyous way as a child eats an orange – lights up, and joins in the excited chat about Kylie. All the crew have been buying new shirts, in preparation for meeting her, he laughs. When it was rumoured she was going to do a BBC Health & Safety course, the course – usually woefully undersubscribed – became fully booked overnight.

'They all think they're going to marry her,' Davies says, lighting a second. 'Even the gays. *Especially* the gays.'

First script read-through, Jim Schmidt Memorial Hall, Tottenham Court Road, London, 2 July

The script meeting is like this: everyone who was at the tone meeting is here, plus the cast, plus – most noticeably – people who've blagged their way in so they can meet Kylie. Everyone in the room is very, very excited pending her arrival. The smell of aftershave is palpable. New shoes squeak. New shirts rustle. Brand manager Edward Russell admits he spent three hours looking for a new shirt yesterday, 'Because if I get the right shirt, Kylie will love me.' He says this with absolute conviction.

Russell T Davies enters the room. 'Kylie! Kylie!' he says to the room at large, waving his hands in the air, and voicing everyone's hysteria. David Tennant enters shortly afterwards, looking rock'n'roll in jeans and a Lou Reed T-shirt, to a general hubbub of 'David!' Julie Gardner bustles into the room with an announcement.

'Guess what!' she hoots, eyes wide with excitement. 'Security found a *Sun* photographer hiding in a cupboard! Trying to get Kylie! They've just thrown him out!'

This provokes an immense, outraged hubbub – topped only a minute later when someone discovers that there are no plastic cups for tea. They're all, inexplicably, in a van on its way down from Cardiff. This is widely considered to be an unforgiveable trespass on human rights.

Five minutes later, Kylie herself finally enters the room – bang on time, and with an 'entourage' of one, her PA. She's in jeans and a silky top and her hair – still short and curly, growing back from the chemotherapy – is pinned close to her head. Her skin is pale and her eyes an extremely unusual, beautiful, mineral-water blue. She looks nervous – fairly under-standably, as she has just walked into a village of people who've known each other intimately for three years – and hovers by the conference table, not quite knowing where to go. David Tennant immediately bounds over, and slaps his script down on the table next to her.

'I'm going to sit next to you,' he says, beaming at her. She smiles up at him, and they sit down together. She puts her pencil box and make-up bag on the desk and fiddles with them – just like it's the first day at school. Russell beams at her encouragingly, and only looks a bit like a huge giant grinning at a tiny sugar mouse.

Jane Tranter, Head of BBC Drama, stands to make a speech, which concludes, 'You're going to have a ball, living up to the public's expectations – which are, frankly, huge.'

Then everyone introduces themselves to the room, from the tea boy up.

'I'm David Tennant, and I play the Doctor,' Tennant eventually says, to huge yells.

'And I'm Kylie Minogue,' Kylie says, to a gigantic roar of approval.

The read-through is a little creaky at first – mainly because, judging from the faces in the room, everyone is preoccupied by thinking 'Kylie! It's Kylie! Kylie gold hotpants Minogue Kylie!' but by shot seventy-eight, where Kylie has a key scene with the Doctor, Tennant smiles a real, tender smile at her, everything judders into place, and there's a sudden spritz of Christmas magic in the air.

The read-through ends at precisely 2pm, and most people in the room gather around the buffet to eat cake, which is of a noticeably better quality than at meetings where Kylie Minogue has not been present.

Suddenly, Kylie – who seems to have got over her nerves, and has been buzzing around and introducing herself to everyone in a very relaxed and charming way – materialises at the table.

'Hello all you clever and high-powered people,' she says. 'I don't want to interrupt your pow-wow, but just to say thank you, and goodbye.'

She then points at James Strong, the director. 'And you need to crack the whip on me. When you *know* me better.' And with a twinkly, minxy finger-wave, she leaves.

'Ooooooh,' Strong says.

'Kylie,' Russell sighs.

*

Cardiff/Swansea, 17 July. On location. In the rain

This is a good day for the employees in the businesses located in the Baltic Building, Cardiff. For despite a heavy security presence, and a series of tarpaulins and screens having been erected, they can see directly into the informal 'green room' of the *Doctor Who* Christmas special – i.e., the car park outside the location shoot. Here, under the gaze of a half-dozen secretaries and clerks staring out of the window and eating yoghurts, sundry cast and crew members of the top-secret show smoke fags and drink tea. There are twenty extras in Edwardian formal-wear standing around, talking about previous work on *Holby*. And there are six angels, with their dresses hitched up to keep out of the mud.

'At least they haven't got their golden masks on,' *Doctor Who*'s brand manager, Edward Russell, says, standing under an umbrella in the rain. 'Last year, on one episode, I had all these people in pig-masks coming up to me and going "Hi, Ed" and I didn't have a clue who they were. You just have to busk it until the penny drops and you go, "Oh, the pig is BRIAN!"'

We join *Doctor Who* stalwart Peter Casey, currently dressed as an angel, but who has, in the past, played every *Who* monster going – Slitheen, Cyberman. He voices his relief that these Christmas Special monsters aren't particularly scary.

'When you're a Cyberman, hardly anyone asks you if you want to go for a fag,' he says, sadly.

On set, and a semi-neglected building has been done up to look like the interior of the *Titanic* – huge Christmas trees, a parquet dance-floor, a delicious, turn-of-the-century, intergalactic buffet.

Down a quiet staircase to the side, one can hear the unmistakeable sound of Kylie Minogue being lovely.

'Wow – are you the guys who did all the sanding downstairs?' she's asking two star-struck council workmen, engaged in renovating a dilapidated staircase. They are in dusty overalls. She is in a thigh-skimming waitress's uniform, with seamed stockings and knee-high boots.

'You've done an *amazing* job,' she coos.

David Tennant comes bounding over, between takes. This morning, he explains, collapsing leggily onto a chair, he and Kylie did the modelling for the *Doctor Who* dolls; already tipped to be one of the Christmas best-sellers. The trick is, he says, to have a completely blank expression when they photograph you. He learned this as a child, playing with his own *Doctor Who* toys.

'If the figures look happy, or fierce, or anything, it's bound to ruin *some* scene you've got going on,' he says, wisely. 'The versatile action figure is the blank-eyed action figure.'

That night – the night with the most spectacular sunset of the year – there is a party to celebrate Kylie's last day on set. The Roald Dahl Suite of the modish St David's Hotel is reserved for the entire cast and crew to let their hair down, celebrate, and give thanks for the beauty of Kylie's sexy legs having been on the BBC for an hour on Christmas Day.

At the appointed hour, carpenters, lighting riggers, camera men, sound men, make-up artists, producers, directors, aliens, the Doctor and Kylie Minogue all filter into the room. Everyone who isn't Kylie is wearing a clean shirt, and has a freshly scrubbed face. Kylie, on the other hand, is wearing a skin-tight dress of gold and silver lace, and Christian Louboutin heels. She actually looks like she's from another planet, where everyone is gorgeous and had their life changed by shagging Michael Hutchence. She looks around the Roald Dahl Suite – a windowless corridor with a small, sad-looking bar at the end of it.

'This is awful,' she says, very reasonably. There is a small pause. 'Everyone follow me!'

Like Maria leading the Von Trapp children over the mountains in *The Sound of Music*, Kylie leads the entire cast and crew down two flights of stairs, across the lobby, heels clicking, and into the beautiful St David's Hotel bar. There are five businessmen in there, having a small, dull meeting over a single beer. When the *Doctor Who* massive enter the room, spearheaded by Kylie Minogue, their jaws drop to the floor.

Edward Russell escorts Kylie to the bar, and addresses the bar manager, who appears to be in a state of mild shock.

'Ms Minogue would like to move her bar-tab to this bar,' he says, with a winning smile. 'There isn't a problem with that, is there?'

'Of course not!' the manager says, the faint sheen of sweat on his brow.

The next six hours pass as some manner of experiment, whereby some undisclosed figure is trying to work out who can party harder – an entire Welsh TV crew out on the razz, or a pixie-sized pop legend.

On the left, we have the show's make-up artists explaining, with owlish, technical passion, why you shouldn't drink flaming sambucas whilst wearing lip-gloss – 'It's made of petroleum jelly. It sets fire to your lips.'

On the right, we have Ms Minogue, working through a steady stream of pink Cosmopolitans, restyling people's hair, and using her 'Gaydar' match-up on various crew members and production staff.

David Tennant – although engaged in a very silly conversation about the potential innuendo contained in motorway signs ('I mean, slip-roads! Really!') – brings his evening to a gentle end after just three whiskies.

'That's enough for me,' he says, quietly leaving the party.

Last week, his mother died after a long illness. He took just two days off filming, so as not to disrupt the schedule.

Kylie finally leaves the party at 1.30am, shortly after dropping her drink on the floor ('Ooops! Better get another!'), spanking people's bottoms and hugging them as she leaves the room. There is a collective sigh as she leaves. It's a bit like when someone turns the fairy lights off on the tree.

The final edit, 28 November. A screening room at the BBC in Cardiff
It is over two months since the wrap party. Someone has decorated the room with two small Christmas trees, a plate of mince pies and a yule log. Russell, Julie and Phil scream when they see them.

Russell, Julie and Phil scream as the theme tune begins. It's a new version, with added drums, which makes it sound a bit like the BBC's *Ten O'Clock News*, but as if the news came from Mars, and headlines were about psychic silver spiders exploding out of a black hole.

'Did you see how many times I cried?' Julie demands, as the final credits roll. She looks to Russell and Phil – only to see they are crying, too. There is a moment of satisfied, contented silence. Then:

'I've got a few notes …' Julie says.

'Me too,' says Phil. 'Pages of them. But let's do a toilet break first.'

Russell slips outside, for a cigarette. He sits in the plastic bus shelter, lights up, and exhales.

'That's all gone very well,' he says, cheerfully. 'I'm quite excited about Christmas, now. I might even fancy an advocaat, whatever that is.'

He pauses for a moment, and then sighs. A process which began almost exactly a year ago, at the launch party of the 2006 Christmas Special, has finally ended.

'Well, I'd better start on next year's now, I suppose,' Russell says, taking another drag on his cigarette, and staring up at the sky. 'I'm thinking of a Victorian theme …'

Last piece for this section – on the curious phraseology of the anti-choice move-
ment in America. 'A gift.' 'A gift.'

This is Not a Gift

There's something disturbing about the idea of someone pressing some-thing unwanted – wholly unwanted – in your hands, saying, 'It's a gift! It's a gift!'

And you demure, politely at first – saying, 'How lovely, but no. I do not want this gun/modern sculpture too large for my house/a sack of oysters – to which I am allergic – thank you. It is lovely that you thought of me: but no.'

But the insistence increases.

'It's a GIFT,' they insist, forcing it into your palm. 'A PRESENT. YOU MUST HAVE THIS GIFT.'

And now your hands are bleeding, and you're truly alarmed, and you try to back away. But you find that the law is changed, overnight, and you are legally obliged to take this gift – even as you stand there with your hands torn, saying, 'But surely a gift is something wanted? Something *suitable*? A stranger's hand putting something into my pocket is the same as a stranger's hand taking something *out* of my pocket. Really, there should be no hand there at all.'

And the gun goes off, and the sculpture is wedged in the doorway, immoveably, and the oysters leak, slowly, onto the floor. Things that would have been wanted elsewhere cause chaos here. They do not fit, and they cause grief. And the stranger walks away from you. Having pressed his gift upon you, his work is done. And you do not understand why he ever came to your door.

Republican candidate Rick Santorum's comment that, if his fourteen-year-old daughter were raped, and became pregnant, he would not want her to have an abortion – but think of the baby as a 'gift' from God – has been one of the defining quotes of the year.

As contraception and abortion become, yet again, controversial – the UK facing the second proposal, in as many years, for pro-life organisations to counsel women wanting an abortion; in the US, Rush Limbaugh and Rick Santorum speaking out against contraception, even for married couples – the idea of babies as a 'gift' becomes a pivotal one.

'Gift' is a key concept. If all babies are a 'gift', then a pregnant woman seeking abortion becomes unforgiveably 'ungrateful'. Similarly, contraception is bad, because it is the rejection of yet more 'gifts'.

Let us think of all the inferences of 'gifts'. If I give you a gift, it is usually a surprise. It is probably something you would not have got for yourself. And after I have given it you, I would not see it again. I leave you with the gift. Gift-giving leaves the person who receives the gift essentially powerless – not a problem if it's an incongruously brightly coloured wristwatch; a great deal more so if it's a human being you bear responsibility over for the rest of your life.

Babies being 'given' to women as gifts makes the women sound powerless. Just something that a present was put into, like a cupboard, or a shelf – rather than a reasoning adult, who decided they were ready to be a mother, instead.

Calling a baby 'a gift' also sounds – let us be honest – like the phrasing of someone who has not spent much time bringing up children. It seems unfair to use visceral language to describe the reality of parenthood – but as anti-choice, anti-contraception campaigners are quite happy to use visceral language themselves ('slut', 'prostitute', 'whore', 'murder'), I have to presume they would be all right with it.

From the shop-floor of pregnancy, childbirth and motherhood, here's what that gift can entail: tearing, bleeding, weeping, exhaustion, hallucination, despair, rage, anaemia, stitches, incontinence, unemployment, depression, infection, loneliness. Death. Women still die in childbirth. Not as many as used to – but notably more than die whilst receiving any other 'gifts', such as scented candles, or mini-breaks. Additionally, 'gift' sounds hopelessly inadequate to describe your children, whom you would die for in a heartbeat, inhale like oxygen, and swoon over like lovers. I have never done this over a foot spa, book token or vase.

The worry of the anti-abortion and anti-contraception campaigners is that women rejecting these 'gifts' are rejecting the gifts of Nature, or God. It is in obeisance to them that we should not turn to contraception, or abortion. But Nature, of course, turns to contraception and abortion all the time: the diseases that make you barren; the sperm counts that fall to zero. Blocked tubes and blown wombs and the thousand sorrows of the infertile. The one-in-three first pregnancies that end in miscarriage – miscarriage which is just like abortion, we must remember – a potential life ended – except miscarriages are unwanted, and often dangerous, whilst abortions are safe, and wanted.

Nature also, clearly, believes in non-procreative sex: for twenty-seven days a month, sex is non-procreative. Sex after the menopause is non-procreative. Statistically, most sex is non-procreative. Clearly, sex *isn't* just for procreation: it's also for the creation of happiness, or excitement, or contentment.

Those things that really are gifts; and are always wanted. Those things that do not scare me, when pressed upon me.

part**three**

Parenting, Politics, Party-bags and Poverty

In which we boggle over Downton Abbey,
mount a defence of parental binge-drinking,
discuss the heaviness of poverty, and call for Lola
from Charlie and Lola *to be rubbed out for ever.*

But before that, a domestic interlude.

Whilst my job involves a lot of brief yet incongruously intimate encounters with all kinds of people, my ability to just 'get on' with anyone – put them at their ease, make time with me a pleasant experience – is never more pertinently exposed than in the late-night conversations I have with my husband. In many ways, I feel these chats encapsulate marriage in a nutshell: one person bursting with ideas they feel they can only share with one, special, most-beloved; the other just wanting to be very unconscious.

All the Ways I've Ruined Your Life

It's 12.04am. I'm on the woozy half-slide of sleep; the cotton-wool duvet of more weightless thought. There's something about my teeth growing bigger. I'm falling, leg-first, into a dream.

'Cate.' It's my husband, sitting up next to me.

'Wh?'

'Cate.' He, apparently, is not falling asleep.

'Wh?'

'I've just found your Mooncup under my pillow.'

For those who have never come across one, a Mooncup is a … ladything, that you use at … lady-time, to do … lady-business. For some reason, I always seem to be losing them – then finding them in unexpected places. The second most embarrassing thing that has ever happened to me is having my best friend's one-year-old son walk into the kitchen, my Mooncup wedged in his mouth, like a dummy. I still can't talk about the most embarrassing thing that ever happened to me. Needless to say, I was not expecting to see that twenty-one-year-old accountant on my landing at that particular moment.

'Why is your Mooncup under my pillow?' Pete asks. Oh dear.

'I wondered where it was!' I say. Maybe my cheeriness at having found it again will infect Pete, and he will be happy for me.

'I'm not happy for you about this,' he says. 'If that's what you're thinking.'

'I am sorry,' I say. 'It is just the way of my Mooncup. It is like all scissors and cheese-graters – I never, ever know where they are. They seem to flit between parallel worlds. It's mad!'

'I don't think your Mooncup has made it to underneath my pillow via string theory,' Pete says, still looking quite awake. 'Because it's one of many, many of your things that have ended up in the wrong place, and I don't think even an infinite universe has that many wormholes.'

'What do you mean?' I say.

Clearly I am not going to sleep any time soon. Pete is obviously a little het up about this. I have to say, I find this desire to chat during sleepy-time somewhat thoughtless. I would never do this.

'Well, yesterday I found a slice of half-eaten bread and Marmite on top of my Pentangle boxed set,' Pete says, sounding genuinely quite annoyed. 'I was going to have a go at the kids – until I recognised the gigantic, foot-wide mouth print of the person who'd been eating it.'

'Me?' I say.

'Well, it was either you or a wandering T. rex,' he says. 'You appear to have the mouth span of something that can dislocate its lower jaw and eat a piano, whole.'

'Well, that's not so bad, is it?' I say. 'Toast on a CD? After all, they do look like coasters. They're easy to wipe clean. In a survival situation, they'd be an obvious substitute for melamine picnic plates. I think that's quite reasonable.'

'You just shouldn't leave your lunch on my records!' Pete says, sounding a little bit emotional. A bit like a woman, I have to say. 'I wouldn't—' He casts around for a comparable event '—put a pork pie in your handbag.'

'I wouldn't mind if you did,' I say, reasonably. I am very reasonable.

'I know you wouldn't!' he says. 'I've seen you put falafel in the side compartment before now! You have very low standards of hygiene! After sixteen years, I accept that in you! I just don't accept it in you on my stuff!'

'Is it so bad?' I ask. I'm rather hurt. I have improved my standards since we've been together. When I moved into his flat, in 1996, I brought two black bin liners of washing-up with me. Dirty washing-up. That was by way of my trousseau. In one bag, there was an ashtray. Full. But I wouldn't do that now. I have changed.

'You leave your dirty tights in the kitchen. I found one of your flip-flops in my computer bag. Yesterday, I took my Oyster card out of my coat and it had one of your Compeed blister plasters stuck to it – I had to stand at Holborn peeling it off. You threw my Le Creuset oven glove out of the window.'

'I've already done a column on that,' I say. 'To my mind, it's been dealt with.'

'I came down after one drinking session and found you'd stubbed your fag out on Nancy's special *Little Mermaid* plate,' Pete continues. 'You try to squeeze the blackheads on my nose when I'm driving; you come in and start conversations with me when I'm on the toilet; you've ruined all the BBC4 reruns of 1976's *Top of the Pops* by repeatedly saying, "I hope when the punks finally turn up, they've got GUNS and KILL J J Barrie."'

'Is this,' I say, hopefully, 'one of those arguments where you list all of the ways I've ruined your life – but, by the end of it, you feel oddly saucy, and the argument segues into some sex? Like in *Moonlighting*?'

'And you compare everything to *Moonlighting*, even though you know I've *never* seen it,' Pete says.

The pleasures in having children are uncountable. The touch of a sticky, star-fish hand on your face. The walk to school where you merrily slag off half their classmates together. The mammalian joy in watching an ill child find comfort, and fall asleep, in your arms.

On top of this, if you're a lighthearted newspaper columnist charged with taking a wry, sideways glance at life until life knows the fuck it's been wryly glanced at sideways, they're always good for rinsing out a quick 850 words on a tight deadline. If anyone calls it child exploitation, you can point out that the Lego Death Star costs £274.99 – and so therefore who, really, ultimately, is screwing over who here?

I Refuse to Make You Party-bags. Leave Before I Summon a Policeman

I am not a curmudgeon when it comes to my children's birthdays. Not at all. I *make* them a card, I *make* them a cake. Let's cut to the chase – I made *them*. I am a birthday originator. If it weren't for me, they'd just be card-less, cake-less, aimless sperm.

But whilst there is no end to the amount of delight I am prepared to shoehorn into my daughters' big days, I do draw the line at one thing: party-bags. I find party-bags unconscionable. I will not hand them out. I think they are the symbol of a decadent and corrupt regime. There is no logical reason why they ever have come into existence, or why we – as reasoning, sane people – should continue to support them.

In the sixteen, peaceful years my husband and I have had together, there are only two subjects on which we come to blows. The first is over his repeated, intolerable desire to own an oven glove – MAN UP AND USE A FOLDED TOWEL. YOU DON'T NEED SOME MANNER OF PAMPER MITTEN TO GET A TRAY OF OVEN CHIPS OUT, YOU THUNDEROUS NANCY.

And the second is party-bags. Twice a year, it is the same argument.

Him: 'Party tomorrow. Better get the party-bags ready.'

Me, reasonably: 'Pete, as those children leave, they will already HAVE a party-bag. The bag is their own heads – and the gifts inside are the memories of a great day, spent violating a balloon-animal man.'

Him, not listening at all: 'I don't want to put the same things in it this year as I did last year. Last year I did mini Rubik's cubes. It's got to be something different.'

This desire for 'unending bag surprise' has led my husband down some unexpected party-bag alleyways. Last year, he made every single kid at Lizzie's ninth birthday a compilation-CD of songs he thought they'd like. We never got any feedback on the ninety minutes of the 'more accessible' works of Stackridge, Kraftwerk and psychedelic folk-jazz titans Pentangle – possibly because kids these days have everything on MP3, instead. They must have been intrigued by the odd rainbow drinks-coaster in their bag. Perhaps they thought it was a duff pirate BlueRay of *Avatar*.

Pete's problem is that he is essentially a good man, trying to make sense of a bad system – but he should never have been pushed into the invidious position of trying to get nine-year-old children into psyche-folk in the first place. Why on *earth* would a child attending a party receive, essentially, a gratuity? It's like we're tipping them on the way out of the door.

Let me make this clear: I am not *thanking* them for coming. I've just laid on three hours of food, amusement and tolerance in the face of Alfie taking over the disabled toilet at Pizza Express, and using it as his own private office-cum-hangout, much in the manner of the Fonz conducting his 'business' from his favourite booth at Al's Diner. I have also had to deal with Emily, who has explained her attitude to pizza thus: 'I don't have the pizzas with tomato sauce, or cheese, on. Not those.'

The message I have, to 24 departing children, is not 'Here is your treasure-bag. I am grateful for this special time with you'. It is, 'You've had your fun – now sling your hook, sunshine, before I summon a police constable.'

I don't believe in children's party-bags in the same way I don't believe in 'the Gifting Room' at awards ceremonies. People rocking up at the Oscars don't need to be taken into a room full of high-end consumer durables and/or 'pamperment experiences'.

By the time you're walking down a red carpet, a kilo heavier from all the diamonds, all your life is basically one big gift. You know – Mariah Carey's had a great day. She's got out of the house, worn a nice frock, had a conversation with John Travolta she probably didn't understand, and now she's going home again. She doesn't need a Diamonique-covered Magimix and some spa vouchers to sweeten the deal.

And yet this pointless giving of gifts continues, unstopped. Parents are brought to the edge of despair by it. You see them, the day before a party, wandering around shops with that 'party-bag look' in their eye.

'I just need a collection of stuff that comes to no more than £2 per child,' their posture is saying. 'It honestly could be anything. I will put an apple, a box of tacks and a copy of the *Express* in there if I have to. I just need a quantity of stuff to weigh a child's hand down as it goes out of the door.'

The honest, untrammelled reaction of a child, meanwhile, reminds you of the pointlessness of the whole thing.

'Oh,' they say, looking inside the bag. 'This rubber is all covered in cake-jam.'

And then they throw the whole lot in the bin.

More parenting fury – this time, over the monolithic merchandising cashpoint that is Charlie and Lola. *At the time I wrote this, it didn't seem appropriate to mention in* The Times *that I've 'got my eye' on husky-voiced, awkward Marv – Charlie's best friend – and would totally Mrs Robinson him when he reaches the age of majority; some four years hence from his age in the books. Somehow, though, it seems OK to say it here. The italics oddly make it OK.*

I Hate *Charlie and Lola*

In the early days of parenthood you aren't, of course, so picky. In those first, panicking years, anything that entertains and diverts your children for ten minutes – allowing you such fripperies as falling asleep face down on the landing, or the time to slough crusts of gack from your unflattering parenthood pantaloons – is gratefully embraced. You would put on a DVD of any old toot for five minutes' respite from a 3pm toddler, who is freaking out, *Gremlins*-style, about contact with sunlight. It's hard to explain to a non-parent how very low your standards – and, indeed, morals – become. Once, on one of the very worst days – when no TV show seemed to please them – I remember thinking, 'Hitler apparently had a mesmeric oratory style. Audiences would listen, silent and rapt. I wonder if I could order something from Play.com.'

But as they get older, it gets easier, and you can, finally, afford the luxury of quality control. You can begin to cast a critical eye over just what it is your children are staring at, saucer-eyed, and evaluate it in the same way you used to evaluate your own collection of music, DVDs and books.

And when I started to do this with my children's very favourite programme – one of the most famous and successful of the last ten years – I had a creeping realisation: I hate Lola from *Charlie and Lola*.

There. I've said it.

For those who've never watched the programme, the set-up is this: Charlie and Lola are two middle-class, bohemian children who live in a world of eclectic Scandinavian textiles and irregularly drawn eyes. Where their parents are, no one knows – judging by their house, Mum is probably appearing on *Newsnight Review* wearing spendy shoes and analysing *Peep Show*, whilst Dad drops some rare Twinkletronica and Humbient grooves at an online nu-rave club, via Skype.

In their absence, bright, chatty, intolerable four-year-old Lola is being raised by her older, put-upon, tousle-haired brother, Charlie. Charlie has a lot to endure. 'I am a fussy eater!' Lola declares, cheerfully – necessitating Charlie to spend a whole show renaming carrots 'orange twiglets from Jupiter', until his sister finally gets her tea down her. He has to rename mashed potato 'cloud-fluff from the pointiest peak of Mount Fuji' because Lola is a child who won't eat mash. A child who won't eat MASH! Honestly, I have more tolerance for the Klu Klux Klan. 'I honestly, totally and completely can look after your dog!' Lola promises Charlie's friend, Marv – immediately losing the dog, and probably getting Marv beaten that night.

'I am too absolutely small for school,' Lola says – crocodilian eyes calculating exactly how long she can play Charlie for a mug, wringing bribes and concessions out of him, before she finally knuckles down and goes through the school gates LIKE SHE KNOWS SHE HAS TO.

Charlie's age is never specified, but he looks around eleven – on the cusp of puberty. That he has to spend his days humouring a girl who opens all his birthday cards, breaks his rocket and thinks she's Mariah Carey at her most mad ('All the world should have rainbows and ice creams!') must, surely, be a ball-ache of titanic proportions. His parents have created a lisping, eating-disordered monster – and then left him to deal with it while they take their Pashleys to La Fromagerie, to choose between their two favourite ash-rolled goats cheeses for supper. Guys! Just get some Dairylea and bail this kid out! Bail *us* out.

For the real basis of my hatred of Lola comes from her terrifying power as a role model to my daughters. She has raised intolerable expectations of what a twenty-first-century child's bedtime might reasonably consist of – demanding tigers drinking pink milk, lions to put the toothpaste on her toothbrush, and three whales in her bath before she'll even deign to put her pyjamas on. This is, obviously, roughly equivalent to pressing a button labelled 'Drive all parents mad NOW'. It's certainly not how I was raised. My bedtime ritual consisted of my mother pointing upstairs, and shouting 'GO THERE'. That was very much a ritual I intended to pass on to my own children, until this … termagant came along.

What will become of Charlie and Lola, in adulthood? Although it's theoretically too early to call it, Charlie's clearly going to be a total hotty by the time he hits sixteen. Given his appearance and upbringing, he'll end up forming an awkward, middle-class, Boards of Canada-type band, tour for a couple of years, then get a gig composing the incidental music for *Skins*. His early experience with a capricious younger sister will make him prime husband material, and his high-achieving wife will happily indulge his twice-yearly snowboarding sessions, and on/off weed habit.

Lola, on the other hand, will be one of the high-profile audition-ees on *The X Factor* who tanks out spectacularly at Bootcamp, wailing 'PLEEEEEASE, Simon – I absolutely completely and totally know I can do this!'

Yes. In thirteen years, Lola will be Katie Waissel.

Still, I'm aware that being a father is just as hard as being a mother. Especially when your kids start talking.

The Horror of Daddy's Special Lemonade

I was sitting at the kitchen table last week, flicking through the newspapers, and observing just how many confusing and/or alarming things I could absorb before breakfast. Here was the news that David Cameron is apparently taking 'anti-posh' lessons – surely an ill-advised move in the middle of an election campaign, given that, were it successful, the Conservative Party would be left with little more than a pair of trousers, and a name-tag reading 'Dave'.

On the next page, another mention of how the Mayans believed the world would end in 2012 – a theory which is now beginning to rattle me quite badly. What, I panic, in the name of *Moses*, is going to go down at the London Olympics? How badly wrong can an opening ceremony featuring Paul McCartney, David Beckham and Stomp go? The only thing that could possibly make the End of Days worse is knowing that its epicentre was in Stratford, and that all the disruption of building the East London Line had, in the event, been a complete waste of time.

But then I turned the page and saw a picture of convicted paedophile Sidney Cooke, and felt suddenly and enormously reassured.

Now he really *does* look like a paedophile, I thought to myself, happily. No doubt about that. He's a *classic* beast. He looks like he's from some putative Nonce Central Casting Agency. If I saw him in a playground, I thought, there would be no doubt or uncertainty. I would be evacuating the swings immediately. So long as there are paedophiles who look as obviously up to no good as Cooke, there is less confusion and worry in the world. He has that certain, unmistakeable, alarming 'something' that sets the nerves jangling. Thank God for Cooke.

I turned the page in the newspaper, finally feeling more relaxed about the world.

But of course, that certain, alarming 'something' is not just restricted to things that actually warrant alarm. Sometimes, we are alarmed by things that shouldn't really be alarming at all.

I was given cause to reflect on this the next day, when we had some friends over. Lizzie greeted them in the hallway.

'I've been helping Daddy make his Special Lemonade!' she said, brightly. My husband does, indeed, make a very good lemonade. As lemonades go, it really is quite special. But as I caught the momentary quizzical looks of my friends, I realised that the phrase 'Daddy's Special Lemonade' has a certain … dubious quality to it.

'I love Daddy's Special Lemonade!' Lizzie continued, cheerfully, as we all went into the kitchen. The situation started to feel bad.

'It's got limes in it,' I said, briskly. My husband, however, had already noticed the glances.

'Oh, I wish I'd never called it that,' he sighed, pouring lemonade out into glasses. 'Daddy's Special Lemonade was a bad idea. It's like that tickle thing, all over again.'

The 'tickle thing' was an unfortunate incident a couple of years ago, when we had to leave a playground after a very young Lizzie shouted, 'Daddy! Tickle me in my special place!'

As it happens, her 'special place' was a particularly ticklish spot under her chin – but the looks on the other parents in the playground suggested they did not believe this to be the case. We actually never went back to that playground again – which was a shame, as there was particularly good mobile reception there, and I used to read all my emails while she was on the slide.

It is a sad fact that, over the last few years, both 'special' and 'Daddy' have taken on a slight tinge of … unsavouriness. Menace. Perhaps it's the racks of misery memoirs that have them in the title – *Please Daddy, No; What Daddy Did; Daddy's Special Girl* – but two ostensibly benign words are becoming loaded with unhappy inference. To the point that, when I see a greetings card with 'To a Special Daddy' on the front, I can barely repress a shudder. A Special Daddy? A Special Daddy must be the very worst. That's some seriously gnarly ominousness. What manner of monster are Hallmark catering to?

As things stand, at this point in the twenty-first century, we're on the verge of losing our innocence towards the words 'daddy' and 'special'. I feel like homophobic bigots must have felt in the 1970s, as they watched the word 'gay' slip from their vocabulary.

Lexical tectonic plates are shifting. Special Branch, the Special Olympics, The Specials, Special K – all will have to be renamed, as the word shifts from 'something unique and significant' to 'a terrible traumatic secret, such as would be a major plotline development in *EastEnders*'. As a consequence, the words 'specialisation' and 'specialist' will sound little better than an outright admission of having studied evil to university-level.

Within my lifetime, I suspect, Daddies Sauce – never a wholly reassuring name for a product, even twenty years ago – will have to be rebranded, having taken on a critical ominousness.

As for Daddy's Special Lemonade – we've told Lizzie to refer to it as Lime Surprise from now on. As a matter of some urgency.

'Mummy's Special Lemonade', on the other hand, is a much different beast. It's a gin and tonic with a massive wedge of lemon.

In Defence of Binge-drinking

According to a BBC *Newsround* report last week, 70 per cent of children have seen their parents drunk – and, of these, 46 per cent don't think their parents should ever drink in front of them.

Before we go any further, let's just tackle the obvious yet necessary points: if we're talking about parents who go completely woo-hoo/Bill Sykes on the sauce; or who are only managing half the school run before sitting down in the middle of the pavement, puncturing a Gaz canister with their keys and sucking out the contents with a 'special' straw, then guys, you need help. I am not interested in 'partying' with you. If you come round my house with a bottle of Lambrini, I will hide in the coat-cupboard, whilst phoning in a perfect description of you to Social Services. You are not my good-time bredren. Consider yourself eschewed and betrayed by me.

Everyone else, however, is welcome to join with me in faintly piqued incredulity at the children of today. WHAT MORE do they WANT from us? Don't they KNOW how this system WORKS? Mummies and daddies have to drink lots of wine down in one go on Friday night – because the schedule doesn't *allow* it the rest of the week. It's called TIME MANAGEMENT. If I don't drink a whole bottle of wine on Party Night, I probably wouldn't get time to drink at *all* – and that, obviously, would be ridiculous. Parents drinking is the reason you came into the world, and if we didn't keep doing it then, by God, it would be the reason you went back out of it.

This is one of those many occasions where adult reason must overrule the ill-thought-out utterances of the young and stupid. You don't want us to drink in front of you? Where, pray, are we *supposed* to drink? Obviously we'd *like* to go to the pub – we'd *like* to go to Harry's Bar in Venice, in 1951 – but we can't, because we're *looking after you*. And, I might add, looking after you in the best possible way: has Mummy ever been more entertaining than when she stood on the patio table, opening and closing the big parasol, and singing 'I'm No Good' by Amy Winehouse? Or when she had a little 'wine nap' at the bottom of the garden, and Uncle Eddie and Uncle Jimmy wrote 'BALLS' on her forehead in marker-pen, and you got to colour in her nose and ears blue? If CLOWNS were doing this in a CIRCUS you'd think it was hilarious. And, let's face it, it's the only time Mummy can be halfway arsed to play Super Mario Kart with you.

But by the skewiff logic of the younglings, my father had a better attitude to drinking – in that we never actually *saw* him drink. Instead, we'd be left outside the Red Lion in a Datsun, engine running so that Radio 1 could entertain us. As we howled along to 'Take On Me' by A-ha, Dad would occasionally reel out of the saloon bar door and push a packet of crisps through the crack in the window – saying 'Remember you're a Womble' – before going back into the pub again.

Three hours later he'd suddenly come bombing out holding something incongruous like a fish tank, say, or a bag of plaster, hissing, 'It's all gone a bit *serious* in there,' and pulling away from the kerb at 60mph. Then he'd pass out on the hall floor, and we'd rinse his pockets for spare change.

Was he ultimately the better parent? The fact that I once watched him throw two litres of petrol onto a bonfire – 'Because *The Two Ronnies* is on in ten minutes'– thus setting fire to our garden fence, means that I can answer this, frankly, 'No.'

But we are, at least, of accord on the issue of parental drunkenness. Look, man. I don't do fox hunting, diamond collecting, spa breaks or that much nitrous oxide any more. My leisure time has to operate within the boundaries of being conducted a) within 40ft of my children b) between the hours of 6pm and 1am, Fridays only, and c) costing no more than £30. Therefore, I like to get a very, very cheap bottle of supermarket whisky – the kind that, when you drink it, turns you into a pirate: closing one eye and shouting 'ARGH!' – then sit down with a couple of chatty people, and get a bit toasted.

If you're of joyous mind, that kind of drinking is like a mini-break – as exhilarating an experience as spending three days sightseeing in Rome, or walking Scafell Pike. You'll have imperially wiggy conversations, solve the world's problems three times over, spontaneously remember all the lyrics to 'I Don't Know How to Love Him' from *Jesus Christ Superstar,* and wake up in the morning feeling oddly cleansed, and cheerful.

And if the kids don't like it? Darlings, you talk this much nonsense, and fall down the stairs that dramatically, *every day of the week.* You haven't got a leg to stand on.

Drinking £7.99 Pinot Grigio in the kitchen, fearlessly reporting on teenage girls eating pasties – in many ways, I am the Orwell of my times. Orwell of The Times. *'Oh well' of* The Times.

Pasties and the Teenage Girl

Teenage girls eat more unhealthily than any other group in the population, government research has revealed. Girls of secondary school age are living on junk food. Forty-six per cent are failing to get the recommended amount of iron or magnesium, and only 7 per cent are eating the minimum recommended five portions of fruit and vegetables a day.

The research was carried out over a year, involved 1,000 adults and children, and included physical measurements, blood pressure checks and urine samples – although, to be fair, I could have saved them the bother by simply phoning them up from outside Greggs, Crouch End, and shouting 'PUT ANOTHER STAR ON THE CHART!' every time a fourteen-year-old girl came out carrying a sausage roll and a can of Fanta. As far as the girls at the girls' school are concerned, Greggs is the official school canteen – sometimes forsaken for KFC over the road, although there is a small, hardcore group who buy their lunches exclusively from the newsagents on Weston Road: Skips and Twiglets for main course, Bounty for pudding, and a hot chocolate, from the machine that looks like a photocopier, to wash it all down.

At the end of the school day, the girls catch the W7 bus home from the stop outside Greggs. If you get on after a flock of them, you often find the interior handrails are covered in a thin film of pastry-fat, and crisps.

Those girls' diet might be slowly giving them heart disease and rickets – but, on the plus side, their hands are constantly being exfoliated and moisturised with salt, and lard. In their coffins, they will have the well-preserved hands of a twenty-year-old.

Being a teenage girl is hard. I could probably argue it's harder than being in a war. After all, the Taliban never pretend to be friends with the British Forces for six months, and have sleepovers at each other's bases, whilst all the time secretly spreading rumours that the British Army has one breast bigger than the other, and an uncle who's a paedophile. Landmines – or everyone on a school coach trip shouting 'LESBIAN!' at you? It's a tough one to call.

There's little to recommend being a teenage girl, really. I reckon that, throughout history's great span, six people have actually enjoyed it, tops. If you have long legs and swingy hair, and your dad is Paul McCartney, *maybe* you'd have a chance. For everyone else, though, it's a period where your body explodes in a vile and alarming way, and you sleep under a pink Power Rangers duvet that depresses you every time you look at it. When it comes to chillax time, your options are severely restricted: there are no flinty Viogniers in your life. Sex involves being in the 'cabin' bit of the tall slide in the park, with a sixteen-year-old boy: in the extremely unlikely event of your achieving orgasm, it will probably be rapidly followed by you sliding twenty feet down, head-first, and landing on a council-approved safety surface. You can't even steal a shopping trolley and throw it in the canal any more, since they put those magnetic security ramps in the exits to supermarket car parks.

No wonder, then, that teenage girls self-medicate on gigantic quantities of sugar, fat and carbs, instead. Sugar to get you high, screaming and giggly on the back of a bus while you sing along to Rihanna on your mobile; carbs and fat to opiate when you're on the sofa with your mum, watching *Take Me Out* and wishing, for the millionth time that day, you were dead. Or, if you're slightly more clear-headed about things, Stella McCartney.

When I was a teenage girl, food definitely wasn't 'food' to me, i.e., something with vital nutrients and energy in. I'm pretty sure I'd heard of Vitamin C. I judge this because, when I started smoking, at the age of sixteen, I remember smugly switching from Coke to Orange Tango, in order to replenish the vitamins I knew I was destroying.

'That's sorted that,' I thought to myself, lighting up.

Other than that – nah. If you'd asked me how much magnesium I was getting, or how many portions of fruit and veg I should be eating, my eyes would have turned into those little rainbow pinwheels you see on Apple Macs, just before they crash.

At seventeen, here were my priorities on food:

1) Does it have prawns in it? Prawns were the modish thing in early nineties Wolverhampton. When Marks & Spencer introduced the Prawn Marie Rose to their sandwich shelf, it caused as much sensation as Raleigh bringing back the potato from the Americas. Wolverhampton prawn-fever hit hard. I can remember a night in the Dorchester night-club where the entire conversation revolved not around who had yet to lose their virginity, but who had yet to eat their first prawn sandwich. My inaugural decision, on reaching adulthood at sixteen, was that I would now spend 20 per cent of my weekly income on M&S Prawn Marie Rose sandwiches – and, later, when I developed a modicum of sophistication, the simpler and more elegant Prawn & Mayonnaise. In lieu of having a car, prawn sandwiches were, for me, totemic of an independent and exciting life. Judging by the trade at Greggs, a Steak Slice seems to fulfil much the same function in 2010.

2) Can I put chips in it? Being a teenager involves a lot of hanging around outside, in the cold – bus stops, street corners, parks. Given this, there's a fairly convincing argument to be had that if British teenagers didn't eat the amount of hot chips they did, we would find dozens of them, frozen to the spot, every morning – like the White Witch's statue-filled court-yard in Narnia. I think it's significant that I only started eating salad at the point where my social life began to revolve around my own kitchen table – rather than an upturned bread crate on some wasteland, where someone

had just made a tiny, carcinogenic campfire out of mattress springs and a car battery.

3) All things considered, wouldn't I rather just have a Malibu and coke and another fag, instead? For much of 1993, the answer to this was 'Yes' – I dropped three stone in four months and had times of wild and high adventure. This whole, pleasing existence was curtailed, however, when I suddenly fainted in the front room at 9.30am on a Tuesday, and couldn't – when frantically questioned by my mother – actually remember when I had last eaten. I was lucky that I had a mother who then grounded me until I reintroduced the concept of 'three meals a day' back into my life. By way of contrast, the first time my friend Sasha fainted from hunger, she got so excited by the high she spent the next five years being tiresomely bulimic. Unlike most teenage girls, she actually did get her daily-recommended portions of fruit, veg and magnesium – but only for twenty minutes, tops.

Want some more about my childhood? Here's the bit where I was in a caravan in Aberystwyth, listening to Night Owl *by Gerry Rafferty and semi-convinced that, when I grew up, I'd marry Joey Boswell from* Bread. *I always enjoy writing about my childhood. It requires absolutely no research and always seems pleasingly improbable – like something I dreamed of when I fell asleep in a wardrobe, looking for Narnia.*

Aberystwyth: the Only Place I Stop Wanting

We first went to Aberystwyth when I was thirteen, at the height of my parents' hippydom. We had no TV, we lived on huge pans of lentil soup, and I ran barefoot across fields so long, the skin on my soles was like cork-tiles.

We were spending our summers in a caravan with no toilet in a field outside Pontrhydfendigaid, near Tregaron: eight kids, two parents, and three huge dogs. In my memory, when you walked towards the caravan, the faces and legs of all the humans and animals were pressed up against the glass of the window, like a terrine. That caravan was very full. When my parents had sex, the van would rock like a fairground ride, and all the kids would sit in the front room, quietly singing 'California Girls' by The Beach Boys – to block out the sounds – until it was over. Our harmonies were terrible. We were not the Wilsons.

But we did not spend much time in that caravan. We had a Volkswagen campervan – the greatest vehicles ever created; a cheery cupboard on wheels – and when my parents had finished noisily co-joining, they would take us on post-coital journeys all across West Wales: up to Port Madoc, down to St David's, right round the yawning pig-jaw of Cardigan Bay. Wide white estuaries, book-stack fishing villages, and bleak, wet-slate hamlets where it always lashed rain against the single, solitary phone-box.

I don't know why it took us four months to finally go to the nearest, biggest town – Aberystwyth – but when it did, some inner room in my heart twanged; some lever was pulled. It wasn't like falling in love – I was thirteen, and had never been in love. I just felt – not unhappy any more. The quiet litany of pubescent frets that I counted, daily, like rosary beads – I was fat, I was lonely, I knew too much about my parents' sex life, I didn't have any shoes, and I wanted, more than anything, to be the best friend of the Duchess of York – all stilled the first time our van drove down Darkgate Street, and turned left onto the seafront.

There was something so perfect about Aber that it halted my life-long internal monologue. I needed silence, to fully take the place in. It had a gothic university like a castle, castle-ruins like a smashed cake, a cliff-top Victorian theme-park that appeared to have been commissioned by a pissed H G Wells (a funicular railway! A camera obscura! A golf course using GIANT golf balls!) and then – slicing the town in half like a fabulous blindness – the cold, hard, glitter-glue of the sea. Apparently, dolphins chased by the rock-pools, at dawn.

Face pressed against the window, wetting it with breath, I wanted to concentrate on this town. And then eat it, whole, like a crisp sandwich, but even better. For the first time ever, my heart stopped wanting.

'This place is shitting brilliant!' I chirped, from the back of the van.

'Don't swear in front of the fucking kids,' my dad replied.

Twenty-three years later, and I'm back with my husband, and my kids, to the only place still that makes me happy and quiet. I came here with Pete when we were first in love, then again with each baby; and now we come every year, at the end of August: migratory creatures that can be followed on a map. We take the same apartment on the seafront, go to the same restaurants, do the same things, have the same days. I think even the conversations are the same: 'No beach has better pebbles!' 'No castle has better views!' 'No freak-shops have a better array of skull-shaped bongs, dude!'

The first day is Arrival – falling from the car on a journey that is always an hour longer than you remember, dehydrated and shrunken-legged. Aber's magic is that – ninety miles from the nearest motorway – it is near to, and on the way to, nothing, except the dolphins in the bay. You only come to Aber if you're going to stay in Aber – a night, at least; a week, usually; the rest of your life, if you're one of the hippies who first pitched up here in the 1960s, or one of the 8,000 students a year who come here for their degrees, then just … don't leave.

We throw everything into the apartment, then walk along the sea front – the sea! The sea! Sailor-blue! Or else, with bad weather, as hard, thrilling and unstoppable as a sword – to The Olive Branch, on the corner of Pier Street. It's a comfortable, higgledy, pine-and-spiderplants joint and, if we're lucky, the window-table will be free. We'll eat good Greek food – my husband is Greek, so he's picky about these things – whilst staring across the bay to the distant shadows of Anglesey, and Snowdonia. Because it's the first day of the holidays, I will have had at least two glasses of wine by the time we finish, and go down to the beach for the first time: Pete and I leaning against each other as the kids fall into the waves for the first, and then the second time; wringing out their shorts, and spreading them on the beach to dry.

It's a fine, pebble-and-shale beach – crunchy, not clacking – and the currents bring a junk-shop variety to the stones on the tide-line. Quartz, slate, igneous Ordovician, meta-limestone from the Lleyn, cider-bottle glass smoothed to emerald – we fill our pockets with the most interesting ones; the ones shaped like letters, or animals or, once, a Volkswagen caravanette, just like the one we used to have.

You can crab, happily, for hours, off the boardwalk; legs hanging into the sea. In summer, the boardwalk is filled with coachloads of Orthodox Jews – hats and curls buffeted by the sea-breeze. It seems right that they'd come here – Barmouth is too normal, Tenby too twee. Aber feels as practical and time-suspended as they are. It's far too windy for urban spores of anti-Semitism to take a hold here.

The sea turns silky, and electric-green, as the sun goes down – tide rising by the minute, and sucking at your knees until you leave the bay and walk home. Safe, from the apartment window, the bay explodes into sunset – fire, fire, pink nuclear fury, and then the utter insanity of Welsh starlight; mirrored in the trawler-lights, heading for Ireland.

The next day is proper beach-day, and we head sixteen miles up the coast, to Ynyslas. There's a picnic in the boot from Ultra Comida, on Pier Street – a jewel-like Spanish restaurant/deli with breads, cheeses, olive oils and pastries – and the drive takes you high enough to see the lion-back Cambrian mountains, chasing you all the way to the end of Dyfed. Ynyslas is a National Nature Reserve consisting of nothing but sky, sand-pools and dunes: over a morning, you follow the tide out, over endless, new, creature-filled sandpools, until you reach a newly revealed sandbar, miles out to sea.

The afternoon is then spent in slow, contemplative retreat back to the mainland as the tide comes back in – racing across the sand, throwing up instantly doomed sandcastles, and writing our names – 'MUMMY' 'DADDY' 'LIZZIE' 'NANCY' – in metre-high letters on the beach, in the way that, two decades ago, my siblings wrote their names – 'CAIT' 'CAZ' 'EDDIE' 'WEENA' 'PRINNIE' 'GEZMO' 'JIMMY' 'JOFISH' – in the same, not-same sand.

The third day will rain – Cluedo – and the fourth rain, probably, too: the Ceredigion Museum, on Terrace Road, is Aberystwyth's old thea-tre, now filled with curious agricultural tools, archeological finds, stuffed animals, maritime oddities and a dinky café, all in a Womble-ish jumble. Then Wasabi – Aberystwyth's sushi restaurant, on Eastgate – before home, and the concluding round of Cluedo.

Day five is probably my favourite: full immersion in Aber. A half-hour walk takes you to the top of Constitution Hill, and Luna Park – the benevolently ghostly Victorian amusements on top of Aber's outcast cliff. A candled, rickety shrine to the Virgin Mary, halfway up the path, is the point where you stop to eat crisps. At the top, it's tea and Welsh cakes. Then the funicular railway down lands you in the centre of town again, and lunch at the Treehouse – another of Aber's jumbled, pitch-pine joints, this time selling soul-cheering local wholefood and chilli hot-chocolate.

You can spend hours here, on a rainy day, as the windows mist up; the smell of fenugreek and jasmine tea and goats cheese making the room pleasingly dreamy as you do the crossword, or stare out of the window at the million greys of wet, Welsh slate rooftops. And then, when the weather breaks, the castle: a green hill overlooking the sea, with the rib-bones of a fourteenth-century castle poking through. The view is the very best, the one I bone-ache for in London: Cardigan Bay from end to end; the full length of Wales visible in one, long sweep. The first time I saw it – thirteen, standing here in a wet, crocheted poncho, holding my squalling two-year-old brother – I felt insane, wild jealousy towards Prince Charles.

'I can't believe he's the prince of all this!' I shouted, into the wind. 'I would KILL for this!'

And then I remembered that, of course, in a roundabout way, he had.

But there's a quiet, stubborn, time-biding, self-contained Welshness to Aberystwyth that makes the idea of being 'ruled' over laughable. This place simply disbelieves it belongs to anyone but itself. In the playground, in the dip next to the castle – sheltered, and lavish with white clouds of hydrangea – the slate gravestones from a demolished church have been laid, like purple flagstones, around the perimeter. So many are in Welsh – the stories of farmers and captains and politicians and priests who would have no idea of England's existence as they lived, and died, here: travelling no further than the mountains behind us, and the sea in front.

As the wind blows across again, and the grass sings lysergic, rain-drowned green, and the bay looks like a billion smashed fish-scales, stretching all the way forever, who could ever imagine England, east of here: flat, dusty, half-coloured, quiet and so, so distant?

In the car home, I cry, like every time since 1988.

The next piece is a heroic plea for everyone to enjoy paying massive income tax bills.

Interestingly, a couple of weeks after this was published, I ran into handsome David Tennant, aka Doctor Who, who appeared to have forgiven me for, the last time I saw him, mentioning his dead mother and ruining an otherwise lovely evening with Kylie Minogue.

On this occasion, I managed to keep the conversation on the cheerful subject of taxation, instead. Tennant spent five minutes agreeing with me on this very subject, whilst I stood there thinking, 'SHIT! It's the Doctor! The sexy Doctor! He's looking at me with his eyes whilst I look at him with my eyes! We're eyeballing! I think I might have just breathed his breath! Oh now I'm thinking too much about breathing and I've forgotten how to do it! I'm going to faint! I'm going to faint on him! And, as I faint, I'm going to wet myself! Oh, I should NEVER have written about income tax. It is a man's game.'

But we both agreed we love paying tax.

This column was prompted by the artist Tracey Emin complaining about her tax bill.

Tax Me. Hard

Look, I can argue in favour of Tracey Emin until the cows come home. I like modern art. I think if men have got away with spending 500 years painting each other on horses, looking supercilious, then the least the ladies should be allowed is some boozy foxine, and her 'Everyone I've Ever Slept With' tent. Tracey Emin is a cool accessory for any modern country to have. She's got ideas! She's got purpose! She's got an absolutely cracking rack! Plus, it is clear to me that, if we ever went out for a couple of cocktails together, we would probably have invented The Beatles by 9pm; and lost our shoes by midnight!

Sadly, however, last week, Tracey said something that threw our close, decades-long, totally imaginary friendship into doubt.

'I am simply not willing to pay tax at 50 per cent,' she said. 'I reckon it would mean me paying about 65p in every pound with tax, National Insurance and so on.'

She then went on to threaten to leave Britain entirely, and relocate to France – where she already has a home – when the new 50 per cent tax, on earnings of £150,000 and over, is introduced in April next year.

Obviously Emin is not the first public figure to get lemon over tax increases. Michael Caine has said he's also thinking of leaving. Guy Hands, the City financier who recently gutted EMI Records, has moved to Guernsey. Phil Collins, Lewis Hamilton, Mike Jagger, Sean Connery, that grinning bloke who owns EasyJet – gone: to the Caribbean, and Switzerland, and Dubai. George Harrison, of course, wrote a whole song about it: 'Taxman'. Although forty-three years have since passed, it does still seem absolutely amazing that Harrison's first big songwriting moment in the spotlight – released at a point where the man was being treated as a demi-God, drowning in a sea of beautiful women, and getting high with Bob Dylan– was him spaffing on about his *accounts*. Fair enough, 95 per cent tax is a trifle steep – but were a young man ever in a position to lie back, sigh and say, 'All things considered, I'm still winning, really. Indeed, to coin a phrase, everything must pass,' it was Harrison.

So yes – moaning about tax is well established as a British celebrity pastime. It's up there with golf, and Botox. But frankly, I just don't understand where these guys are coming from. Personally, I love paying tax. Really. Maybe it's my upbringing – I am the first Moran *ever* to pay tax. Well, a 'money-tax', rather a 'potato and mud-tithe' tax. When I got my first ever drearily written, implicitly threatening, standard letter from the Inland Revenue, I was *thrilled*. Getting stuffed by the taxman means you're *earning money*! You're not going to go to the workhouse, after all! No more throwing the weaker siblings onto the fire, for warmth, for YOU this winter! Should you consider the population of the world for just one second, you will observe that a British citizen, earning enough to pay income tax, is in the top centile of success. Yes, the paperwork is a downside – but the not-being-an-indentured-child-labourer-in-China-making-lightbulbs is a definite plus.

So given that only 0.6 per cent of British workers earn £150,000 or over, complaining about having to pay what is effectively a You Really Are Winning Tax comes across as an act of querulous, caviar-maddened ingratitude. You're basically being Chandler in *Friends*, when he wails, 'My wallet's too small for my fifties, and these diamond shoes are too tight!' I think it's actually a repressed, British form of showing off – like when the aristocracy complain about how draughty their castles are, and how difficult it is to find an undermaid who'll tolerate being raped, and then sent away to a home for unmarried mothers in Devon.

This is not the way I roll. Every time I write out a gigantic cheque to the Inland Revenue, I get a bit excited. Woooo! I go. What a seriously grown-up thing to be doing! It's like drinking whisky, buying an engagement ring, or chopping down a tree. In a world where nearly every other signifier of adulthood – fighting Vikings, dying during childbirth, growing a beard, nurturing your own yeast-culture, having a leg ripped off in a horrific agricultural accident – has been replaced with an unending childhood of telly, jogging bottoms and strawberry-flavoured medicine, writing a single, bracingly large cheque once a year is pretty much the only adult duty we have left. On this basis alone, I find it exhilarating. I kind of *want* it to hurt a bit. I feel like the Joker, facing down Batman: 'Come on – stick National Insurance on top of it! I can handle it! VAT me! VAT ME!'

But I am not wholly unsympathetic to the point that Tracey Emin is making. We have, after all, been best imaginary friends for over a decade now – so when she says, 'So much here is simply not working. We're paying through the nose for everything,' I kind of know where she's coming from. You give the government a cheque that could buy a really nice three-bedroom caravan – and then, the next day, the bin next to the bus stop is overflowing. It's hard not to draw your own conclusions.

But you know what would, in a single stroke, make tax paying much more popular in this country? And might even keep my incredibly close friend Tracey here?

A receipt. After all, whenever I've just blown £227 in Waitrose and feel a bit alarmed by it, it's oddly comforting to read through the receipt and say to myself, 'But at least I have a lot of yoghurt, now.' Similar comfort would be experienced by the tax payer if, in exchange for a large cheque, one was simply issued with a printout of what you'd just bought yourself: £2,000 for the NHS, £600 for streetlights, £2 for Prince Andrew, etc.

And of course, once you've got a receipt, it's much easier to claim a refund …

It's not just David Tennant I turn into a stuttering div around. In my seventeen years as a journalist, I've been a total tit in front of many of this nation's best-loved figures. You think of them, I've probably said something inappropriate to them. You're talking to a woman who met Paul McCartney and asked him, 'What would you do if your face got horrifically mashed up in a car crash, Paul?' PAUL McCARTNEY FROM THE BEATLES.

Listing all the people I've twonked up in front of would be too dispiriting – for me, obviously; I'm aware everyone else would find such a Roll Call of Failure quite amusing – but suffice to say, I watch most BAFTAs going, 'It went badly with her, fucked it up with him, acted like a prize prannet with both members of that double act. Yeah – I've got the full set here.'

It's why I don't watch the BAFTAs any more.

In this following piece, I make it clear how very badly nearly every meeting with one of my heroes, Eddie Izzard, has gone. It's been nearly two decades of me making every encounter with him slightly more awkward than it needs to be; mainly because I love him so much it all goes wrong and I end up – as in this case – showing him a piece of lettuce I've knotted with my tongue.

And do you know what the amazing thing is? In 2010, I was voted 'Interviewer of the Year'! For talking to famous people! Hahahaha! HAHAHAHAHAHA!

Eddie Izzard: 'I Keep Going Because I Think She'll Come Alive Again'

We're four rows from the front of the Manchester MEN Arena. With 13,000 people sitting behind us, these are pretty much the best seats in the house – yet, still: we can't see Eddie Izzard's eyes.

Well, more specifically, there's no time to look at Eddie Izzard's eyes whilst he's humming and buzzing across the stage, like some super-bright sunshine kid in full-on 'delight' mode. You only really have time to register his grin – like a predatory Cheshire cat – as the characters fall out of his one-man phantasmagorical ensemble-pieces.

Here comes a traumatised squirrel from Brooklyn; a raptor in a pork-pie hat being pulled over for speeding; a Persian soldier very slowly impaling himself on Spartan spears at Thermopylae. Caring sharks. An entire swarm of bees.

You simply presume that Izzard's eyes are twinkly, warm, Father Christmas-style eyes. You know what I mean. Tom Hanksy. Like the dog you loved the most from your childhood.

So the jolt when you meet him in the flesh is all the more intense.

'Hello,' he says, at the aftershow, appearing at your shoulder – and, up close, the eyes are glittery, hard; like a silver clockwork owl. The thumb-smeared kohl and eyeliner – sigils of glamour, and possibly decadence – merely underline how ferociously present he is. He has eyes like guns.

This contrast between ostensible glamour and decadence, and the true purpose beneath, is echoed in the room we're standing in. Somewhere in the intestines of the MEN, a room has been swagged to looked like a harem. But who is here? It's not the usual line-up of hangers-on, surly local scenesters, dealers and birds. Instead, it's just Eddie's cousin-in-law, Johnny Vegas's manager, and the heavily pregnant Lucy Powell – Labour Parliamentary candidate for Manchester Withington.

I've been interviewing Eddie Izzard for sixteen years now. Not continuously, obviously – that would be weird. No – I just pop in every couple of years, and see how he's getting on; plug his new thing. As an invention – a boy in heels as charming as a robin, and as remorseless as gravity – I think Izzard is amazing. I like watching what he does.

Nearly every time I meet him, however, I make a total arse of myself. At a wedding we both went to in 1997, I offered him a cigarette – and then another, with the words, 'If one is cool, then surely two *at the same time* would be even cooler. It's like a … circle of coolness.'

Ten seconds later – after he'd walked away, looking bemused – I realised that was pretty much word-for-word a routine he was famous for doing at the time. I think I even did it in his voice, a bit. But then, most people who meet Izzard come away reporting that they end up talking to him in his voice – going all 'Um' and 'Ah' and 'Yeah but'. His speech-pattern is insanely catchy. There's practically a Survivors Support Group of people who've done an impression of Eddie Izzard to Eddie Izzard, then cringed themselves into next Christmas at the memory.

Today, at the Manchester aftershow, I had been amusing myself by showing my sister a trick I learned off Audrey Horne on *Twin Peaks*. In a pivotal scene in the drama, she gains employment in a local brothel by displaying how she can tie a cherry-stalk into a knot, using only her mouth. Prompted by my sister's goading that I would not be able to do this, yet stymied by the lack of cherry stalks in the room, at the point where Eddie finally comes over to say 'Hello', I have just tied a strip of frisee lettuce into a knot in my mouth, and triumphantly spat it out into my palm. It is covered in saliva.

'Hello,' Eddie says, all pewter-pupils.

I explain to him what I have done.

'And is that ... useful?' Izzard asks, looking bemused. I am so mortified at my continuing intention to exude the Fonz at Izzard, only to end up as Ralph Malph, that I make my excuses, and drag my sister from the aftershow party.

We leave through the Arena's loading bay. There – lined up like the start of a dinosaur derby – are six, huge, articulated lorries. Each has the official 'Stripped' tour shot of Eddie on the side: Izzard in a dinner suit, torn open to the waist. His eyes are smudged with glitter, and he's sexily kissing his fingers. As a convoy, the trucks must look pretty spectacular whenever they hit the M6. This immense, 'sexy truck', European and US tour will eventually play to 380,000 people – including 20,000 at Madison Square Garden alone. He really has not wasted the last sixteen years at all.

It's become beyond a cliché to refer to comedy as a 'serious business'. Clearly, the business here is immense – even at an Izzard-stipulated, non screw-over, £35-maximum per ticket, Eddie isn't heading back to Covent Garden – where he spent the 1980s performing on a unicycle, for pocket-change – any time soon.

But the *seriousness* is the interesting thing. In a year where he's conducted a massive, technologically innovative, sell-out arena tour, marketed as the thinking-woman's pin-up, Izzard also ran forty-three marathons in fifty-one days, and then – on the last day of running, at a reception in Downing Street – announced he suspects his eventual future lies in politics. He will stand – presumably for Labour, to whom he is a major donor – in either two or three elections' time. When he talks admiringly about Barack Obama's technique with large crowds – 'He does this ... *big intimacy*' – it's not only as a showman admiring the chops. It's as a future statesman studying the form. His ambition is inexorable and amazing.

'I'll have to kill my career for it. But sometimes, you just have to ... stand up, and be counted,' he says, shrugging in an excitingly determined manner. 'Because if you don't do it – who will?'

In the documentary *Believe: The Eddie Izzard Story* – which has just done the international film festival circuit, and gets a limited theatre release here from 11 December onwards – there is a key, 'Oh! now everything makes sense!' moment.

Over the last fifteen years, Izzard has scarcely been reticent about discussing what a big impact the death of his mother, when he was five, had on him. Aside from mentioning her both on-stage and in interview, he named his production company, Ella, after her. We know about the young Eddie Izzard losing his mother in the same way we know about Madonna losing hers.

In the documentary, however, director Sarah Townsend – Izzard's former girlfriend – keeps pushing Izzard on why he seems so driven: taking fifteen years of rejection before becoming a successful stand-up; then learning French so he could gig in French; then relocating to America to pursue a film career.

In response to her questioning, Izzard finally says – in an uncharacter-istically desperate burst – 'I keep thinking that if I do all these things, and keep going and going, then – she'll come back.'

And then he starts crying.

Today, over breakfast in Manchester, Izzard recalls the shooting of that scene.

'I didn't know I was going to say that, because ... I didn't know I thought it,' he says, simply. 'That's why it's weird. That's why I start crying.'

Breakfast is black coffee, Special K and toast. Izzard is in a rather beautiful, blue, borderline-Mod suit, and wearing glasses, which he's needed since the beginning of the year.

'Shall I show you a picture of my mum?' he asks. He gets his iPhone out, and starts scrolling through the pictures. When he finds the shot, he holds up the phone: it shows a blithe woman with a chatty, wonky-looking mouth, and soft dark curls, in a cotton print dress.

'She's pregnant with me, there,' Izzard says. There's a pause. We look at the picture. He continues, with immense gentleness: 'She was a singer. She sang with amateur opera groups. There aren't many pictures of her. I'm trying to find them all. Last year, a Swedish family contacted us with footage of the entire family just sitting there, having a holiday. That was ... amazing.'

Izzard scrolls through the few more pictures he has – his mother and his brother in Yemen, sitting in the garden of their house. His mother on stage, dressed as a ballerina in tiny, tiny shoes.

'I have small feet, too, like her,' Izzard says. 'Six and a half.'

He looks at the photograph again. It's an odd sensation – looking at a photograph of someone's mother, with someone who knows not a huge amount more about them than you do.

'Most of the memories I have are from the cine-film, and photos,' Izzard says, still looking at the picture. You see that the awful thing about losing a parent at such a young age is not that the memories unsettle you, but that there are no memories at all.

In *Believe,* there's a moment where Izzard finds a letter his mother wrote, where she refers to him as 'Edward'. Until that point, he hadn't even known what she called him.

It reminds me of something that occurred to me the night before, as I watched Izzard onstage: that his material and demeanour – slightly woozy retellings of history, science and nature – is that of a bright primary-school child coming home, and telling its mother a phantasmagorical version of what it learned that day; just to delight her.

Izzard is scrolling through the rest of his pictures. 'This is me in my football team!' he says. 'When I was twelve. I've just started playing again – because you should reclaim all the things you enjoyed from your child-hood. I really believe that. I'm training to be a striker, because – I'm a striker in everything else I do. I like to attack things, and push push push. Because anyone can do anything, can't they? World War Two showed us that. Bankers were made into commandoes. Women were taken from Cheltenham Ladies' College and put on anti-aircraft batteries. Everyone can do way more than they think.'

Izzard loves the Second World War. As things stand, he is still the only person to play two speeches by Churchill on prime-time Radio 1.

A fan comes over to get her breakfast menu signed – she is shaking with nerves. Izzard gives her his big T. rex beam, and scrawls away.

Breakfast finished, we wander round the back of the hotel, to Izzard's tour bus – 'And there it is!' Izzard says, triumphantly, pointing at a skip. Next to the skip is a massive, sky-blue tour bus. Inside, Izzard cruises through the lounge area, past a healthy dish of roast seeds, and then stiff-ens when he sees a plateful of Milky Ways and Love Hearts next to them.

'Where did they come from?' he asks, almost peevishly, pointing.

'Someone left them here,' Sarah, his tour manager, says, vaguely.

Izzard sighs, as if burdened.

'Is it a problem?' I ask.

'Weeeell,' he says, already looking pre-defeated by them. 'If I could, I would just sit down, and spend the rest of my life with a straw stuck in a fifteen-kilo bag of sugar, sucking. They just … mmmm.'

'Is that why you ran forty-three marathons?' I ask. 'So you'd have an excuse to kick back, and stuff your face with Haribo every evening?'

'I ran forty-three marathons,' Izzard says, pertly, 'so I'd have an excuse to live to 183. I'm currently thinking of my peak fitness age as being ninety. Do you want to try one of my gels?'

We go through to Eddie's bedroom, at the back of the van, and sit on the bed. It's unbelievably tidy. Not a single item has been left out. It looks like *either* borderline compulsive behaviour, *or* that he just removed everything before the journalist turned up, in order to prevent prying. Personally, I favour the compulsiveness theory – when he sees I'm hold-ing a small piece of rubbish, he holds his hand out for it, silently, to put it in the bin. He also seems mildly distressed about shoes on the bed.

Izzard brings a bag of energy gels out of a cupboard, and we sit there, sucking them. They taste like orange spaff. I gag on mine. Izzard knocks his back in one, like a tequila-shot.

Izzard survived on these during his still-unlikely-sounding forty-three marathons in fifty-one days, for Sport Relief. As a country, I think we're still kind of in denial that these marathons ever happened. David Walliams swam the Channel – *once* – and we didn't hear the end of it.

Izzard, on the other hand, spent the whole summer holidays running a twenty-six-mile marathon pretty much every day, and everyone kind of went, 'Er, yeah, um …' and changed the subject.

'It was a bit surreal,' Izzard admits. 'I think it was like saying I'd eaten a car. "I've just eaten a car. I've eaten a whole car." People just wouldn't believe me.'

Izzard would pass the time imagining the history in the places he was running through – at the Battle of Naseby, he tried to work out just who was fighting on behalf of the Royalists, 'since the Parliamentarians were, like, the people'. He would get sudden, unexpected company on sections of the run – one woman who appeared at his side had driven all the way from Slovakia, just to lope along next to him.

'I feel like I own the road now,' he says, 'in the same way I feel like I own the stage. In that visceral sense. I can turn it up, turn it down. I get it.'

Two days after the last marathon, Izzard was booked to appear on *Friday Night with Jonathan Ross*. He ran all the way from Piccadilly to the BBC studios – 'It was nothing.'

For all his talk of 'killing his career' for politics, he's still got at least a decade of comedy left in him yet: not least his recent idea for a comedy festival – a big one, like Glastonbury, or Glyndebourne.

'Rain and comedy don't work, so we'd have to work out how to cover it all. And we've got to nail the sound – because if you miss just a word in comedy, that could be a whole build-up screwed. Maybe headphones – or a drive-in thing, where you could sit in your car. But then, we can't hear the laughter, and we need the laughter. Perhaps people could flash their headlights, for a small chuckle ...' he starts musing. 'Or we could mike the car park, and people could wind down their windows, and laugh in a designated direction ...'

But he's still restless – a restlessness that it's borderline disconcerting to be around, when you consider the weekends-off, and non-marathons, and quiet compromises of your own life.

'The thing about the realisation in *Believe*,' I say, 'is that if you really *are,* ultimately, doing all this to bring your mother back, there is, obviously, no end to it all. It is infinite. There is no ... satisfaction.'

'I don't *want* to be satisfied. I don't *want* to get there,' Izzard says, reasonably. 'Do you know what I mean? You've got to be four steps ahead – because if you're just one step ahead, that's very close to standing still. Or even going backwards. You stop for a *week*, and ...' He splays his hands.

And he goes to put his trainers on, and run the seven miles to that night's gig, where 13,000 people have paid to watch him think.

One of the reasons I'm such a dick around Eddie Izzard is because he's a self-taught, auto-didactic, preternaturally curious person, and I like to kid myself that I am too – and this is why we could *be great friends if I could just stop behaving like a monumental div around him for nine minutes at a time.*

As me and all my siblings were taught at home, the local library was the extra room of our home: it was our schoolhouse and our playground. Oh, it was a million more things beside – not least an easily accessible toilet if you were caught short on Warstones Drive – and so when the coalition started closing libraries – shooting out their lights and leaving the buildings to rot – I wrote this piece, which got the biggest response of any piece I've ever written for The Times. *It ended up being included in a very worthwhile anthology about libraries,* The Library Book, *whose proceeds went to a pro-libraries charity, and included entries from Stephen Fry, Nicky Wire from the Manic Street Preachers and Zadie Smith – all of whom, to pleasingly prove a point I was just making, I've behaved like an idiot in front of, too. FULL SET! YAHTZEE!*

Libraries: Cathedrals of Our Souls

Home educated and, by seventeen, writing for a living, the only alma mater I have ever had is Warstones Library, Pinfold Grove, Wolverhampton.

A low, red-brick box on grass that verged on wasteland, I would be there twice a day – rocking up with all the ardour of a clubber turning up to a rave. I read every book in there – not *really*, of course, but as good as: when I'd read all the funny books, I moved onto the sexy ones, then the dreamy ones, the mad ones; the ones that described distant mountains, idiots, plagues, experiments. I sat at the big table and read all the papers: on a council estate in Wolverhampton, the broadsheets as incongruous and illuminating as an Eames lamp.

The shelves were supposed to be loaded with books – but they were, of course, really doors: each book-lid opened as exciting as Alice putting her gold key in the lock. I spent days running in and out of other worlds like a time bandit, or a spy. I was as excited as I've ever been in my life, in that library: scoring new books the minute they came in; ordering books I'd heard of – then waiting, fevered, for them to arrive, like they were Word Christmas. I had to wait nearly a year for *Les Fleurs de Mal* by Baudelaire to come: even so, I was still too young to think it anything but a bit wanky, and abandoned it twenty pages in for Jilly Cooper. But *Fleurs de Mal*, man! In a building overlooked by a Kwiksave where the fags and alcohol were kept in a locked, metal cage, lest they be stolen! Simply knowing I could have it in my hand was a comfort, in this place so very very far from anything extraordinary or exultant.

Everything I am is based on this ugly building on its lonely lawn – lit up during winter darkness; open in the slashing rain – which allowed a girl so poor she didn't even own a purse to come in twice a day and experience actual magic: travelling through time, making contact with the dead – Dorothy Parker, Stella Gibbons, Charlotte Brontë, Spike Milligan.

A library in the middle of a community is a cross between an emergency exit, a life-raft and a festival. They are cathedrals of the mind; hospitals of the soul; theme parks of the imagination. On a cold, rainy island, they are the only sheltered public spaces where you are not a consumer, but a citizen, instead. A human with a brain and a heart and a desire to be uplifted, rather than a customer with a credit card and an inchoate 'need' for 'stuff'. A mall – the shops – are places where your money makes the wealthy wealthier. But a library is where the wealthy's taxes pay for you to become a little more extraordinary, instead. A satisfying reversal. A balancing of the power.

Last month, after protest, an injunction was granted to postpone library closures in Somerset. In September, both Somerset and Gloucestershire councils will be the subject of a full judicial review over their closure plans. As the cuts kick in, protesters and lawyers are fighting for individual libraries like villagers pushing stranded whales back into the sea. A library is such a potent symbol of a town's values: each one closed down might as well be 6,000 stickers plastered over every available surface, reading 'WE CHOSE TO BECOME MORE STUPID AND DULL'.

While I have read a million words on the necessity for the cuts, I have not seen a single letter on what the exit plan is: what happens in four years' time, when the cuts will have succeeded, and the economy gets back to 'normal' again. Do we then – prosperous once more – go round and re-open all these centres, clinics and libraries, which have sat, dark and unused, for nearly half a decade? It's hard to see how – it costs millions of pounds to re-open deserted buildings, and cash-strapped councils will have looked at billions of square feet of prime real estate with a coldly realistic eye. Unless the government *has* developed an exit strategy for the cuts, and insisted councils not sell closed properties, by the time we get back to 'normal' again, our Victorian and post-war and 1960s red-brick boxy libraries will be coffee shops, Lidls and pubs. No new libraries will be built to replace them. These libraries will be lost for ever.

And, in their place, we will have a thousand more public spaces where you are simply the money in your pocket, rather than the hunger in your heart. Kids – poor kids – will never know the fabulous, benign quirk of self-esteem of walking into 'their' library and thinking, 'I have read 60 per cent of the books in here. I am awesome.' Libraries that stayed open during the Blitz will be closed by budgets.

A trillion small doors closing.

Shall we do a couple more righteous columns? While I've got my serious face on? These are the ones I think of when people go, 'Oh, I read your stuff! You're not bad! I think my dad likes you!,' and I'm all like, 'Yeah, I'm changing your life with my Marxist/feminist dialectic! Check out my rad moves!'

Then it turns out, further into the conversation, they were just thinking of the funny one where I try to get Pete to call me 'Puffin', instead.

Unlike Most of the Coalition, I Was Raised on Benefits

Unlike most of the people voting on the proposed £18b cuts to the benefits budget – as it shuttles between the Commons and the Lords – I was raised on benefits. Disability benefits – collected every Tuesday from the post office, in a shuffling queue of limpers, coughers, and people with their coat hoods pulled right up.

Perhaps if you drove past the queue, you would presume the ones hiding their faces were doing it because they were on the fiddle – 'playing the books'. In reality, they were the scared kids with mental problems on Incapacity Benefit, who you'd see trying three times, and ultimately failing, to get on a bus. Good luck with getting them on a Re-Start scheme, you would think. Good luck with trying to funnel that terror into a cardboard hat in McDonald's.

A council estate on benefits isn't what you think – if you must imagine it, rather than remember, or just look out of the window. Popular imagination has it that it's full of obese, tracksuit-wearing peasants smoking Rothmans on the front doorstep, rehearsing for their spot on *Jeremy Kyle* whilst spending their fraudulent benefits on a plasma TV.

Benefits spent on plasma TVs is the totemic fury-provoker of the professionally angry social commentator – 'They're spending YOUR taxes on A FORTY-TWO INCH SONY!!! You couldn't MAKE IT UP!' – ignoring the fact that if you live somewhere with broken-glass parks and looming teen-clusters on each street corner, and gave up on the idea of having a car or a holiday long, long ago, then staying at home, safe, together as a family, and watching fifteen hours of TV a day is a peerlessly cost-effective, gentle and harmless way of trying to buy happiness.

Besides, they almost certainly won't have spent 'your' taxes on it. They'll have got a massive overdraft, like everyone else in the Western World. They'll have got your telly the way you got your telly. People on benefits are just people – on benefits. Some of them are dodgy, most of them are doing their best, and a few need more help than we could ever imagine. The mix is about the same as on your street. If you are having to imagine it – rather than remember it, or look out of the window.

What's it like, being on benefits? Being on Disability Benefits – 'I've had a hard day's limping, to put that tea on the table!' my dad would say, as we sat down to eat something based around a lot of potatoes, and ketchup. Well, mainly, you're scared. You're scared that the benefits will be frozen, or cut, or done away with completely. I don't remember an age where I wasn't scared our benefits would be taken away. It was an anxiety that felt like a physical presence, in my chest – a small, black, eyeless insect that hung off my ribs. Every Tory budget that announced a freezing of benefits – new means-testing, new grading – made the insect drill its face into the bone. They froze benefits for four years in a row, as I recall: 'freezing' being the news's way of telling you that you – already poor – will be at the checkout, apologising as you take jam and squash out of your bag, put them back on the shelves, and ask them to add it up again. Every week you fear that this is the week the pennies won't stretch any further, and something will disappear: gas, food. Your home.

Eventually – and presumably to the endless gratification of Richard Littlejohn – they did take the telly away; halfway through *Twin Peaks*. All the kids cried and cried and cried. There wasn't really anything left to do. I invented a game where you lay on the bed staring at the telegraph lines outside the house for so long, without blinking, that you would start crying. The house was very cold. Dad spent whole days in bed – a huge white plastic jar of painkillers on the floor beside him, looking like the New Schmoo.

All through history, those who can't earn money have had to rely on mercy: fearful, changeable mercy, that can dissolve overnight if circumstances change, or opinions alter. Parish handouts, workhouses, almshouses – ad-hoc, makeshift solutions that make the helpless constantly re-audition in front of their benefactors; exhaustingly trying to re-invoke pity for a lifetime of bread and cheese.

That's why the invention of the Welfare State is one of the most glorious events in history: the moral equivalency of the Moon Landings. Something not fearful or changeable, like mercy, but certain and constant – a right. Correct and efficient: disability benefit fraud is just 0.5 per cent. A system that allows dignity and certainty to lives otherwise chaotic with poverty and illness.

Certainty, that is, until you cut the budget so savagely, some benefits disappear altogether. Then, you bring back all the fear of the alms house, and the parish dole. Then, you cut this country back to Victorian times.

I remember it, from my childhood. I can feel the dreary terror from here.

And another. After this column was published – about my schizophrenic friend, Richey, losing his flat, due to Housing Benefit cuts – I was bombarded with calls from news shows, wanting Richey to come on and talk about his experience. But, of course, schizophrenics rarely want to go on live TV and talk about how they feel – the terrible Catch-22 situation that means we still know so little about mental illness, until it happens to us, or a loved one.

A Thousand Rooted Lives
Sliced Through with a Spade

It's the nearest thing to magic, really – legislation. Bills before Parliament. A document is written somewhere in London, a room full of people agree to it, and suddenly the country shimmers: concentric circles travelling outwards at 1,000mph, blasting through Birmingham and Liverpool and Aberdeen. Hospitals open, or close. People put down roots, or move away. Anxiety and nervous tension is either created, or alleviated. One document, blasting through Manchester and Swansea and Plymouth. One document blasting through Brighton.

Brighton is where my friend Richey lives. I've known Richey all my life – both when he was a kid, dressing up as Robin Hood, obsessed with *Daley Thompson's Decathlon* on the Commodore 64; and when he was a teenager – when the fever of schizophrenia burnt him up one winter, and left him lying on his bedroom floor, fists buried in his eye sockets, listening to a radio tuned to static.

Everyone who knew Richey at that time – Christmas 2001 – had to make the biggest promises of their lives: that they hadn't drugged him and put bugging devices in his brain; that we didn't secretly hate him; that we weren't trying to turn him into a man he kept dreaming of – 'Evil Simon', with a monobrow, 'Like a crow across his forehead.' No, we didn't do that to you, Richey. We would never have done those things to you. We love you so much.

That was eleven years ago. Richey's on medication, now, and he's good. The pills made him 'well' enough to get a degree – 2.1 – although he could never socialise with his fellow students, because any room filled with voices would necessitate him having to clarify conversations with polite, yet nervous, questions like, 'Did you just call me a dick?' and 'Did you just say I'm evil?'

Obviously there are very few jobs where one can ask those kind of questions on a daily basis, so Richey's on benefits: Disabled Living Allowance and Housing Benefit. He didn't, as he planned, grow up to be Robin Hood or Daley Thompson, after all.

In a world seen only in numbers, Richey is useless. He draws his benefits from the State, and the only 'trickle down' effect he contributes comes from cheap rolling tobacco and tinned curries. Any government department with a calculator would declare him a deficit in Britain's budget. But that's only if that department had – inexplicably, against all we've ever discussed about what it is to be human – decided to only see people as 'profit' or 'loss'.

Because in the undeclared statistics of people – on the black market of love – Richey is a peak in Brighton's accounts. Captain-hearted, he holds together his troubled family like a shy sheepdog: his single-mother sister, his emotionally fragile mother. And this is whilst working on the full-time job of keeping himself together: performing the thousand daily exorcisms he must to keep thinking in a plain, straight line.

But the concentric circles of benefit reform move towards Brighton, now. In panicked phone calls, Richey tells me about the coming awfulness of May: when the new Housing Benefit legislation kicks in, and he will be left with £75 per week to find a home in Brighton. Single people under thirty-five no longer qualify for one-bedroomed accommodation:

everyone must now cohabit – a cruel and unusual punishment for some-one who needs to be able to count the amount of voices in the room, as all his case-workers agree.

So now Richey has just two options.

The first is to lie: to claim his symptoms have got worse, which would qualify him for higher housing benefits, and keep him in Brighton, with his family. Of course, the advisability of someone with medical-level para-noia doing this is deeply questionable – the fear of being busted would probably, and ironically, genuinely worsen his symptoms. This option has the second irony side-note that the increased medication he would be prescribed costs the NHS more than it would for him to stay in his tiny, calm, quiet flat; plus knock him out for twelve hours of the day, leaving him like a zombie.

The only other option is to go. Relocate to another, cheaper city – as tens of thousands of the poorest people are now doing, as the benefits reforms shimmer across the country, and make whole cities unafforda-ble. Maybe he could move to – I don't know – Croydon or Leicester or Dudley – find a small room, and, totally alone, die, and start again.

For when we talk about people having to leave a town or a city, what we're really asking them to do is leave their whole lives, and make another one. And the people being asked to do this – ill; poor; with children, settled in schools – are the ones least fitted to it. This isn't like asking a generation of boisterous young fellow-me-lads to up sticks, and seek their jolly fortunes elsewhere. This is herding the shamblers and the scared through the streets – and then shutting the city gates on them. Tiny little rooted lives, sliced through with a spade. A whole country changed, with a single shiver – circles radiating out from Westminster.

After publication, the response I got to the previous column was vast, varied and astonishing. I felt I had to write about some of the most recurring comments.

The People You Never Hear From

A third of the people in this country are dependent on benefits.

Of course, you wouldn't know that was the figure from television, media or literature. Judging by the lives of our popular fictional characters, you'd presume that if a third of the country *were* anything, it would be either a) maverick coppers, b) high-class call girls, c) pairs of whimsical post-grad kidults in urban flat-shares, or d) Jamie Oliver – not people signing on. You never really see people on benefits. You never really hear about them – apart from as statistics in newspaper reports, or as cast members of *Shameless*.

Perhaps due to the odd, ongoing mysteriousness about the bedrock of this country's class system, writing about benefits prompts a very mixed, and often confused, response.

Two weeks ago, I wrote about my friend Richey – a schizophrenic whose Housing Benefit is being cut, in May. I wrote about how this means he must leave Brighton – where his friends, family and support system is – pick another, cheaper town at random, and begin his life again.

The comments, emails and letters I received were intriguing. By and large, people who were sympathetic to Richey's situation were people who had experience of a similar situation – either personally, or with a loved one.

Those who were unsympathetic, meanwhile, tended to be speaking theoretically – discussing figures and reports that they'd read, rather than actual people they knew.

For the unsympathetic, one idea seemed paramount – encapsulated in: 'If I were a well-paid columnist, I would help [Richey] out – instead of taking to my column and whining about it.'

The presumption here is that there's only about six poor people in Britain – and if all their broadsheet columnist friends just bailed them out, we could dismantle the welfare system tomorrow. And for those who are genuinely worried, let me assure you: I've bailed out as many as I can. I am like Bob Geldof with a typewriter, except with much better hair. I have thrown UNICEF bags of grain and powdered milk at every troubled friend I know.

But the problem with this solution – let's call it MoranAid – is that a) I don't personally know everyone who needs financial help, and b) many of the people who need help aren't as charming and accidentally well connected as Richey. Let's face it – a lot of disabled/mentally ill/ poor people are grumpy, or charmless, or shy, or friendless. Probably the same proportion as in 'normal' society. They just aren't going to persuade nearby people to support them, financially, unfailingly, until they die.

That's why I like the Welfare State – which helps everyone: even people with terrible personalities, or who don't know broadsheet columnists – rather than the Big Society, which is wholly optional and ad hoc, i.e., the situation we had right up until 1945 – paupers' graves, workhouses, parish handouts and all.

From a purely selfish point of view, as a British citizen, one of the things I particularly like about the Welfare State is the lack of admin: instead of seeking out local, winsome widows and pressing bread into their grateful hands, I pay my tax bill, get someone else to source needful widows, and use the time now freed up to watch *Masterchef*, or give the kids a bath.

I guess if I were a bit richer, I could hire a PA, and get *her* to do it – that would be my only hope at contributing to the Big Society. Using a

PA – but in the meantime, I'm pretty happy with the way the DSS does it.

I had a similar kind of postbag a few months ago, when I wrote about how me and my eight siblings were brought up on benefits – how poor we were, and our constant terror that these benefits would be taken away.

Again, several people asked why their taxes should have been used to pay for my parents' decision to have eight children 'that they couldn't afford'.

Well, I can't speak for my parents now – just as I couldn't alter their decisions then. What I *do* know, and can say, is that the principle of the welfare system was that I should not suffer from the decisions, or fortunes, of my parents. That as soon as I was born, the State stepped in, and acted like the well-paid columnist our social circle so sorely lacked, in Wolverhampton, in 1986 – bailing me and all my siblings out.

It clothed me and fed me, and gave me glasses when I squinted, and opened a library where we all read so much, we all subsequently went to university, and now pay taxes of our own, that bail out other children – who, in turn, will bail out other children, with equally unfortunate parents.

In this respect, at its best, the Welfare State is like some fabulous Electric Boogaloo – the current passing from one citizen to another, making us all body-pop joyfully into education, and up the class system.

And when we get here – onto pages like this, into newspapers like this – we can, finally, tell people about it.

So the country hears a little bit more about how one third of us live our lives.

One more.

I Know What It's Like to be Poor. They Took Away the TV, and We Cried

We've recently heard a lot about the gulf between the rich and the poor – the difference between those with money, and those without.

Well, I've been poor, and I've been rich. When I was poor, I knew I was poor because we lived on benefits, slept on mattresses on the floor, and would share a Mars Bar between ten for pudding.

Now I'm rich, I know I'm rich because I've got underfloor heating, and could afford to eat out at Pizza Express up to three times a week, if I so chose. I'm basically living the life of a billionaire. I am loaded.

So, having been a rich person and a poor person, what I notice is how similar they both are, really. There's not that much difference at all. Everyone cheerfully plays the system they find themselves in.

In Wolverhampton, when you needed a dodgy MOT for the car, an uncle's mate would be given a tenner 'for a pint', and an exhaust-pipe would magically appear out of somewhere – to the ultimate financial detriment of the garage it had been lifted from, but hey-ho.

Now I'm in London, friends of friends recommend good accountants who will 'sort out' your VAT problem for a pint-equivalent fee – to the ultimate economic detriment of the country, but hey-ho.

We're all just monkeys using sticks to get grubs out of logs, really. However. There is one, massive difference between being rich and being poor, and it is this: when you are poor, you feel heavy. Heavy like your limbs are filled with water. Perhaps it is rain-water – there is a lot more rain in your life, when you are poor. Rain that can't be escaped in a cab. Rain that has to be stood in, until the bus comes. Rain that gets into cheap shoes and coats, and through old windows – often followed by cold, and then mildew. A little bit damp, a little bit dirty, a little bit cold – you are never at your best, or ready to shine. You always need something to pep you up: sugar, a cigarette, a new fast song on the radio.

But the heaviness is not really, of course, from the rain. The heaviness comes from the sclerosis of being broke. Because when you're poor, nothing ever changes. Every idea you have for moving things on is quashed through there never being any money. You dream of a house with sky-blue walls; wearing a coat with red buttons; going out on Saturday and walking by a river. Instead, you see the same crack in the same wall, push-start the same car down the same hill, and nothing ever changes, except for the worse: the things you originally had are now slowly wearing out – breaking under your fingertips, and left unreplaced.

This has the effect of making your limbs feel heavy; like you're perpetually slightly drowning. You're dragging ten years of non-progress behind you like a wheel-less cart. Perhaps there's something out there you would be superlatively good at – something that would give you so much joy, you feel like you are flying. But you'll never find out: the world is a shop and it is closed to your empty pockets, and you are standing still, heavy, in the dead centre of your life. You look around, and start to suspect you might not exist. After all, you appear not to be able to make an impression on the world – you can't even change the colour of your front door. Twenty-six years, now; forty-two, and you've never even been to your neighbouring town – it's too far away. And so you sit. You sit still. Because your limbs are so heavy. They are full of rain.

If you've never been poor, I don't think you could imagine what it's like – simply because of the timescale. You could envision a day, maybe, or a year – but not a lifetime. Not generations of it, passed down like drizzle, or a blindness. Not how, if kids from a poor background achieve something, it's whilst dragging this weight behind them. How it takes ten times the effort to get anywhere from a bad postcode.

My children can't imagine it. They love to play at their Sylvanian Family rabbits being 'poor': they love the ingenuity of a sofa turning into a bed for five rabbits; of having only one thing to wear.

'It's all cosy,' they say. 'It's all – little.'

I can see how if you were – say – a coalition government consisting of public-school kids and millionaires, you could convince yourself that the poor are snug in their Sylvanian caravans. That all they need to bridge the 'gulf' between them and the rich is for things to be less cosy. That making *their* life harder – withdrawing benefits, and council housing – incentivises them in a way making life harder for the wealthy – imposing higher tax-rates – would apparently *disincentivise* them.

But the last thing – the very last thing – anyone poor needs is for things to be harder. These limbs are full to bursting.

There's something to be said for the more misty aspects of human behaviour. People operating on less coherent, yet still surging, instincts. People just ... gathering.

The Occupy London movement set up camp outside St Paul's Cathedral in September 2011, and stayed until they were finally moved on in March 2012. Many commentators derided their well-meaning incoherence. I loved it.

I Love a Protestor. You Don't Need Answers – Just Questions

I love a protestor. We all protest, of course – getting out of bed with 'My back!', shouting at the television: 'You ASS!', reading the headlines with furious exclamations of 'We did WHAT?'

But that's just a sentence or two – a minute of remonstration, and then back to wiping paintwork, stacking papers and talking about the profound oddness of the people next door. We protest for the benefit of our own blood pressure, then forget again.

But a protestor – a proper protestor; someone out there, protesting – I find to be a beautiful thing. An objection made flesh, a whole body made over to do one thing – voice disapproval, simply by standing somewhere.

In a world where a minute's remote dabbing at your computer can transfer thousands of pounds, order a car to your door or petition against a death sentence, there's something so simple, elegant and forceful about putting your shoes on, walking out of the front door, and going somewhere where your body is a vote, instead.

There's a group of Chinese Falun Gong protestors who've taken it in turns to man a small table, covered in leaflets, outside the Chinese Embassy on Portland Place, since 2003. Every time I walk past them I think of how there are no elections in China at all: this is the only vote they have; standing in the rain, trying to protect the bright yellow table-cloth with a spoke-spined umbrella, for eight years. Just standing.

If I'd had two gins and felt a bit whirly, I'd claim occupation-protesting lay on the borderline between politics and art – that by placing yourself, say, outside a cathedral, you mean, and become, something wholly differ-ent to when you are placed in a supermarket, buying veg. You put yourself somewhere you shouldn't be. You are the odd thing out. A misplaced item in the bagging area. And this is how you want to change the world: just by being a misplaced particle. Difficult to tidy away.

And, so, to the protestors outside St Paul's Cathedral, objecting to the global banking crisis. Their presence has caused so much commentary – and from so many different viewpoints – that it is clear they have stopped being merely a news item – a fact to be told – and have crossed over into being an infinitely malleable metaphor for whatever the commenta-tor wishes to project on them, instead. Toby Young in the *Telegraph* saw them as 'preening narcissists', only protesting because they 'want to be on the news – that's all they care about'. Richard Littlejohn, meanwhile, saw them as 'a gormless rent-a-mob ... layabouts from Mickey Mouse universities'. I could spend hours suggesting why it might be that those particular people chose those particular epithets. Actually, I couldn't – it would take less than a minute and consist of shouting 'POT! POT! POT!' over and over again, until my Kettle Black Timer went off.

Anyway. Nearly all those who protested against the protestors commented on two things: how unwashed and scruffy they are, and how the protestors have merely 'vague slogans', and have failed to say what their solution to the banking crisis would be.

To the first comment, one can only reply, 'But dudes – they are in tents. It would be alarming and disconcerting if people sleeping on roll-mats in central London emerged from their bivvies at breakfast, box-fresh, and sporting a crease down each leg of their slacks. Your insistence that the revolution be "smart-casual" suggests a lack of any pictorial reference points to previous revolutions. They tend to be fairly "festival chic".'

With the second caveat, I would be a little more disappointed that it had ever been voiced in the first place. Is this now the entry qualification for voter-protest – that we must have all the answers, before we are allowed to speak? That when it comes to a global banking crisis so severe and complex that the combined powers of the European Union cannot come up with a solution – other than going 'Text China! They're LOADED!' – voters can't comment on it unless we've got a massive folder full of maths with 'SOLVED! The Banking Crisis' written on the front?

If we insist protestors must shut up unless they have answers, we are confusing them with columnists, academics, advisors, politicians. And, at root, protestors exist for a wholly different reason to these people. It misses the point of why people put on their shoes, leave their houses, and stand in the wrong place for a long, long time. Protestors don't have the answers. They would never pretend that they have. What they are is a question mark. St Paul's currently stands over a square full of question marks – each tent a black punctuation mark in the middle of the City. A huge black question mark we now see every night on the news, and in the papers.

And the question being asked, over and over again, 'What are you going to do about this?'

They don't need to be anything more than that. Asking questions is beautiful. Asking questions is enough.

I found it one of the more incongruous coincidences that the slow dismissal of the underclass came at the same time as ITV1's massive them-and-us, upstairs/downstairs, master-and-servant blockbuster, Downton Abbey. *I have a complex relationship with* Downton. *Well, not really. I think it's stupid – like a big dog in a dress, galloping around – and I delight in boggling at every demented, over-blown, eye-rolling move it makes. It's the period drama equivalent of Crufts.*

I'd been writing about how enjoyably dumb Downton *is for a year before I started to be quite good friends with Dan Stevens, who plays the show's Matthew Crawley – or 'Handsome Cousin Matthew', as I always like to refer to him in print, because I know it makes him a bit awkward, even though he cannot deny he is handsome. Incredibly handsome. Honestly, sometimes it's like sitting in a bar with the sun.*

Dan – and I know he won't mind me saying this, mainly because he's too busy to read this, and so will never know – is a skilled party-maximiser. A dedicated and joyous boozer with some manner of supernatural, endlessly forgiving liver. I once saw him accidentally fire a champagne cork at a tramp in Soho – but he subsequently apologised so profusely and literally handsomely that, in the end, I think the tramp felt flattered to have been assaulted by someone so facially perfect. That was the night that ended with him and Michelle Dockery – who plays Lady Mary in Downton, *also a bit of a dude – crunking to Blackstreet's 'No Diggity' in a nightclub at 2am. As I watched them, my mind made them wear corsets and World War One military garb. Given the amazing plotlines of* Downton, *it may well be something that actually happens in a subsequent series.*

My favourite night out with Dan was when we attended an Olympic Ball together in West London, and vowed not to tie one on, as it was a school night. Everything went well until – on our way out of the venue, pretty sober – we passed a bar.

'We need cider. For the taxi,' Dan said, decisively. And bought four bottles.

Obviously, by the time we'd chucked that down like Vimto in the back of the cab, we were wasted before we were even halfway home, and ended up going back to my house, and drinking half-pints of port whilst listening to records.

At 1am I failed to find the record I was looking for – a bootleg of Elton John singing Nick Drake demos. Amazing – and went upstairs to wake my husband, who knows the location of all the records in our house.

'Pete,' I said, cross-eyed on port. 'Downton wants Elton Drake. Semergency.'

He's still in my mobile as 'Downton'.

Downton Abbey Review 1: Lady Mary's Haunted Vagina

Downton Abbey returned – finally, finally – on Sunday night. I'm sure you're aware of this. You would have to have been on a spiritual retreat down a deep well, with your eyes closed, to have missed it – in the matter of promotion, ITV1 have been acting like a gangster-made-good, parading its beautiful-yet-spoilt daughter around a Mob restaurant, boasting about how beautiful she is.

'Have you seen her? Look at her! Look at her! She's *gorgeous,'* all the channel's full-page ads in the national press screamed. 'Look at my little *Downton.* She's real classy. Nominated for Emmys and everything. She's my princess. Nuffink's too good for her. *Nuffink.* If you touch her you're dead, sunshine.'

But then, who can really blame ITV's pride? *Downton* is currently in the *Guinness Book of Records* as 'the most critically acclaimed television show of all time' – a fairly astonishing accolade when you bear in mind a) *Twin Peaks*, say, or *Life On Earth*, and b) *Downton*'s much more urgent deserving of another record: that of Guinness's 'silliest television show of all time'.

Honestly, *Downton* is off its chanks. Sometimes it plays as if writer Julian Fellowes sits at his writing bureau – overlooking his extensive lands, including *three rivers* – sucking on a helium balloon, and giggling as he starts bashing at his typewriter. This is, after all, the drama where an evil, chain-smoking maid caused her mistress to miscarry by deliberately leaving lilac-scented soap on the floor, which she slipped on. Yeah, that's right. She killed the unborn Earl of Downton with soap. This is a plot twist not even *Dynasty*, at its most gibbering, considered.

So here we are in Episode One, Series Two. It is 1914. All we can see is a nightmarish vision of mud and barbed wire. Shells whistle and explode as men fall to the ground, broken. In the trenches, men no more than boys weep, lighting cigarettes with bloodied, muddied hands. There's no two ways about it: this dinner party is going really badly.

Through the labyrinthine tunnels the cameras roam, until they find the man they seek: Matthew Crawley, played by Dan Stevens. In many ways, Crawley is the centre of *Downton*'s world: as the middle-class solicitor now unexpectedly due to inherit Downton itself – plus one half of the Lady Mary/Matthew Crawley on/off love story – Crawley's character touches on every issue of class, destiny and desire.

More importantly than this, however, Crawley is unbelievably handsome. It is notable that, in this Stygian quagmire, he alone is immaculate. Whilst everyone else looks like a bog-troll, he is blond, burnished and pristine. Perhaps the mud – being French – is aesthetically highly tuned enough to respect his beauty, and refuses to cling to his astonishingly well-cut trench-coat and buttermilk skin, out of sheer love.

Either way up, Julian Fellowes knows the assembled nine million viewers haven't rocked up to ITV1 for *Wilfred Owen: The Movie*. There are nine million Cup-A-Soups going undrunk as the audience shouts, 'This is a bit of a downer. Where's Maggie Smith looking snooty about someone using the wrong boot-buttoner?'

To this end, two minutes in, Matthew Crawley stares out into the mid-distance of WAR.

'When I think of my life at Downton, it seems like a different world,' he says, impossibly yearning, as the scene fades to black.

And so we're back to lovely old reassuring Downton itself, where all the things *we* yearn for occur: flighty maids making up beds with billowing linen; frisky footmen standing to attention as ladies alight from carriages; posh girls setting down their tortoiseshell-backed hairbrushes and weeping over thwarted love affairs. Life is carrying on at Downton, despite the war – or 'this DAMNED war', to give it its full name.

And its full name is being used often. People are referring to the war a lot. Despite the First World War being, surely, one of the Top Ten Events It's Unnecessary to Back-Ref to, it seems any slight change to the domestic routine since Series One must be contextualised with a quick mention of the ongoing worldwide conflagration.

Whilst this is amusing during a scene of overdue cushion-plumping in the drawing room – 'There's a war on. You cannot keep standards as high' – it reached its apogee when Lady Sybil bumped into Lady Cora in the hallway.

'This is early for you to be up, Mama.'

'War makes early risers of us all.'

This begs the viewer to ask, 'Really? Is the sound of shelling in the Dardanelles carrying all the way to Yorkshire?'

As well as being a hindrance to cushion-plumpness, war, we discover, is also a massive bummer. Lady Sybil receives a letter telling her a former beau, Tom, has caught it in Flanders.

'Sometimes, it feels as if all the men I've ever danced with are dead,' she sighs. Darling, I've been to works Christmas parties too. I know exactly how you feel.

And it seems love is being thwarted left, right and centre. Sexy DILF butler Bates looks like he's finally going to get it on with housemaid Anna, after spending all of Series One mooning after her like a calf on Wobbly Eggs. He even gets around to telling her his plans for their future life:

'I want to open a little hotel, in the countryside,' he says, holding her hand outside the scullery.

The Bates Hotel? Really? That's honestly his plan? You can imagine Julian Fellowes taking a particularly huge hit off his helium tank as he wrote that line. As fans of the show will know, Fellowes seems to reserve all his most wiggy helium-moments for Bates. Bates, let us not forget, was the one who wore a 'secret leg-stretching contraption' in Series One – until he wearied of the pain, and hurled it into a lake.

Anyway, Bates' Series One Secret Leg Contraption Agony is as nothing compared to the torments Fellowes has for him in Series Two: seconds after announcing his Bates Love Hotel plan, Bates's evil, estranged wife turns up to banjax everything.

Understandably, one-legged love-calf Bates is initially unwilling to receive her – keeping her waiting in the kitchen for half an hour.

'Sorry to keep you waiting, Vera,' he says, finally arriving. 'I've been … up in the lofts. Sorting out … some cupboards.'

One look at Vera Bates's Super Evil face tells you that, with excuses like this, Bates is gonna be dog food. She will screw him over, right into Series Three. All housemaid Anna can do is run off, and cry into her apron near a butter churn.

Upstairs, and love is equally complex. Home on leave, the luminously handsome Matthew Crawley attends a fund-raising concert at Downton, allowing him to bump into Lady Mary for the first time since she dumped him, then he dumped her back (it's complicated. Just go with it).

Despite Matthew now being engaged to the sappy Lady Lavinia, and Lady Mary being pursued by Richard Carlisle ('You mean Sir Richard Carlisle? Who runs all those ghastly newspapers?' Lord Crawley expositions, handily. Often, *Downton* might well be renamed *Exposition Abbey*), we know Lady Mary and Matthew Crawley will end up together, eventually. Their love is real and true – for Matthew still loves her, despite her Terrible Secret: a brief fling with a Turkish diplomat, which ended with him dying in her bed.

Although I'm not certain of all the technicalities, I think this means Mary's private parts might now be haunted by the ghost of Mr Kemal Pamuk. I keep waiting for it to jealously go 'WoooOOoooo' every time she looks at Matthew Crawley.

Alas – as Episode One finished, I was still waiting. There's no dice as yet – but with another seven episodes to go, and *Downton* reliably demented, I'm pretty confident that I'll hear Pamuk's muffled 'WooOOOooo' by the end.

I went through a spell of reviewing Downton *every single week – just because simply describing what was happening often made me senseless with laughter. This review also encompassed one of the BBC's big break-out shows,* The Great British Bake Off, *in which shy, flour-covered Brits competed to make jam tarts against the clock.*

I loved the show anyway – but in this particular episode, I noticed a cut-away shot to the gardens the show is filmed in featured a very ... special squirrel. I won't be coy – it's not my way: it had a cock and balls like a flesh wheelbarrow.

Tweeting about the outsize squirrel genitals in advance of the show, I was thrilled beyond measure when it got picked up as a news story ('Great British Bake Off Viewers shocked by "explicit" image of male squirrel' – Daily Mail. *'Viewers Go Nuts Over Squirrel' –* Guardian*), and I was quoted as 'TV critic Caitlin Moran tweeted, "This can only be topped by* Coast *featuring a badger with huge tits."'*

In terms of personal, professional pride, this was a moment that was only beaten by the odd day on Twitter when it seemed as if convicted child molester Gary Glitter had opened an account, and had started tweeting about a forthcoming tour. As the Mail *put it, in its story on the subject, 'There is understandably some doubt as to whether the account is real. Journalist Caitlin Moran suggested "Wave a kid in front of him" as a potential test of the profile's validity, and noted his reluctance to talk about any subject other than himself by calling him 'a Ming-browed ourobors nonce'.*

These are the things I live for.

There's a bit on The X Factor, *here, too.*

Downton Abbey Review 2:
'SEX WILL BE HAD! SEX WILL BE HAD!'

Yeah, we're British – and one of our most talked-about programmes of the year is people competing in a rainy marquee to make perfect Victoria Sponges, brandy snaps and scones. So what? You going to make something of it? We don't need to be defensive about this – right, lads? We invented DNA and the Dyson and Heston Blumenthal and Radiohead – we've proved that the entire British Isles isn't just some adorable village in which vicars on bicycles deliver the clinking-clanking milk bottles to a post office run by the pig from *Babe*. We've been all fierce and modern. We're having an Olympics. We've got a fast-train to Paris *under the sea*. We've got the biggest Topshop in the world. We're totally twenty-first century.

This, then, gives us the leeway to enjoy a show which is basically *Calendar Girls* – but with every single scene taken out apart from the bit where Helen Mirren says, 'We're going to need considerably bigger buns.'

The Great British Bake Off was BBC2's surprise hit last year, and finished its second series this Tuesday. Its joy is simple: in watching a bunch of amateur bakers in aprons make cake, we become, once more, kids sitting at the kitchen table, watching Mum breaking eggs into an earthenware bowl.

Well, to be honest, I don't – my mother was a terrible cook. Her thirteenth birthday cake to me was a baguette from Sainsbury's, with ten candles stuck in it. I have no cosy kitchen memories at all. I just get Proustian flashbacks to Ma Larkin making bread and butter pudding for Catherine Zeta-Jones, instead. But this is the wonderful thing about being brought up on television – it is exactly the same thing. Exactly the same thing.

This year's stand-out contestant on *Great British Bake Off* was Rob, the Sexy Indie Baker from Preston. Week after week, Rob whipped up tarte au citron, macaroons and profiteroles – huge pouty lips clamped in concentration – as viewers marvelled over the construction of his hair. How was he keeping a fringe that luscious, lavish, indie and immense from collapsing in the heat of the bake off? Had he blind-baked it first? Was it in some kind of bain marie? Maybe Rob's hair was, in fact, made of spun sugar – semi-cooled toffee flicked repeatedly over a greased broom handle to make long, fine strands of beautiful indie-boy hair?

Either way, Rob was finally dismissed at the end of Episode Five, after judges Paul Hollywood and Mary Berry insisted he'd supplied a disappointing ratio of jelly-to-pastry in his hand-raised pork-pie, and booted him out of the marquee. Many viewers will have been outraged by this decision: he's just a kid, Paul and Mary! Just a really sexy kid! A kid who wants to bake his heart out! Isn't this what Broken Britain needs – troubled teens (he's actually twenty-five and a photographer, but sshhhh) who want to bake love, not war? More puddies – and less hoodies? DAVID CAMERON, WHAT ARE YOU DOING, YOU SCONE-SMASHING BASTARD?

But you can't argue with the judges on *Great British Bake Off*. They are, quite possibly, the most terrifying judges on British television. Mary Berry has published over forty books on baking, and has the iron-spined air of a seventy-six-year-old woman who last suffered a fool gladly before the old king died. If you questioned her judgement of a junket, she'd probably shoot tiny pewter bullets out of her eyes.

Paul Hollywood, meanwhile, has inspired a whole nation to ask the question, 'Who the fuck is Paul Hollywood?' Deeply tanned – indeed, possibly glazed, with an egg-and-milk wash – Hollywood has piercingly blue eyes, like those of a Bond villain, and a bristlingly alpha air about bakery.

'The interior of that is *revolting*,' he told Mary-Anne, of her Everlasting Syllabub.

'The bake is GOOD,' he told Jo – turning her white chocolate and pistachio pie upside-down, and examining its tiny brown bottom like a paediatrician. On Googling Hollywood, one discovered that he is, in fact, the baker responsible for creating Britain's most expensive ever loaf: an almond and Roquefort, sold for £15 a loaf in Harrods.

Whilst creating Britain's most expensive loaf is not ostensibly an impressive thing to do – I could stick a 42-inch Sony flatscreen in a bap and charge you £699, bread-buying idiots – the combination of extravagance and, let's face it, vileness of a £15 marzipan and blue-cheese loaf merely adds to Hollywood's menace. On several occasions, during the baking, I expected the camera to find him in the corner of a marquee, with the legs of one of the show's runners hanging out of his mouth. He just … looks like a people-eater. I know you know what I mean. One of those men who just puts people in his mouth, and they never come back out again.

The finale was fought out between Jo, Holly and Mary-Anne, on the battlefield of three modern petit fours, 'with a theme of British Summer Time': not a bucket of rainwater with a dead frog in it, as many of us remember the summer, but something to do with strawberries and stuff.

In the end, perfectionist Holly lost out on her ganache (Mary Berry, sternly, in the manner of Lady Bracknell: 'It should be poured – not *spread*') and glorious carb-battleship Mary-Anne blew it with her over-vigorous mixing of whipped egg white into melted chocolate (Paul Hollywood, like a murderer: 'There's *flecks* in this').

It was won by Jo – a sweet housewife from Essex who had 'never done anything for herself', and had the nervy, low self-esteem of an ex-race greyhound, despite baking like an angel. The show finished in a flurry of feel-good Blighty core values and cake, and remains one of the few shows I watched without fail, cheering all the way. Tuesday nights will be genuinely bereft without it, and I want the BBC to cook up another series as quickly as possible. In the microwave, if necessary. Ping. Get a move on.

Be all of this wonderful, heart-gladdening, flour-speckled stuff as it may, however, I must note the extraordinary moment, forty minutes into the finale, when we cut to a jolly 'and so time passes' exterior shot of a squirrel, bounding across the lawn.

The squirrel paused, went up on its haunches – and then brazenly displayed the most gigantic pair of squirrel testicles I have ever seen in my life. I cannot overstate their size enough. They were bigger than its head. They were bigger than *my* head. I'd like to pretend otherwise – but the truth is, when we went back into that marquee for the last ten minutes of baking, I found the final decorating of the petit fours had been completely railroaded by a freakishly large pair of squirrel knackers. It was just impossible to concentrate on Mary-Anne's lemon-icing feathering with the memory of those outrageous mammal nuts hanging around outside.

The crew were clearly just as astonished by it as I was – because, two minutes later, we cut back to the same squirrel, in the same louche pose of ample display.

The final message was unequivocal. Yes. Yes, we might be a country that loves a twee baking competition held in a marquee – but our Squirrel Nutkins has balls like David Bowie in *Labyrinth*, world, and don't you forget it.

'Do the plots in *Downton* move too quickly?' is the question many are asking at the moment. And with good reason. After all, as we realised last week, the entire First World War has only taken five episodes of *Downton*. At this rate, Maggie Smith could be making imperious comments about the etiquette of Neil Armstrong landing on the Moon ('But has he been intro*duced* to the Clangers? Does he know their *family*?') by Christmas.

But you know what? As long as you just strap yourself in – and maybe partake of a medicinal sherry beforehand – the rapid pacing is fine. It's a hoot! Just think of an episode of *Downton Abbey* as a 'Haunted House' style ride – such as you would find at a fair, or on a pier. You burst in through the double doors to find the Earl of Grantham (Hugh Bonneville) kissing a widowed housemaid, mount a gantry to view Ethel's illegitimate baby in the pantry – then take in a final straight that includes an elopement, a miracle-cure and a revelation of unrequited love before the final credits. Put your hands in the air, and scream if you wanna go faster! It's only two quid, fun for aaaawl the family.

Of course, some fast-plots are bigger than other fast-plots. The mega-plot that *Downton* currently revolves around is the state of Cousin Matthew's (Dan Stevens) trousers. It is all going off in Cousin Matthew's trousers, these days. That's where all the narrative is being stored.

Cousin Matthew, you may recall, is the preternaturally beautiful blond heir to Downton Abbey, who bravely went off to the hell of war to serve his king and country – only popping back to Downton half-a-dozen times for key concerts, balls, scenes where it just generally felt good to have him around, and angsty forbidden-love stare-offs with Lady Mary (Michelle Dockery).

At one point, Cousin Matthew popped back from the war halfway through Lady Mary singing 'If You Were the Only Boy in the World' at a concert – then joined her in a loving duet for the last verse, before immediately going back to the war again. It's the scene Vera Brittain never had the balls or insanity to write in *Testament of Youth* – but, now, finally brought to life by Julian Fellowes in *Downton*. Hurrah! If the thinking remains as blue-sky as this, Season Three of *Downton* – set in the Depression – can have Bugsy Malone with a splurge-gun, or even – fuck it! – Scarlett O'Hara escaping a burning Atlanta in a horse and cart, with Miss Melly giving birth in the back. You might as well go for it, that's what I say! Scream if you wanna go faster!

Anyway. Matthew's trousers. In a war full of unspeakable atrocities, the Hun's most beastly move has been an attack on Cousin Matthew's – possibly literal, given his poshness – crown jewels. When he returned from the front in Episode Five, it was in a wheelchair – 'An impotent cripple, smelling of sick,' as he called himself, clearly on a bit of a Downton downer.

For a few, amazing moments, it seemed as if *Downton* might have gone the whole hog, and written in a character who'd had his nads blown off in the heat of battle – only the second-ever drama to attempt this, after the BBC's ground-breaking, testicle-exploding *Lilies* in 2007.

And, indeed, the first scene of last Sunday's episode seemed to confirm this: the Earl of Downton watching solemnly as a car departed down the driveway, his sombre expression suggesting that the vehicle contained Matthew's balls on a tray, being taken off for a decent burial.

But – to infinite rejoicing – we found this was not the case. Not the case at all. Matthew was, in fact, *trousioso intacta,* as I'm sure the Latin would have it. The contents of his orangery were all present and correct – it was merely the 'sexual reflex' that was missing. Or was it? Ten minutes later, sitting in his wheelchair, Matthew stared out into the mid-distance.

'Bates,' he said to his valet. 'If I were to feel a … tingling, what would that mean? The doctors keep saying it's the memory of a tingling – but I keep feeling it.'

'If something is changing, it will make itself known,' Bates said, with all the wisdom of a man who'd had a broad country upbringing.

Although it sometimes felt like it, *Downton* was not all about Cousin Matthew's trousers, of course. My favourite sub-plot involved the villainous Mrs O'Brien and Thomas entering the post-war black market economy – and trying to rip off the Downton estate by selling hooky foodstuffs to Cook.

Whilst initially keen on sourcing such luxe ingredients – 'I've not seen this since before the war!' Cook exclaimed, holding up candied peel as if it were an unquestioning attitude of deference towards the upper classes – Cook found, on tasting the resultant cake, that Thomas had been sold a pup.

'This is plaster dust!' Cook shouted, spitting cake all over the floor; then getting all *Watchdog* on Thomas's ass.

Thomas eventually returned to his warehouse full of now-unsellable, poisonous ingredients, and – furious – started to trash the lot. As he repeatedly punched a massive sack whilst shouting 'NO!!!', it occurred to me that this was the first time I had ever seen a man fighting 'some flour' – and I gave thanks, yet again, to the mad majesty of *Downton*.

But, in the end, Sunday's episode ended as it had begun: in Cousin Matthew's trousers. Post-Tinglegate, we were all on high alert for further developments in Matthew's pelvis – but were aware that the breakthrough he needed might come at a high cost. Previous cases of people in dramas 'spontaneously' recovering from paraplegia seem to centre around high drama – suddenly finding the power in their legs when a loved one is in danger, say; or when their own lives are at risk.

In the event, Matthew's miracle recovery didn't quite play out like that.

Joining Matthew in the drawing room, Lavinia – his current, wrongful fiancée – noticed something was seriously awry at Downton:

'Look!' she said, pointing to a table, with six cups and saucers on it. 'They've forgotten to clear the tea things!'

Walking over to correct the servants' heinous mistake, Lavinia was given fair warning by Matthew.

'It's too heavy for you!' he said, as she picked up a tray.

But, too late! Lavinia had – inevitably – paid the price for the lower orders' carelessness: tripping over an ornately embroidered footstool, and having to steady herself by putting her hand on the marble fireplace, next to the ormolu clock.

'Heavens! That was a near thing!' she exclaimed, breathlessly – before they both realised that this moment of peril had jolted Matthew out of his paralysis: he was now standing next to her; broken spine a thing of the past, future now rosily re-filling with the possibility of rumpy.

On discovering the happy news about his heir, the Earl of Grantham rushed around Downton insisting everyone come and see Matthew in the drawing room at once. Really, he appeared one whisky away from ringing the bells in Downton chapel and shouting 'SEX WILL BE HAD! SEX WILL BE HAD!' to the entire cast.

I'm sure the staff were subsequently instructed to bring out the special 'Heir's rediscovered sexual reflex' dinner service, as has been in the family for generations, in order that all of Downton might celebrate in the most Downton way it knows how – with the maximum of formality, oddness, and washing-up for the peasants.

Of course, there are other TV shows on at the moment. Well, one other, really: *X Factor*, now at a curious point in its 'journey', having sloughed off two million viewers since the departure of Simon Cowell.

People are saying *X Factor* is 'all over' – but, clearly, it's not. Really, losing two million viewers is neither here nor there in an unseasonably warm October, when you're a show that still has ten million viewers, and still dominates the tabloid agenda. *X Factor* remains, whichever way you slice it, an enormously popular show.

But it is also, increasingly, an odd one. On Saturday's show, it was announced that Ashley, member of boy band The Risk, had decided to leave the competition. It was the kind of hasty departure one usually associates with someone remembering they've left the iron on – rather than the life-changing revelation that, actually, they don't want to be a pop star, after all. Let us not forget, three weeks ago, Ashley had been at Boot Camp weeping, 'I want this 110 per cent – this is my *dream*,' like a child begging for bone-marrow. This was a fairly epic sea-change, 110 per-cent-wise.

What made things even odder was that Ashley was then immediately replaced by 'Ashford' – a member of a band who'd been kicked off the show two weeks previously, and was, presumably, in band-mentor Tulisa's mobile, just after 'Ashley'. He was recruited into the band, rehearsed, then brought on stage in a VT package that took under a minute.

The remorseless speed of the whole thing was redolent of those Cecil B DeMille epics showing the building of the Pyramids – where, every so often, a slave-worker would get crushed to death under an enormous marble block, but construction would not halt for a second, and anyone who mourned over him was whipped. Onward! Onward! Build *X Factor* back up to twelve million viewers, for the glory of the great Pharaoh Cowell!

The disconcerting replaceability of everybody was reinforced by the absence of judge Kelly Rowland, formerly of Destiny's Child. Either 'too sick' (official line) or 'too full of hatred for fellow-judge Tulisa' (tabloid line, but possibly fed by the official line people, for extra press traction) to attend the show, she phoned in her vote on Sunday night in a whispery, 'ill' voice many of us will have recognised from hanging our heads over the edge of the bed whilst phoning in sick at work, before getting dressed and having a long lunch with a friend from out of town.

With competitors coming and going like commuters, and the actual physical presence of judges seeming optional, *X Factor* is starting to look like a gigantic, light-bedecked eighteen-wheeler bombing down the motorway, panelling and engine-parts flying off everywhere. Will it make it to Christmas intact? I genuinely don't know.

We make a good team, Pete and I. Both journalists, both into carbohydrates, both agreed that the perfect baby-sitter for the children during the summer holidays is a man of dubious qualifications and reputation touting some massive see-through hamster-balls, in which you can place your children.

Summer Is an Emergency

'The thing about summer is, if you work and you've got kids, it's an emergency,' my husband says. 'A total emergency.'

Today is the worst day of August, so far: both of us are sitting next to a 40ft paddling pool, on the sea front, in Brighton.

A cheerful, chain-smoking goblin from Manchester has set up some manner of novel amusement here: gigantic plastic 'hamster balls', into which children can be inserted, then launched onto the paddling pool. Our children have taken to this activity with all the enthusiasm of genuine hamsters. They keep tumbling past us, upside-down, screaming, 'THIS IS AWESOME, DUDE!', and flashing peace-signs.

Sitting at the picnic tables we wave, shout things like, 'You look totally deranged! We're going to leave you here, and go home alone!', then go back to typing, furiously. My husband is trying to write the definitive overview of UB40's first, politically outraged, critically revered album. I am writing a stirring 4,000-word pro-feminist refutation of waxing: both Brazilians, and Hollywoods.

Every so often, my husband stares at me blankly, and says 'Dub'.

I stare back at him, equally blankly, and say 'Pubes'.

The children wheel past in the background, screaming 'COWA-BUNGA, MAN!'

Today – having run out of holiday allowance, two weeks into the summer holidays – this paddling pool is our office. An office with no ceiling, in which drizzle is falling onto our laptops. It's far more exciting than it sounds, though: for with Brighton council being inexplicably heel-draggy about providing free power-points on any part of the seafront, we also have a thrilling, against-the-clock element of trying to finish writing before our batteries conk out.

'How long have you got left? I'm on thirty-seven minutes,' I will say, anxiously checking the stats.

'I'm down to seventeen,' my husband replies. 'I've turned the "Screen Brightness" down so low, it looks like a window onto eternal night.'

It is like an episode of *24* centred around Jack Bauer sending a single, very important email.

Of course, to complain about this would be to suffer a gigantic loss of perspective. We are, by no stretch of the imagination, the most stressed parents this summer. We aren't even the most stressed parents on Brighton seafront – earlier, I had passed a child jack-knifing on the floor, wailing 'I don't WANT Nanna to be dead forever!'

At least, I tell myself, cheerfully, we're dandy, teleworking media nobs who *can* bring our work to a giant inflatable paddling pool in Brighton.

'Imagine having to bring your *lathe* down here,' I keep thinking. 'Or your *furnace*. Or the *mountain* you had to climb – because you are a professional mountaineer, like Chris Bonham. We are the lucky ones.'

If you're working parents, the fact is simple: the holiday maths don't add up. You, the parents, have four weeks of holiday a year. Your children, on the other hand, have thirteen. Ergo, you are about to lose your mind. It's not a system anyone would come up with now. It's a vexing remnant of the patriarchy – a society in complete denial that both a) MUMMY IS ON A DEADLINE TOO, NOW, and b) MOST CHILDREN DISLIKE GOING TO A THREE-WEEK-LONG DRAMA WORKSHOP WITH A LOAD OF RANDOMS AS MUCH AS YOU WOULD. The solution to two-parent-working families is *not* to get thousands of kids to learn the *Bugsy Malone* songbook – although, as I write that, I do realise how much my core beliefs have changed since I was twelve, and wanted to be Blousey Brown.

Two weeks later, it is the first day of autumn term. The school gates resemble the first assembly-point after a plane crash. Slightly stunned parents stand around, waving goodbye to their children, with the auras of people who've recently spent so much money, and begged so many favours from Grandma and Grandpa, that they might now have to go home and lie very, very still for five days, before they can feel normal again.

'You got through, then?' one says.

'Yeah. Don't quite remember how, though. I appear to have spent over £6,000 on *Doctor Who* DVD box-sets and bags of Mini Cheddars.'

They then get on their mobiles, and start wearily arranging the transportation of their lathes, back from Polperro.

But you know what? Secretly, this is why I love the summer holidays. Unlike my husband, I get off on an emergency. In the summer, you can basically pretend it's the Second World War – running out into the street in your rollers, clutching a kettle, screaming 'THE GERMANS ARE COMING!', smoking black-market fags.

Now it's autumn, however, you can't get away with that kind of stuff any more. There's no more putting the kids to sleep in a cardboard box under the patio table. No more gin on the lawn at 2am. No more giving everyone KitKats and apples for breakfast. You just have to retrieve your shoes – from the lavender bush, where you threw them, in July – put them back on, and go back to being normal, and sensible, again.

Until Christmas, anyway.

Here is pretty much my entire life story in 830 words. Note a return to the justification of not going abroad. I don't know who I'm aiming all this 'I will not travel' ranting at, really. Maybe the Thomas Cook in my head.

Time Travel in the Same Four Places

I'm not a great believer in 'travelling'. Every holiday I've ever had somewhere 'novel' seemed to consist of repeatedly walking past much nicer restaurants than the one we'd just eaten in, whilst crying, 'Oh! That place looks delightful! There's no feral one-eyed cats under the table *there*.'

And that's ignoring the actual travel of 'travel': a thing so awful it warrants its own insurance, sickness, and tiny hairdryers. Every time I think of some distant wonder I might quite like to see – Sydney Harbour at night, for instance; or Venice from a bridge – I ask myself, 'Do I want to see it so much that I would take my shoes off at Heathrow security at 6.55am?'

And every time the answer comes back, 'No. I would rather keep my shoes on and watch a documentary about them instead, thank you.'

So instead of travelling, I just … go to places, instead. The same four places, for the last twenty years: Aberystwyth, Brighton, Gower, Ullapool. That's it. Nowhere else. Over and over, repeat and return. Like a casting-on stitch done over and over in the same spot – but at slightly different angles. When I go back to these places, I see can my ghosts from every previous visit. When I go to these places, I don't travel in space – but in time, instead.

So when I go to Ullapool, in the Highlands, I walk the main street seeing flickery, analogue broadcasts from earlier parts of my life. The timecode on the oldest ghost is 1986. August – the August we bought a campervan. We've been driven off every other campsite in the area, as the owners think – what with my seven siblings, and rainbow-coloured wellies – that we are travellers, displaced from Stonehenge. It's a miserable holiday: the rain is solid, cold. All we can do is eat sausage soup and read *Kidnapped* aloud to each other in increasingly risible Scottish accents. Everyone is angry. The dog nearly drowns. I want us to climb a mountain or swim in the sea, but we spend five days in a space the size of a wardrobe, staring at running windows, and then go home.

A decade later, and the ghosts from 1995 are of better quality – a brighter picture. I am nineteen, now. I've convinced a friend who has a car to drive me back to Ullapool, so I can finally see it in the sunshine – or at least through the rainy windows of somewhere more spacious, like a hotel. In the day, we both climb a mountain *and* swim in the sea, because I'm in charge of me now. At night, after drinking the most expensive wine we have ever ordered – £22! – we realise we're probably in love, and walk to the same bedroom without saying a word. Four years later we come back on our honeymoon, and spend the first night crying, even though we love each other, because …

Here I am on the seafront in Brighton, in 1994. I have just told my best friend that we shouldn't go out with each other.

'We were meant to be just friends,' I am saying. I have read about love in novels, and am sure I know all about it. This is one of the cleverest things I have ever done. I am eighteen. I exhale my cigarette, like a grown-up.

Here I am four years later, on the same stretch of seafront, with the same friend. We are on a bench. My head is in his lap. We are talking about what to call our baby in my belly. My wedding dress is in a bag at our feet. We get married in three days. Since we were last here, I have learned that I knew nothing at the age of eighteen. I know now that love can be a quiet, sure thing – like the first April sun on your arms – and not the pyroclastic blast I was waiting for.

In nineteen hours, we will find out the baby is dead. The grief that is coming for us has five blades on each hand: it will fall on us like a blizzard, and leave us on the floor.

We will weep on our honeymoon in Ullapool – so lost I could not tell you if it did rain at all, that time. At the time, I thought the deep-sea pressure of sorrow was so great, it would crush my heart smaller, forever. I was sure I knew everything about it.

This morning, at the start of my holiday in Brighton, I watched our two daughters – eight and ten – on the beach.

'My heart is even bigger now,' I thought. 'And I know what love is, and I don't smoke, and the grief did not kill me, and I know I still know nothing, and I'm in charge of me, now.'

A casting-on stitch done in the same place, over and over again, gets stronger. In Ullapool, Gower, Aberystwyth and Brighton, I don't travel to broaden the mind.

I return – something completely different.

part**four**

Euthusiasms, Advices and Deaths

*In which I meet Paul McCartney FROM THE BEATLES
and ask him what would happen if – 'Heaven forefend,
Sir Paul' – his face got smashed up in a horrific
car accident, mourn the deaths of Amy Winehouse
and Elizabeth Taylor, open the 'Nutter Box'
and nobly resist sniffing Sherlock's pillow.*

But, first: back to a small domestic misunderstanding.

My French Dress

It is 7.48pm. I am just about to leave the house, for a night out with friends. I have checked I have a spare pair of tights in my handbag, ensured that the working remote is actually in the oldest child's hand – no more panicked, 10pm 'WE CANT FID [sic] THE CONTROLLS!!!' texts for *me* – and now, the last thing that needs to be done is to bid my husband adieu.

I walk into his 'study', where he is listening to a reggae compilation, whilst contemplating his new Fotheringay mug, which is full of tea. He has a happy look on his face.

'I'm off now, love,' I say.

'Have a great night,' he says, taking his headphones off, and beaming.

There is a pause. I kind of … stand at him a bit. Loom, maybe.

'I'm off out, now,' I say, again, more purposefully. 'Off into London. To see people.'

'Make sure you've got your keys!' he says, cheerfully. 'Have a great night. Send my love to … whichever bunch of arch, chain-smoking homosexuals you're on loan to tonight.'

There is another pause. I stare at him quite intently. He stares back, confused. Pete can tell there is some manner of urgent business left unattended here – but he does not know what. I can sense his heart-rate accelerating, like a panicked lab-rat on sighting a speculum. The rat does not know exactly what is going to happen next – but it knows it's going to be bad.

'Do you … want a lift to Finsbury Park?' he asks, eventually.

'HOW DO YOU THINK I LOOK?' I shout.

Pete is immediately both contrite – 'Sorry!' – but also back in charted territory again.

Twelve years ago, shortly before our wedding, I told him – with the kind of fearless honesty that lovers can afford – that I would only ever impose two rules on our marriage. 1) That he must never, ever throw me a surprise birthday party in our front room again. And 2) that every time I appear in front of him in a new outfit, he must say, without hesitation: 'You look so thin in that!'

'You look so thin in that!' Pete says – delighted to be back on firm ground.

He puts his headphones back on. He clearly thinks all the business has been concluded.

'Phew. Have a great night out,' he says – going back to staring at his Fotheringay mug, which depicts the whole band as fifteenth-century minstrels. 'I'll see you in the morning.'

Unfortunately for Pete, 'You look so thin in that' is *not* the droids I am looking for in this particular conversation. The dress I am in is a bit of a new development, in terms of my 'fashion range'. It's a 1950s tea-dress in shape – but in pattern, it's got an African-textile theme going on. I'm wearing it with zebra-skin sandals, and a snakeskin clutch-bag. Basically, I need to know if I look like some manner of 'Lady Ace Ventura – Pet Detective' in it. I don't know if this 'lysergic safari' thing is working.

Were I with any of my female friends or relations, they would have understood this instantly. My sister Weena, for instance, would have greeted me with, 'You're perverting the assumed prejudices of post-war chicks, with some kind of "demented gay Ghanaian disco" vibe. It's *Mad Men* vs Brixton Market. You're essentially saying you're a liberal – but with big tits. Nice. Catch that bus with confidence.'

This is what women do – tell each other what story their outfits are projecting, by way of confirming that the wearer has got it right. The women who love you recite back to you the aspiration and impact of your 'look' – hence a group of eight of us being able to greet our friend

Hughes with, 'Post-divorce slutty secretary – but with unexpected neon rave-stilettos! You're a sexy lady who will not cling to one man tonight, but seek the communal ecstatic uprising of a room full of party-goers, instead. In this Pizza Express we are having dinner in.'

Women speak the language of clothes. Everything we wear is a sentence, a paragraph, a chapter – or, sometimes, just an exclamation mark.

Unfortunately, however, Pete does not speak the language of clothes. My dress and zebra-sandals are essentially shouting at him in French. Unable to make out a word they are saying, he panics.

'It's a top-notch item,' he says, staring at it. 'Unusual. It's, ah, amazing that "they" keep coming up with innovative things – even in 2012. That's … got to be good news for the fashion industry!'

There is a small pause – then he starts laughing so hysterically at the desperation of what he has just said that he slides off his chair, headphones still in hand, and kneels on the floor, red-faced, and weeping.

He's still there when I leave the house. Which is a bit annoying, because I did actually want a lift to Finsbury Park. My zebra-skin sandals are chafing.

Obviously they knew it was a bit of a security risk – but, for the second series of Sherlock, writers Steven Moffat and Mark Gatiss let me see how they made the show – following it from the first script meeting to the triumphal premiere on the South Bank, over the course of summer 2011.

I had to sign so many forms: 'I promise I will not scream during a take.' 'I promise I will not sob loudly during a take.' 'I promise I will never again lick a prop or major cast member, or major cast member's prop.'

It was worth it alone for the interview I did with Martin Freeman, which contained so many filthy stories and expletives that my transcription service formally complained, and charged me extra – for emotional distress caused to their typist.

The transcription service also supplied the interesting statistic that, in conversation, Steven Moffat and I had, at one point, hit 249 words per minute – but I think that's less to do with the fact that we're both gabblers – which we are – and more to do with the fact we were just talking over each other, without listening to each other at all, in the way that writers do on the very few occasions they socialise with other humans.

Sherlock Feature: The Making of 'A Scandal in Belgravia'

July 2010. It is three weeks before the first series of *Sherlock* broadcasts on BBC1, and show-runners Steven Moffat and Mark Gatiss are panicking. The BBC have suddenly brought forward the slot for their show 'by a substantial amount'. As summer is already a difficult time to launch a show, Gatiss and Moffat are bewildered as to how they will promote it.

'We were sitting around with our heads in our hands,' Steven Moffat remembers, 'going, "There isn't enough time to do this. It will broadcast to *no one*."'

This was when they joined Twitter.

'It was really only one step up from individually knocking on people's doors and shouting "*Sherlock* is coming!" through their letterboxes,' Mark Gatiss explains. 'We were almost ... desperate.'

'What did we think we'd get?' Moffat muses.

'Four million viewers,' Gatiss replies. 'Four million viewers, tops, and a couple of nice broadsheet write-ups. That was our best-case scenario.'

On the night the debut episode – 'A Study in Pink' – went out, the core cast and crew assembled at Steven Moffat's house, in Kew, to watch it, in a state of nervous tension.

Gathered around the wine – 'a lot of wine' – were Martin Freeman (Dr Watson), Benedict Cumberbatch (Sherlock Holmes), Mark Gatiss, Steven Moffat and Sue Vertue, the show's producer, who is, handily, also married to Moffat, 'Which has, over the years, saved us a fortune on cabs.'

In the event, when *Sherlock* began, the Moffat party had to immediately pause it, as Benedict Cumberbatch still hadn't arrived.

'He called us – he was stuck in a traffic jam on Baker Street,' Moffat recalls. 'Sherlock Holmes, stuck on Baker Street! We couldn't work out if that was a good sign or not.'

'I think he might have made that up, to be honest,' Mark Gatiss says. 'But it's a really good lie.'

When Cumberbatch finally arrived, the party who made *Sherlock* watched the show ten minutes behind the rest of Britain.

'But we knew when the climax happened,' Mark Gatiss beams, 'because suddenly all our phones were going off, everyone texting, everyone phoning. I mean, *exploding*.'

'An hour later, I went and sat in the garden,' Moffat says, 'and looked at Twitter. I saw that Benedict was trending worldwide on Twitter, Martin was trending worldwide, *Sherlock* itself was trending worldwide. And people were talking about it with this ... *passion*. As if they were lifelong fans – when, of course, they'd not *seen* it ninety minutes ago. Everything had changed in ninety minutes.'

He pauses for a minute, still looking surprised.

'Everything.'

July 2011. A shabby-looking rehearsal room in Noho. This is the first read-through for the first episode – titled 'A Scandal in Belgravia' – of the second series of *Sherlock*. Almost a year to the day of its first broadcast, it is now the most anticipated show of 2012.

For a *Sherlock* fan, it is impossibly exciting to be here. A table bears a huge pile of pristine, newly printed scripts – each full of mysteries, corpses, grandiloquent scene-setting and bullet-train dialogue.

To the left, Mark Gatiss – who not only writes *Sherlock,* but also stars as Sherlock's upright older brother, Mycroft – sips tea. To the right is Watson (Martin Freeman) eating a banana. I go to the toilet and, whilst washing my hands, express my joy at being in a building which will soon see the arrival of Mrs Hudson, played by Una Stubbs.

'Who's talking about meeeeee?' says the unmistakeable voice of Una Stubbs from the next cubicle.

Since the broadcast of the first series of *Sherlock* – for which Gatiss and Moffat nervously prayed for four million viewers – the show has racked up a devoted 9.2m viewers, won two BAFTAs and Best Show at the Edinburgh Television Festival, was nominated for an Emmy, and promoted a slew of think-pieces about how it had single-handedly made Sunday night TV 'the new Friday night'. Sales of Sir Arthur Conan Doyle's books went up 180 per cent in the same month, and Belstaff – designers of the 'instantly iconic' great-coat Holmes wears in the show – had to put the previously discontinued design back into manufacture. At one point, the waiting list for the £1,000 coat was six months long.

Most notably of all, however, it made an overnight star of its Holmes, Benedict Cumberbatch. Previously the kind of well-respected theatre actor who popped up in award-winning thinky dramas on BBC2, Cumberbatch – with his clay-white skin, sexy-sloth face and pub-time jaguar growl –

became instant pin-up totty; eventually going on to win *GQ* magazine's 'Man of the Year', and be hailed by Steven Spielberg – who then cast him in his forthcoming *War Horse* – as 'the greatest onscreen Holmes'. *Sherlock* has changed Cumberbatch's life.

Entering the room today, the discrepancy between Cumberbatch and Cumberbatch-as-Sherlock is notable. Holmes would enter the room in a swirl of £1,000 coat, rattle off some nail-gun comment, analyse the contents of the biscuit tin to deduce that it's someone's birthday, then go into a high-grade petulant intellectual sulk.

Cumberbatch himself, on the other hand, is wearing a faded band T-shirt, and exudes the air of an indie-kid in his late teens/early twenties. He's bright and enthusiastic and friendly – his is the air of someone who helps mums carry buggies up stairs.

When the read-through starts, however, this gonky teenager disappears, and he slips, effortlessly, into the stiff-backed, cold-eyed, Pentium 20 brain of Holmes. His delivery can still the room – even in his T-shirt, in this bright summer sunshine. Spielberg was not wrong.

When the read-through ends, everyone claps.

'I love that we've all applauded ourselves spontaneously at the end,' Moffat says, dryly. 'Well done all of us. Now we've just got to make the damn thing. Better than the last series. No pressure. Off you go.'

Out on the street, Cumberbatch is fiddling with his phone. Tomorrow is his birthday, 'And I can't get a restaurant reservation,' he says, mournfully. 'They won't call me back. I should have said my name was Sherlock Holmes.' He squints down the street. 'I guess I'll just have to ... have a picnic.'

It is a uniquely dolorous delivery of the word 'picnic'.

August, 2011. We are in 221b Baker Street. It is raining outside, hard.

Inside 221b, however, it is cosy – Mark Gatiss and Steven Moffat are lolling in the armchairs of Holmes and Watson, looking perfectly at home.

We're not *really* in 221b Baker Street, of course – this is the set, in a hangar in Wales. After a few minutes, someone outside turns off the rain – it's just a hose, pointing at the window.

'Come and look around!' Gatiss says, springing up from his chair.

Seeing Moffat and Gatiss here, in domestic repose – giving the impression of being a Holmes-loving Bert & Ernie – seems very fitting. Much of *Sherlock*'s potency comes from reconfiguring the friendship between Holmes and Watson – Freeman's Watson is more than equal to Holmes.

And it is the joy of the game that binds Moffat and Gatiss, too. When they were both working on *Doctor Who* – Moffat as the show-runner, Gatiss a guest script-writer – they would while away the long train journeys from London to Cardiff by talking about their favourite Holmes books and films. Today, they quote classic lines to each other – tripping over each other to be the first to finish. This zodiacal steeping in the canon is what powers *Sherlock*'s astonishing pace and zip: Moffat and Gatiss abstract the existing Sherlock movies and books with the extravagance and hook-hungry eye of hip-hop producers ripping beats. Their *Sherlock* is like some turbo-charged, bass-heavy, super-smart mash-up of all that has gone before.

Their delight in the show's set is palpable. They fly around showing off Holmes's collection of 240 different kinds of tobacco ash, Holmes's bust of Goethe. In this series, we see Holmes's bedroom for the first time – I note it has an en suite bathroom, and is very tidy ('Holmes is the kind of flatmate who would keep his room tidy by throwing all his mess out into the front room,' Moffat notes). I bounce on the bed a bit. I feel I owe all of womenkind this action. I refrain from sniffing the pillowcase. That feels undignified.

The level of nerd-detail is high: there are seventeen steps up from the hall to the front room, as specified in the books. The Christmas cards in the hallway have all been filled out inside, to the landlady, Mrs Hudson. On the set, however, there are no actual quarters for Mrs Hudson.

'She doesn't have a room,' Gatiss explains. 'She just … stands at the end of this corridor, and hibernates until the front doorbell rings.'

It's interesting that – given this level of obsession with Holmes – Gatiss and Moffat found one aspect of their Holmes wholly mysterious until very late in the process.

'We didn't know if he was gay or not until the [first] series had actually finished, did we?' Gatiss muses. 'We kind of had to … work it out. It wasn't *obvious*.'

Wander outside, and you find Benedict Cumberbatch, in all his Holmesian glory, sitting at a picnic table, smoking a fag. Today is a good day for Cumberbatch, he reflects, as he sips from a polystyrene cup of coffee marked 'Benedict' ('I try to get them to write 'Sir Benedict' on it. Occasionally they oblige').

Yesterday, however, was a bad day. Holmes's trademark, tack-tack-tack-tack monologues are one of the most high-profile, technically arduous tricks in the business – as Holmes's extraordinary deductive skills are presented as 'a super-power – an achievable super-power', the deductive monologues are the bits where Cumberbatch has to, essentially, pull on Holmes's underpants over his tights and fly. He has to look like the cleverest man who ever lived.

'I had a non-stop monologue and I just … fell off the edge of the cliff,' Cumberbatch says, sighing. 'I couldn't remember all the words. I just … stopped. It's *horrible*. Sometimes feels like, rather than acting, you're being a machine. I don't mean that in a negative way. Holmes is just very … still. Still but fast.'

Cumberbatch isn't one for dwelling or moaning, though: today is a better day, and he's pretty sure he won't get a RETRAFTA.

'A RETRAFTA? It's something Martin [Freeman] and I made up. Where you act so badly, they come and take your BAFTA off you.'

On set, they turn the hoses back on. It starts raining again on Baker Street. Cumberbatch tamps out his cigarette and, about halfway between picnic table and the sound stage, starts walking like Sherlock Holmes again.

August 2011. Battersea Power Station. Over fifty crew members, actors and sundry personnel are gathered here today, on a location shoot. Ostensibly, they are here because the dilapidated early-twentieth-century grandeur of the power station – with its glowing walnut parquet floors,

20ft windows and rows of clockwork chrome dials – makes one of the most exquisite TV location-shoot interiors in Britain.

In reality, however, it's hard to shake the suspicion everyone's here because Moffat and Gatiss could not resist the lure of a single one-liner: summoned to Battersea by Mycroft, Watson notes, drily, 'He's got a power complex.'

Standing outside a location trailer is Martin Freeman. He is notably not wearing the safety helmet that is mandatory for everyone else on set, and is in the middle of explaining to one of the show's runners – who is wearing her safety helmet – just why this is.

'I'm a big fish, you see, love,' he says, sipping at his tea. 'I'm ... Johnny Big Bollocks. And you're ... you're ... what's that stuff whales eat? Krill. You're krill. Location krill. Krill wears a helmet.'

Freeman is on very good form today. Incredibly funny and incredibly filthy, he makes a comment about Una Stubbs that it would be inappropriate to repeat in *The Times*. ('I've been flirting with Una,' he concludes, after the bad story. 'Well, it's actually sexual aggression, but I often find the line between the two quite blurry.')

This season of *Sherlock* has been scheduled around Freeman's Watson. Having committed to a second series of *Sherlock*, Freeman was then offered the role of Bilbo Baggins in Peter Jackson's forthcoming, multi-million-dollar, blockbusting *The Hobbit*. A man of honour, Freeman had to – agonisingly – turn down *The Hobbit*: only for Jackson to declare Freeman was the only man for the job, and shift the entire, gigantic production schedule around him.

This time next year, after the release of *The Hobbit*, Freeman will be one of the most recognisable men on the planet. In the meantime, it typifies *Sherlock*'s embarrassment of riches that he's sitting in a car park in Battersea, drinking tea, and waiting to play Dr Watson.

'This is harder than *The Hobbit*,' he says. 'That's a half a billion dollar operation. The way they look after you is ... nuts, really. I mentioned that I'd seen this gig with these two great DJs, doing Northern Soul, then a couple of weeks later, I go into the lunch tent, and they'd got these two blokes with their turntables, with their speakers, and a bit of lino so they could do their Northern Soul turns. Just for me. It's a weird thing being incredibly grateful while you're eating your lunch, stone cold sober, in what is essentially a nightclub.'

Freeman does *Sherlock* because he loves it. He regards Cumberbatch incredibly highly: 'He's sweet and generous in an almost childlike way. He's very easy to screw over. I could take advantage of him playing cards. Actually, I *must* take advantage of him playing cards. But as an actor, he's one of the very few people I've worked with whose taste I don't question. Even subconsciously I'm not going, "Well, I wouldn't have done it like that." He commits.'

Freeman is called out for a shot. I wander over to Benedict's trailer. He's dressed as Sherlock, and looks a bit bored.

'Is my eye spasming?' he says. 'I can feel it spasming. Is it spasming? Look! Look! It's doing it now.'

I can see nothing.

'I've never been this near a power station before,' he frets.

'It's been decommissioned since 1969,' I remind him.

Cumberbatch pretends to dislike Freeman.

'He's always doing kung-fu on me,' Cumberbatch says, mock-peevishly. 'We'll be standing around, and I won't be paying any attention to him, and then he suddenly goes "HYYYYMMMNNNNN" and his hand is right next to my windpipe.' He pauses. 'On the other hand, before now he's asked to have jokes for Watson taken *out* of the script, because he says it's taking the attention away from me doing Holmes. He'll be doing some subtle, Mike Leigh thing, and I'll be ... the posh talkative one with the flouncy coat.'

Cumberbatch goes on to talk about how *Sherlock*'s overnight success has changed his life. 'In my career, I hadn't really made myself a target [for the media]. I had played Stephen Hawking, Van Gogh, William Pitt the Younger, Frankenstein ... and now ...' He sighs, and tries to think of an example.

'One woman came up to me,' he says, eventually, 'and asked me about my favourite cheese. I told her which one – how you chisel away so you can get a little shard that tastes so good, because you've worked so hard for it. Then she said, "Can you *draw* the cheese?" and I'm afraid I said no. You know,' he says, both despairingly and indignantly, 'it's *really difficult* to draw cheese.'

We then move on to what I think is the most devastating piece of revelation I've ever got from an interview subject: Cumberbatch does not like his Sherlock hair.

'I was short and blond in *Tinker Tailor Soldier Spy*, and I really, really didn't like coming back to this hair for this second series. I can't think of a wittier or even accurate comparison, but I just think it makes me look a bit like … a woman.'

November 2011. Air Studios, Hampstead. As part and parcel of the lavishness of *Sherlock*, it has a proper score – written by the Grammy-award-winning *Bond* soundtrack-composer, David Arnold, and Michael Price.

I walk in just as the orchestra is syncing to the emotional denouement of the episode. Benedict's face looms, huge and pale, on the screens; the piano and strings fall like sad rain. Sherlock's own violin motif rises and falls, like a bird dying of heartbreak. It's impossibly affecting. You just don't get this on *Midsomer Murders*.

Arnold – a man of martini-dry humour – also composed *Sherlock*'s theme tune, too.

'If you look at the score to the theme tune,' he says, in his rumbly murmur, 'the notes spell out "SHERLOCK".'

'Really?' I ask.

'No, you tit,' he replies. 'That's *Morse*.'

Between takes, all the talk is of the forthcoming *Sherlock* premiere, to be held in the BFI on the South Bank. It is becoming an increasingly big deal – the blogosphere is in a state of mild hysteria about it.

'There are tickets being touted for £350 on eBay,' David Arnold says. '£350.' He pauses. 'If I can get them up to £500, I'm having a skiing holiday. And I can't even ski.'

December 2011. The Sherlock premiere at the BFI. Dedicated *Sherlock* fans have been camping outside the BFI since 5.30am, in the bitter cold, hoping for returns.

It's now 5pm, and the BFI have let them inside, where the fifty most dedicated clutch cameras, and presents for the cast. Well, Benedict, really. They're all here for Benedict. When he walks into the room, there is proper, fan-girl screaming – followed by low, communal moans over his beauty. You don't usually get this for stars of classy BBC Sunday night dramas.

Sitting on a bench, observing all the pandemonium, is a slight figure in a woolly hat. On closer inspection, it becomes apparent it's Una Stubbs.

'Why aren't you in the Green Room, with the rest of the cast?' I ask her.

'Oh, I don't want to make a fuss,' she says, cheerfully.

In the cinema, there are whoops and screams as Mark Gatiss, Steven Moffat and Benedict Cumberbatch enter, and take their seats. The opening credits to 'A Scandal in Belgravia' begins in a room full of love and excitement – but what you notice, as you watch it, is how much more love and excitement there is on the screen.

However much the fans of *Sherlock* love *Sherlock*, it is dwarfed by the passion and obsession of the people who actually make it. On a tiny BBC budget, on schedules that nearly broke everybody, the new series of *Sherlock* looks like a love affair with possibility and ambition: visually dazzling and vibrating with unexpected neural leaps, it spends half its time being the funniest show on TV, and then casually cracks your heart, right across the centre. And, oh, the sheer *brightness*: I have seen audiences clap for things that move them, or make them laugh – but this is the first time I have ever seen a plot-point so clever and unexpected that it prompts a whole room to applaud it.

Sherlock's instant eminence, the first time it broadcast, seems obvious: it does only take ninety minutes for everything to change when you're moving this fast. This kind of velocity is inarguable.

Three minutes into it, Mark Gatiss leans over to Steven Moffat, and whispers something. Moffat starts to laugh – and then looks quite sombre.

Afterwards, in the bar, I ask him what Gatiss said.

'That it's never going to get any better than this,' Steven replies. 'I started to laugh, because I thought it was a joke – and then I realised he was right. It probably *won't* get any better than this.'

He pauses.

'Until we write the next series, obviously.' He looks down into his wine. 'That's going to be *amazing*.'

Of course, I couldn't write about any of the plot in the feature, as it was published before broadcast. Here is the plot, in my review – so LOOK AWAY NOW if you've still not seen it, you baffling Holmes-hater. The first part of the review was about EastEnders, *which I've left in, because it's Pat dying, man. It's a part of history.*

Sherlock Review 3: As Good as Television Gets

New Year's Day, *EastEnders,* and – in the Cockney barmaid equivalent of gunslingers dying with their boots on – soap legend Pat Butcher was dying with her earrings on.

As the most famous huge-earring-wearer of the last three decades, Pat's Earrings of Death had clearly been chosen with care. Who knows how many the wardrobe mistress had gone through before deciding, finally, on these: a white plastic drop-pendant, evocatively shaped like a tear. The appearance it gave was as if Pat's head was crying out one final, big accessory. A huge, clip-on sob.

'Yes,' you thought. 'Unless she had chosen a pair shaped like tomb-stones, or maybe ghosts, they couldn't be more apposite.'

As is the death-bed tradition of *EastEnders,* former cast members came to say their final farewells to Pat's earrings – including David Wicks (Michael French), Pat's estranged son, who left the show in 1996.

As he had then gone on to play Dr Nick Jordan in *Casualty,* his initial arrival caused momentary confusion. Had he turned up to intubate and defibrillate Pat? Or was this just a social call? And anyway, are you even *allowed* to come back to a soap when you've gone off to another one? Could Cindy Beale (Michelle Collins) now, theoretically, come back from her new perch as Stella Price on *Coronation Street*? Surely that's like moving between parallel worlds in space. You'll shatter the Time Vortex. Particularly since Cindy died. Or is the Time Vortex just in *Doctor Who*? I get confused.

Either way, by the end of New Year's Eve, Pat had died, too, after some superlative weeping in the rain from David Wicks's daughter, Bianca (Patsy Palmer). No one in soap has ever cried in the rain as well as Palmer. She weeps like a child left behind as the Ark sails away. At one point, Wicks looked like he was going to leave without having made things up with Pat.

'Daddy, don't go – I need you,' Bianca sobbed, face wetter than rain, inhaling lungfuls of deluge as her cardigan slowly saturated. For all her rain-sobbing, Bianca has never, ever worn an appropriate rain-sobbing outfit. Usually she's in one of those Puffa jackets that are about as rain-proof as a duvet. One day, she'll finally acknowledge just how much rain-sobbing *EastEnders* has in store for her, and will keep a Cag-in-a-Bag by her front door, with a packet of tissues in the pocket, just in case.

Until that eventful day, there's still Pat's funeral to look forward to. Perhaps, when they put Pat in her coffin, instead of placing pennies on her eyes, they'll put her earrings.

Straight after *EastEnders* it was *Sherlock* – the drama so evidently the most anticipated of 2012 that the BBC were airing it just twenty hours into 2012; perhaps scared that more excitable *Sherlock* fans might expire from heart weakness if kept waiting any longer.

In many ways, *Sherlock* doesn't really come across as a TV show. The levels of fandom it inspires are what you'd more readily associate with a pop star, or a rock band. People queued at 5.30am to get tickets for the premiere screening at the BFI. There are whole websites devoted to fans' imagining of sexual encounters between Holmes and Dr Watson. There are women who cry when you say the words 'Benedict Cumberbatch' – and not simply because they are trying to spell it in their heads, and failing.

And so to 'A Scandal in Belgravia', the first of three new feature-length *Sherlocks*, charged with the tricky task of topping one of the most triumphant debut series of all time.

Within the first two minutes, writer Steven Moffat made it clear he wasn't intending to start things off quietly, whilst he found his feet: a pearly-arsed dominatrix known as 'The Woman' entered a bedroom, holding a riding crop, asking: 'Have you been wicked, Your Highness?'

'Yes, Miss Adler,' a posh voice replied.

And then the opening title-sequence rolled. Yeah. That's right. The first episode of the new series of *Sherlock* was about a Kate Middleton S&M blackmail scenario. In your face, *Waterloo Road*.

The next hour and a half were, to be scientific, as good as it's possible for television to be: other programme-makers must have been biting their wrists in a combination of jealousy and awe. Not only does *Sherlock* have a cast list that reads 'Benedict Cumberbatch, Martin Freeman, Lara Pulver, Rupert Graves', but its episode subject was the potent one of 'Sherlock Holmes and love'.

Having spent the first series setting Holmes up as one of the fore-most men of the twenty-first century – all milk and ice and billion-dollar synapses blinking – this series seems to be about examining his weaknesses, instead. They've built him up – now they're going to knock him down. Or, in this case, blow him up, by throwing a fantastic pair of tits at him.

For Sherlock cannot fathom Irene Adler – 'The Woman' – a high-class dominatrix with incriminating pictures of Middleton (it's hinted, anyway, if never made obvious) on her phone.

Played by Lara *True Blood* Pulver, Irene Adler lives in a beautiful house of monochrome damask, and her lipstick is as red as damask roses. On the orders of the palace, Holmes is sent to the monochrome house to retrieve the pictures, and Adler prepares for his arrival.

'What will you wear?' her lover/assistant, Kate, asks.

'The Battle Suit,' Adler replies.

When Holmes arrives – pretending to be a vicar, ridiculously; he's already acting like a div – she greets him naked. The Business Suit. He's poleaxed by her – not just by the quiet authority of her bare arse, swishing past him on the sofa; but her face, too. He cannot read her. Holmes, who can read everyone – he glances at Watson, for reassurance: notes his shoes mean he has a date tonight, his stubble that he used an electric shaver – cannot decipher a single thing about Adler. She can hide herself wholly, even when naked. Particularly when naked. After all, as she reminds Holmes, 'However hard you try [with a disguise], it's always a self-portrait.'

Holmes is so stupefied by the novelty of being out-smarted that he doesn't even realise he fancies her, at this point.

And Adler, against all her judgement and nature, fancies Holmes, too. Adler is as clever as Holmes, but also as damaged: she keeps blackmail material on her phone because she 'makes her way in the world' with a series of deals and dodges; she has 'friends' she regularly sedates with the syringes in her bedside cabinet. Nearly everything in the world bores her. Sex isn't fun – it's just a job. What really excites her is detectives, and detective stories. Despite being a lesbian, what ultimately excites her is Sherlock Holmes.

And so 'A Scandal in Belgravia' was an hour and a half of two odd, fast, hot people being confused by each other: not quite knowing why they jangle when they're around each other; not quite knowing what to do with their feelings. Both have jobs that involve crushing their emotions: should they continue doing that – or actually trust each other?

In the end, their cataclysmic meeting results in a plane full of corpses rotting on a runway as Mycroft, the British government and the American government despair. 'Holmes and Adler' really aren't the new 'Hart to Hart'. She's betrayed him, he's betrayed her, and all Holmes's suspicions about love – 'The chemistry is terribly simple. And very destructive' – have been borne out. Love will never do for Holmes. He likes things to have conclusions, and endings. Love has no conclusion or ending at all. And, also, he fell in love with a mental. That was quite a big error.

From 8.10pm to 9.40pm, it was often hard to tell which part of you was being stimulated more by *Sherlock*: the eyes, or the brain. For whilst the script bounced along with a winning combination of screwball, rat-tat-tat dialogue and parkour-like plot-leaps, Paul McGuigan's direction was of movie-like sumptuousness. You lost count of the moments that looked a million dollars. A shot from above of Mycroft (Mark Gatiss) closing his umbrella, and ducking into a café, out of the rain, had a sense of choreography to it; 221b Baker Street has never looked more sumptuous.

McGuigan seemed to particularly revel in the scene where Adler – trying to retrieve her phone – jammed a syringe into Sherlock's arm, and he floated off into a wiggy state of narcoleptic wooze. As Sherlock collapsed backwards, drugged, the camera rotated once, twice beside him – sometimes you couldn't tell if he were falling up, or down. As he finally came in to land, his face was the same colour as the white-waxed floorboard he was bouncing off.

Here, in a dream, Holmes found himself on a moor – Adler beside him, on a chaise longue. They were two incongruous, pale, elegant town-creatures in all this brutal, wet green. Holmes could still not speak: insensible on barbiturates, his bed rose up out of the moss like a benign tombstone, and Holmes fell upon it, winking out of consciousness, carried into the next scene.

It was as distractingly beautiful a piece of cinematography as you're ever likely to see, and – accompanied by David Arnold and Michael Price's lush, weeping soundtrack – left you walking away from the television after ninety minutes, feeling like you'd just been fed lobsters, champagne and truffles through your brain.

The day after broadcast, an ill-tempered, Bank Holiday-blue kerfuffle kicked off across a couple of blogs, accusing Moffat's script of misogyny. Irene Adler had ended up being rescued by Holmes, the argument went. She fell in love with him and then had to be rescued by him, like some courtesan Snow White. Obviously, as a strident feminist, my 'Misogyny Alarm' is always on red-alert – but I have to say, it didn't ding once during *Sherlock*; save for a momentary sigh over just how many high-class call girls I've seen on television over the years (approximately six million), compared to the amount I've actually met (none).

For *Sherlock* is a detective story, not *Panorama*. It doesn't care about statistics, and nor should it. All I could see were two damaged people making a mess of each other's lives, whilst Martin Freeman did his patented 'Martin Freeman eyebrows' from the sidelines. And, obviously, some of the best television this country has ever produced.

Monday, and Channel 4 was remixing itself with the *Channel 4 Mash Up* – where C4's flagship shows swapped presenters, as part of C4's thirtieth birthday celebrations.

On switching to *River Cottage* – taken over by the Channel Four News team – I had my first 'when I woke this morning, I would not have put money on seeing that' moment of 2012: Jon Snow hammering a massive nail into a live crab, while Krishnan Guru-Murthy watched, wincing.

Tally-ho, 2012! Let's see if you can beat that by March!

Two of the biggest-hitting columns in this book – on my hair.

I Wish to Copyright My Hair

I cannot, in my life, claim to have invented many things. No medicinal breakthrough. No plastic compounds. No movement in figure-skating. True, I was part of a committee of fat children in the Midlands who conceived, in 1988, of the Cheese Lollipop – around 50g of cheap Cheddar speared on a fork, and sucked on during marathons of CBBC classic *Cities of Gold* – but I was just a cog, a fifteen-stone cog, in amongst other equally gifted and gigantic cogs. It's also true that I was part of that same committee of fat children who, having all moved into their adolescence, came up with the Sherry Cappuccino one desperate Christmas. The curdled layers of Nescafé and Somerfield Ruby will live on in the minds of all those who experienced it. Indeed, they probably also live on in the cups we used. It was viscous stuff.

That aside, however, it's clear that, in a version of *It's a Wonderful Life* where I took the James Stewart role, and plunged suicidally off the bridge, Bedford Falls would simply shrug, and carry on with the eggnog, same as they always did. I haven't really contributed to mankind's magnificent struggle one iota.

However, there is one meagre, paltry innovation I feel I can lay claim to in my otherwise uncreative life, and that is my hair. On Halloween 2003 – note the date, hair historians, as I'm sure there must be, somewhere. Maybe at De Montfort University, Leicester – I made drunkenly merry with a can of spray-in grey hair paint. On waking in the morning,

I looked in the mirror, and was astonished at what I saw. What I saw was The Hair of My Life. The Hair of My Soul. I had one icy whoosh of hair over my left eye. A blue-grey streak. A frosted lock. It looked a bit Eleanor Bron, a bit Morticia, a bit the wise monkey elder in *The Lion King*. Clearly, this was the Recipe of Me. I went to the hairdressers, and got them to make me semi-grey permanently.

For the first three years, me and my hair were very happy. True, old people were apt to come up to me at bus stops and commiserate ('Ooooh, you're like me. I went completely grey at twenty-nine, after I had shingles. You want to get yourself one of those dye-jobbies from Boots'), but I felt I was on some kind of Hair Quest. I felt I was pushing the boundaries. I felt I was creative.

Then the bomb fell. Last summer, my brother Eddie – the maverick Cheese Lollipop committee member who, in 1988, had suggested we concentrate our cutlery research solely on the fork – rang me from Brighton.

'I've just seen a woman with your hair,' he said. 'In Peacocks,' he added. 'Buying leggings.'

Initially, I was flattered. I visit Brighton quite a lot. It was not outside the realms of possibility that this woman had seen my hair, and simply been inspired. I couldn't blame her. I am in the possession of hair dynamite.

Then my sister, also in Brighton, rang a month later.

'I've seen FIVE WOMEN with your hair,' she blurted out, immediately.

At this point, I must admit, I felt bad. These women had, fairly obviously, not copied their hair from me. They had copied it from the woman who copied me. They did not know their hair history.

I felt a little like Elvis Presley might have, on seeing someone with a quiff and wobbly legs whose primary influence had not been him, but Shakin' Stevens, instead. The way things were going, there was every chance that my hair would go down in history as 'origin unknown'.

Then, a week before the end of the school term, things escalated dramatically, albeit mainly in my mind. Outside the school gates one morning – as startling as the sight of a polar bear – there was a mother *with my hair*. On my own patch! Bold as the slightly brassy grey tone her – clearly inferior – hairdresser had come up with!

Whilst dealing with the fear of dying in hair-dying obscurity had been unpleasant, this new scenario was a different kettle of fish altogether. I think all women know what another woman stealing your signature style means. I recalled, from my teenage years, my friend Julie's fury on noting that a female classmate had appropriated her then-trademark – a Puffa jacket, worn with badges on the elasticated hem.

'It's war,' she said, flatly, smoking a cigarette in Burger King, as you could, in those days.

And of course, this hair-stealing woman was, indeed, declaring war on me. For who would ever copy the hairstyle of someone they saw every day, if they thought they looked *worse* with it? The hair-stealing mother believed my hair looked *better* on her. That it was, by and large, a good hairdo, but *ruined by the addition of my face*. She was dissing me. This was clearly the act that would lead to the outbreak of war.

But just how does one fight a Hair War? Unsatisfyingly, this is the question I am currently stuck on, with another five weeks of the summer holidays to go, until I face my follicular nemesis again. The way I see it, I've got only three options. 1) Kill her – the sensible, but possibly immoral option. 2) Kill myself – irresponsible, given my prominence in the pick-up rota. 3) Get an entirely new do – frankly, I might as well be asked to traverse to Mordor to cast the One Ring into the Crack of Doom. I'm thirty-two. I'm too old for that kind of quest. This is the hair, for better or worse, I will die with.

So here I am, backed into a hair stand-off I never asked for. I can't believe there aren't government guidelines on this kind of thing. I'm tearing my hair out.

So that's the colour. But what about the size?

Chicks with Big Hair Are My Chicks

Until the age of twenty-five, the biggest fear in my life was that I would go bald. If I considered it for even one second, I had the kind of sweaty, spiralling panic that other people describe on being stuck in pot-holes, or standing at the top of the Empire State Building.

My fear of hair loss was based in cool analysis of fact: as a teenage girl, I was quietly unappealing.

'You have a round, ruddy face, such as a peasant's,' my sister told me, at one point, using her 'helpful' voice. 'Like a Halloween pumpkin – but not as sexy.'

As we were also poor, I didn't have the resources – such as fashion, make-up, or cocaine – to increase my allure to the viewing eye. Simply, then, my hair was a precious commodity – as I could grow it very, very long. Long hair is pretty much the only beauty you can acquire if you have no money at all.

By the time I was thirteen, my hair was down to my hips. I had tended it assiduously. Nothing was too good for it. I would sit around, eating jam sandwiches, whispering 'Grow! Grow!' at my head, in what I deemed to be a voice encouraging to follicles.

At one point, I read in a nineteenth-century guide to beauty that rinsing with a beaten, raw egg would add lustre and shine. Consequently, I spent nearly two years walking around with an eggy, slightly sulphurous air. I was less 'nymphette', and more 'omelette'.

Over these years of intense hair cultivation – I was essentially a 'hair farmer', tending the hair-field on my head – my focus shifted, slowly but significantly, from having 'long' hair, to wanting 'big' hair.

'This is basically a "hair cape",' I realised, looking down, when I was around fifteen. 'I look like Captain Caveman. I don't need *length*. What I need is *width*. This hair needs to be predominantly based on my head. I'm going bouffy.'

Turning, again, to my nineteenth-century guide to beauty, I noted that Victorian women would achieve their gigantic up-dos by padding out their hair with 'rats': tiny pillows they would pin to their heads, and then arrange their own hair over, in a series of billows, knots and waves.

Keen to have my hair in an up-do the size of a hat, I started to use 'rats' myself. At the time, however, the only things I could find in the house that approximated 'rats' were the tissue-paper inter-liners for the terry-towelling nappies my mother used on the babies.

Whilst seeming, at first, to be securely fixed to my head, these liners would regularly fall out while I stood at bus stops, walked through parks, tried to purchase goods at a till, etc. Then I, and anyone else around, would all stare at what appeared to be a giant sanitary towel on the floor, which had just fallen out of my head.

'My rats,' I would explain. It never seemed to make things better.

In the years since, I have, thank God, worked out how to satisfy my Hair Larging urges in a slightly more practical way – essentially by taking half the length off, then backcombing for ten minutes solidly every morning, in the way other people do yoga, or walk the dog.

As I joyfully embiggen myself into the vague silhouette of Chewbacca, I have time to reflect on just what it is about big hair that I find so elementally appealing.

Firstly, there is the obvious matter of perspective. By having big hair, it makes my body look smaller, in comparison. As far as an aid to looking slimmer goes, this is the easiest one ever conceived of. No fad diets, corsetry, optical-illusion spray tanning, or artful couture: just a massive do.

Secondly, when it comes to wanting to look glamorous, there's something winningly practical about having huge hair. Heels cripple you; the bugle-beading on an expensive dress will chafe. Huge hair, on the other hand, can't fall off. You never leave your hair in the back of a cab. It's unbreakable, unstealable, and, most importantly of all, costs nothing. Armed with a comb, you can whip your do up like egg whites into a gigantic hair meringue, without it costing you a penny. Big hair is the party-do Marx would have backed, for sure.

And finally, whilst I am not prejudiced against people with small hair – as far as I know, there has never been any 'small hair on big hair' violence recorded on 'the streets'; we are not in conflict – there's something about big-haired chicks that makes me instantly inclined to like them. The iconography of big-haired women is compelling: cackling barmaids in tight leopardskin; Rizzo in *Grease*, backcombing in the school toilets; Tracy in *Hairspray* wailing 'But our First Lady, Jackie Kennedy, rats her hair!' when the teachers condemn her beehive. Dusty. Alexis Carrington Colby. Winehouse.

It's the hair of the working-class girl on the make; on the town. A party-helmet. A gigantic hair-aura, indicating holy razziness – such as the Virgin Mary would have had, if she'd been The Ronettes.

Hair takes us, naturally and easily, to the most famous hair of the twenty-first century. Not my own, alas – although it is something I am working on all the hours that God sends – but that of the Duchess of Cambridge, née Kate Middleton, our future Queen of England.

The Royal Wedding in April 2011 was one of the big media events of the last ten years. Broadcasters and newspapers the world over wondered just how they could make their coverage truly reflect the grandeur, history and emotion of this occasion. On the one hand, this was something which would be included in encyclopedias, and be thought to reflect upon the age. On the other – two young, cheerful people in love. How best to report on this juddering disparity? How? HOW?

Thankfully, I knew: just write down everything Martin Kemp from Spandau Ballet said on Twitter throughout the ceremony.

The Best Royal Wedding Ever

It might have been a Royal Wedding but, really, there was no pressure.

Should William and Kate have turned on ITV1's *Six O'Clock News* the night before their wedding – perhaps in their dressing gowns, in face-packs, eating Shreddies – presenter Julie Etchingham would have soothed their nerves:

'This wedding,' Etchingham said, standing outside Buckingham Palace, 'is an opportunity for optimism about the future – in a moment our history is marked by tough economic times at home, and DISASTER and DEATH *all around the world*.'

Well. That is quite an implication to take on board: that your wedding will, in some way, negate the effect of the Fukushima nuclear plant leak. However confident in your frock, finger-buffet and vodka ice-luge you may initially have been, it's got to be a bit of a jolt when *the news* tells you that your nuptials have the perceived ability to counteract radioactivity.

But the joy of something like a Royal Wedding, of course, is that everyone *does* go a little bit nuts around it. Last week *wasn't* a normal week. It was like the last day of term, or Friday at Glastonbury: everything upside-down. Nothing usual. The shops ran out of bunting, lager and charcoal, the news disappeared from papers and TV, and what would normally be a work-day turned into a holiday where it was perfectly acceptable to be sitting on the sofa at 11am, blind drunk, using an enormous foam-rubber Union Jack hand to ferry peanuts to your mouth.

And so it was that the eve of the Royal Wedding had all the novelty of the day you move house – displacing all your usual objects and routines, and ending up with a supper of sardines and marmalade in the front garden, using only tablespoons. Odd conversations happened. On Thursday's episode of political show *This Week,* for instance, Richard Madeley claimed that the next day would see the marriage 'consummated' at Westminster Abbey – an event inexplicably left out of *The Times'* souvenir fourteen-page order of service.

Later in the show, presenter Andrew Neill asked him if he, Madeley, would 'get rid of Charles, and make William king?'

Madeley replied, 'Well if he was gaga, obviously,' with the kind of breezy certainty that suggested that, should our heir apparent actually 'go gaga', Madeley would step up to the plate and finish Charles off with a spade, as if he were an old badger knocked down by a car.

As the sun set on 28 April 2011, it was clear that this was a day that would live on in everyone's mind as the day Kerry Katona [@KerryKatona] tweeted, 'Best of luck Kate and Wills. Hope it doesn't end like my last 2,' and Jeff Brazier [@JeffBrazier] (former boyfriend of the late Jade Goody) made his big Royal Wedding statement: 'Wills, I think your missus is fit. And for that reason, I just want to say, "Well done".'

Friday 29 April, 2011

8.35am. It seemed that Kate Garraway had got the short straw: ITV1 had sent her out of London, away from the wedding, to Buckleberry – home of the Middletons. This is Middletonia. Middletonaria. Middletonton.

In a strapless dress and slightly incongruous furry bolero cardigan – it was colder than everyone thought it would be – Garraway was sitting outside Buckleberry's pub, surrounded by locals. One of them was holding a giant rabbit, which was wearing a Union Jack top hat.

'Buckleberry has become the centre of the universe!' Garraway said – patently not true either in terms of the wedding (those international news crews aren't camped outside Westminster Abbey for nothing) or the composition of the universe (it has no observable centre).

We cut away from Garraway to the crowds lining the Mall. A huge cheer had gone up, and the director clearly wished to see what it was. Alas – it was a huge Portaloo-emptying truck, at which the crowd were cheerfully and ironically waving their Union Jack flags. British crowds know exactly how to behave on a Big Day such as this, when the eyes of the world are upon them. You cheer the oomska-wagon with just as much fervour as you would cheer Princess Michael of Kent. It's one of the sly perks of being a subject.

Class-based bitchiness, meanwhile, is one of the sly perks of being a TV news anchor. Alastair Stewart had been outside the Goring Hotel since 6am, reporting on the nothing-happening emptiness that would, eventually, be stepped into by Kate Middleton on her way to the Abbey.

'The police presence is marvellously understated here,' he smoothed. 'Sometimes it's difficult to work out if it's a Middleton – or a member of staff.'

Another one of the great things about this wedding is that it is happening so early. As a nation on a public holiday sets the cafetiere up and argues over the last Coco Pops variety pack, the King of Swaziland and Elton John are having to get into central London on a day with limited public transport options, then queue up for twenty minutes to get into Westminster Abbey.

Look – it is only 9.15am, and there is David Beckham, stuck in a celebrity-and-dignitaries traffic jam, and practising his 'staring into the distance looking noble' face whilst the crowd outside shouts 'Becks! Becks! Becks! Becks!'

Perhaps it is the sheer shock of the early hour, but Beckham's eyebrows appear to be verging just ever so slightly towards 'Ming the Merciless'. Next to him, his heavily pregnant wife Victoria stands in four-inch Louboutins, a ticking human time-bomb. With the time currently 9.16am, and the service not due to end until 12.15, her pregnant bladder will be a matter of fretting concern to all the mothers watching on television.

'That poor cow still on that pew?' they will ask, as they themselves take advantage of their own, immediately-to-hand toilet facilities. 'Let's hope she doesn't sneeze, or it's game over.'

Last night, before the wedding began, there were a couple of things you would have felt incredibly confident in betting on. 1) The recurrence of the phrases 'that dress', 'fairytale wedding', 'what Britain does best', 'the eyes of the world,' 'Diana's boys' and 'Princess Beatrice, there, wearing a … thing'.

2) Most women in the country crying quite heavily at some point during the ceremony.

And, finally, the most certain of all, 3) The BBC providing the definitive coverage of the event: solemn, reverent, knowing, stately, informed, and wholly befitting a royal occasion.

In the event, however, the BBC's coverage *is* solemn, reverent, knowing, stately and informed – and it doesn't befit this royal occasion at all. While the BBC gives us a thorough behind-the-scenes tour of the Household Cavalry's schedule today ('These boys have been shining their boots since 5am!') and thoughtful talking heads in the studio, who marvel over the architecture of Westminster Abbey, ITV1 gets right in there: forcing milliner Stephen Jones to comment on other milliners' creations as they walk through the Abbey doors ('It's very … pretty,' he offered, eventually, with a cat's bum mouth), giving us the money-shots of Earl Spencer turning up ('There he is with his new fiancée – there's always a new one, isn't there?'), and zooming in on Prince Harry's girlfriend, Chelsy Davy, the minute she emerged from a car ('The wonderful thing about Kate is that she's so natural,' Julie Etchingham mewed, as Chelsy's cheerfully bright-orange face moved up the aisle).

In what was perhaps the definitive editorial decision of the day, at 9.30am, ITV1 cut from a live interview with David Cameron, who was being rather shiny and pious ('I know the whole nation wishes those young people a very great deal of luck') to show Tara Palmer-Tomkinson's arrival at Westminster Abbey, instead.

The only possible reason for this newsflash-like urgency – Cameron was literally mid-sentence – was to see if Palmer-Tomkinson had, as had been speculated in the press, got her 'new nose', following the recent collapse of her septum: thus making it abundantly clear that, for today at least, a minxy aristocrat's nasal integrity out-ranked anything the Prime Minister could say or do.

ITV1 had grasped what the BBC hadn't, or perhaps couldn't: that the way this country views the Royal Family has changed, and for the better. The ridiculous, childlike deference we had when Charles and Diana married – an era where there was the assumption that Diana would be a virgin, outrage at the creation of a *Spitting Image* puppet of the Queen Mother, and my father told me, in all seriousness, that I should never criticise the Queen in public 'because you might get a punch in the face'. I was seven – has gone, and it is better for all of us that it has. Opinions on what the national reaction to the life and death of Diana 'meant' are two-a-penny, but I can't help but think that what we all learned, along the way, is that princes and princesses can be as lonely, hopeful, confused, unfaithful, devious, lost, simple, kind-hearted, silly and breakable as the rest of us, and that demanding that they be anything other than fallible and human is apt to work out extremely badly for everyone involved.

The healthiest way William and Kate's future 'subjects' could deal with watching their wedding, then, was to approach it as they would attending the wedding of a friend, i.e., turning up in all good faith, having a couple of drinks, then cheerfully spending the rest of the day taking the mick out of the décor, food, music, location and fellow guests. Watching this just as they would watch *X Factor* – cheering the 'good guys', slagging off the ridiculous or amusing elements on Twitter. And this, in the event, is just what ITV1 did: perhaps most perfectly summed up with Phillip Schofield's [@Schofe] simple yet oddly appropriate announcement of 'Ed Miliband's arrived! Hahaha!'

Twenty minutes later, a tweet from Miliband [@Ed_Miliband] himself merely served to confirm Schofield's reaction. 'Walked down The Mall to the Abbey – because of the crowds,' Miliband said. Poor Ed. Nothing goes right for him.

By 10am, all the celebrities and dignitaries were assembled in the Abbey, and it was time to reflect on whose presence was sorely missed, due to the limited guest list. Personally, I yearned for Bill Clinton – old Big Dog. He was brilliant at the Olympic Bids – always in the background of a shot, mine-sweeping the room for poon and canapés. Tony Blair, similarly, would have been a good booking – or, failing him, Michael Sheen, who could have done the ceremony as Blair, then gone to the reception as either Brian Clough, or David Frost.

Guy Ritchie's arrival, meanwhile, underlined how awesome it would have been if he and Madonna had kept it together, and she was now stalking around the Abbey like Cruella de Vil with abs, making Nick Clegg cry with terror. And who didn't want George Michael there – a little bit stoned, having valet-parked his Jeep into a nearby tree? Thank goodness, then, that he could appear by proxy, via Twitter, whilst watching the ceremony from home – where, he informed us, he was wearing 'Union Jack pants'.

10.10, and Huw Edwards on the BBC was getting very stressed about the day's schedule. 'Prince William has *ten seconds* to appear,' he said; making it all sound a bit like an episode of *24*.

10.11, and – a minute behind schedule – William finally emerged in the bright red uniform of the Irish Guards. As pop critic Tim Jonze [@timjonze] put it on Twitter, 'He's come dressed as Pete Doherty, circa 2003!'

Over CNN, horror instantly broke out amongst the American pundits with the advent of the mini-buses, which were ferrying the wider royal family to the Abbey.

'These are airport shuttle-buses!' one wailed – presumably labouring under the belief that the only way royalty and the aristocracy can be transported around is in a gigantic hollowed-out pumpkin, pulled by unicorns. What the American commentators failed to understand is that one of the things that Britain does best is putting loads of people on a bus. Look at *Summer Holiday*. Away matches. Pakistani weddings in Wolverhampton. With this bus thing, we were playing to our strengths.

Martin Kemp [@realmartinkemp] from Spandau Ballet didn't think so, though: 'Minibuses? Gimme a break,' he snorted on Twitter. 'Spandau or Duran wouldn't get in one of those. I bet Elton won't be going to the party in one. Off with the head of who organised that.'

On the BBC, Kate Middleton had finally emerged from the Goring in a white-out of flashbulbs. Even though we could not really see her, womankind had noticed one thing and was punching the air: the dress was sleeved! Yes! Finally the reign of evil sleevelessness is OVER! GOD BLESS YOU, MIDDLETON! FASHION WILL NOW ALLOWS US TO HIDE OUR UPPER ARMS AGAIN, AS GOD INTENDED. Were the BBC to have a Body Dysmorphia-O-Meter, it would have registered an instant 40 per cent drop across the nation. Our future Queen's biggest legacy had begun.

Sleeves aside, these first shots of Middleton in the car were not ideal. The framing of the telephoto lens was such that both her head, and her lower torso, were cut off from view, and all we could see was Ms Middleton's décolletage.

'It's a limited view, but a delightful view,' Huw Edwards intoned, solemnly, as if he were now the BBC's Official State Perver. As the bride's father, Michael Middleton, fussed around, placing the dress and train into the car, Edwards continued, 'He is making sure everything is unsoiled, and undamaged' – an unfortunate narrative accompaniment to a man on his knees, half-buried under his daughter's dress, on the morning of her wedding.

*

11.05am, and the country's patriotism was peaking. This wedding looked *brilliant*. China must be *so jealous*. In your FACE, France. *No one* could do this better. America might have a funnier leader – Obama's take-down of Donald Trump involved clips from *The Lion King* and adroit political side-swipes; David Cameron does an impression of Michael Winner in a car insurance advert – but when it comes to doing the best ever gigantic ceremony full of princesses, and people wearing uniforms, this wins. It's even better than the last scene in *Star Wars*.

William and a bed-headed Harry were joshing around at the altar like Luke and Han. The chief bridesmaid – Pippa Middleton – had a smokin' ass. The Archbishop of Canterbury's eyebrows were voluminous enough for him to be Chewie, and David Cameron and Nick Clegg could be C-3PO and R2-D2, if they wanted. This was amazing.

As if to confirm everyone's thoughts, Wayne Rooney [@WayneRooney] tweeted, 'Congrats to prince William and Kate. Wow what a turnout.' Rooney could appreciate the box office here as much as the next man.

As William pushed the ring onto Kate's finger, accompanied by an odd, squeaky sound – I think it was his shoes – and the couple tried not to giggle, one thing became pleasingly clear: this wasn't that much-touted thing, 'a fairytale wedding', at all, thank God. It was just … human.

Because it's not just the public who have changed their view of the royals since the last wedding of an heir – the Royal Family itself has changed, too. Charles and Diana's wedding felt like something arranged by the elders and their advisors, into which Charles and Diana were para-chuted, as the token meat in a vast machine. On that day, Diana – in her too-big dress – and Charles – with his heart somewhere else – looked like they were being eaten alive by St Paul's Cathedral. In some ways, it's like they never came back out of there.

This wedding, however, feels like it's been imagined by a much younger and more confident generation: these glossy-haired girls and flush-cheeked, slightly awkward boys; this confederacy of tight-knit brothers and sisters and cousins. There is a sense of freedom, simplicity, camaraderie and fun here that one imagines Prince Charles watching from the pews in a slightly bittersweet way. These young royals seem to have a much better handle on being royal than their parents ever did.

Who would not enjoy this day?

Unexpectedly, the answer was: 'Stephen Fry'. Halfway through the ceremony – around the time of that hymn that sounded like the song the teapot sings on *Beauty and the Beast* – Fry [@stephenfry] incongruously tweets: 'Ding's let Trump in. This 12th frame is beginning to look huge. Nerve-wracking times.'

At first, everyone presumed it was a joke – but when Fry followed it up with 'Mid-session interval and they go in 7-5 in Judd Trump's favour. No one yet pulling out in front, both these semis could go to the wire...' it became clear: Stephen Fry – friend of Prince Charles – really *was* tweeting the snooker during a Royal Wedding.

Someone needed to do something about this – and that someone was 1980s magician Paul Daniels: 'WHO CARES?' Daniels [@ThePaulDaniels] asked Fry, as Twitter held its breath. Was Daniels about to take Jeeves into the Bunco Booth?

Daniels had been very passionate about this Royal Wedding: he had already castigated all the 'snidey shits for coming out of the woodwork' who had dared criticise the day, definitively stated 'WOW. That is what a Princess SHOULD look like' at Kate Middleton's arrival, and informed us that his wife, Debbie McGee, was 'sobbing' from 10am onwards. And in his Musketeer-like defence of the royals, Daniels found an unlikely ally: legendary 1980s puppet Roland Rat.

'I can't believe this English guy is so cynical!' Rat [@rolandrat] tweeted Daniels; presumably whilst wearing shades and a pink blouson bomber-jacket.

'Off with his head!' Daniels agrees. The world's most unlikely Cavalier online militia had started to form.

Indeed, sorry to relate, in the interregnum between the ceremony and the kiss on the balcony, the mood had started to sour right across Twitter. A slightly boozy bar-room belligerence had taken hold. One sensed that, across the country, there were a series of street parties at which celebrities were grudging participants – having been forced to 'get out the house and stop being such a miserable git' by non-famous spouses; only to spend the rest of the afternoon at a half-empty trestle table, grimly downing multi-pack can after multi-pack can of Fosters and tweeting their distress to the world as their neighbours began a conga.

Pulp front-man – and recently divorced – Jarvis Cocker [@really jcocker] tweeted, rather dolorously, '10% of marriages end in divorce. Trust me – I know what I'm talking about'.

George Michael [@GeorgeMichael] seemed a bit … hazy: 'The greatest tragedy was Alexander McQueen not being around to make a fabulous creation for Kate,' he tweeted – only to have to hastily clarify, minutes later, and presumably after some fairly irate replies, 'Of course Diana's absence is the greatest tragedy – but it really goes without saying.'

Things, however, had clearly degenerated most rapidly in the day of philosophical essayist Alain de Botton. Having remained silent on Twitter all day, at 4pm, de Botton [@alaindebotton] suddenly weighed in with, 'Women tend to miss the distinction between women who are beautiful, and women one would want to sleep with.'

Ten seconds later, the follow-up tweet clarified what was on de Botton's mind: 'Kate vs. Pippa'.

As the world got its head around de Botton choosing to issue his Middleton Family Shag-Order list on the day of the Royal Wedding, Jade Goody's widower, Jack Tweed [@JackTweed], finally issued his statement on this global event: 'Not botherd about this wedding in the slightest everyone tweeting like they care is lying!!!'

He was wrong, of course – just like he was wrong that time he attacked that sixteen-year-old boy with a golf club, and got sentenced to eighteen months in jail. People had cared a great deal. They cared about the idea of an event as big as the Olympics, or the inauguration of a President – but about love, rather than sport, or power. They cared about this rather serious young couple making their vows, in the way we care about all young people making vows. And they cared about the rather slash-fiction-ish idea of Pippa Middleton and Prince Harry getting it on. By 1.30pm, the nation was roaring 'Come on! KISS! KISS! You KNOW YOU WANT TO' at Pippa and Harry on the balcony as if this were *Seven Brides for Seven Brothers,* but with a much shorter cast list. And no beards.

As the new Duke and Duchess of Cambridge drove off in their Aston Martin to the reception – where they apparently danced to 'You're the One That I Want' from *Grease,* and Prince Harry began his best man's speech with 'Pippa – call me', before stage-diving off a windowsill into the crowd – you were given pause to reflect that – audience of two billion aside – they had given themselves just the wedding that they wanted.

And they had given us the wedding we wanted, too: heartfelt, worthy of a global audience, with David Beckham in it, and over early enough for everyone to get to the pub by 2pm.

Back to the TV, with a couple of stand-out shows from 2011. Writer Abi Morgan is turning out to be one of the great British talents of the twenty-first century: writing both The Iron Lady *and* Shame *for cinema, in the space of two years.*

She could have worked on anything, and gone anywhere – but instead, she brought The Hour *to the BBC: all unrequited love, bum-freezer jackets, proto-feminism, spies, crosswords and rain, on a TV in the corner of all our living rooms. Texturally,* The Hour *was one of my favourite dramas ever. I wanted to live in it. I loved all the characters so much, I dreamed about eating them. That's normal, isn't it? Wanting to eat fictional characters. We all do that, yeah? Yeah?*

Cometh *The Hour*, Cometh Me

What did I think *The Hour* was going to be? From the trailers, I thought I knew. It seemed to be an open-and-shut case of the BBC going, '*Mad Men?* Fast, clever, lavishly stylised period-drama – which has been exported all over the world in a million box-sets? That's *classic* BBC territory! We should have been all over something like this like a pigeon on a chip! *Knackers!* This has been a *massive* operational failure!'

Pause.

'Miss Mountshaw! Order fifty pencil skirts, nineteen ashtrays, two trench-coats, a wind-up record player and a cocktail shaker. ALAN! Call casting! I need a chick with an ass, and a fella with a lantern-jaw who'll appeal to both women *and* gay bloggers. RORY! Check Twitter and see if George Michael's slagged off Jeremy Clarkson again. It's nothing to do with this project – I just find the fellow amusing. Right! RIGHT! Let's show those sons-of-bitches at Lionsgate TV how we do things in downtown White City! ACTIVATE THE MULTI-MILLION-POUND BUDGET!'

But in the event, those BBC trailers for *The Hour* – heavily stylised; all Saul Bass-esque graphic design, sliding split-screens and fruity 1950s winking – turned out to be a bit of a red herring. Twenty minutes into *The Hour*, and you wouldn't have been comparing it to anything at all. The BBC might have commissioned it in the wake of losing the broadcasting rights to *Mad Men*, but *The Hour* is too much its own creature to be seen as 'the spoiler from Blighty'.

I'll square with you: I got to the end of the first episode, and then gorged on the preview DVD of the second episode. And when I got to the end of that – having watched two hours back-to-back – I rang round TV critic friends, to see if they had Episode Three. When they didn't – or were *lying* to me, because they didn't want to give up their Precious – I was so disappointed and deflated that I just gave in, and went to bed an hour early. The rest of the day seemed too inevitably whack to bother with. The last time I had something new and craved more of it as badly was with *Sherlock*, I think. And, unlike *Sherlock*, I don't even fancy anyone in *The Hour*. Well, not much.

So what is *The Hour*? Well, first off, it's pacey: there's stuff going on all *over* here. A man stabbed in the throat on the District line; a debutante weeping in a phone-box: nose bleeding as she dabbed at it with a silk glove. There's secret messages in crosswords; working-class kids trying to take over the BBC; Kennedy running for Vice President. In the last minute, we find the debutante dead: hanging from the shower-rail with a broken neck.

'*They* are everywhere,' she had told her oldest friend, TV reporter Freddie Lyon (Ben Whishaw), hours before she died. 'They will kill me if they know I am talking to you.'

When he finds her, she's still twitching: a foot off the floor, wallpaper clawed to shreds around her.

'Cut her down! Give her CPR!' you shout.

But it's 1956. No one knows CPR in 1956. All Freddie can do is shout her name as she dies in his arms – kick-starting his off-the-books investigation into who '*they*' are.

So yes, *The Hour* is a thriller: there's a mystery here that, by the end of the series, needs to be solved. But what will almost certainly take *The Hour* to a second series is that, at heart, it's a love-triangle in a BBC news-room, at the time of the Suez crisis. They might as well have subtitled it '*Two Boys, a Girl, a Channel & a Canal*'.

All-round alchemic casting has *The Wire*'s Dominic West as Hector Madden – a lantern-jawed, privileged, musky but ostensibly dim news-reader. *Brideshead Revisited*'s Ben Whishaw is the nervy, gobby, Scrappy-Doo journalist Freddie Lyon – all bum-freezer jackets and outbursts. And *The Crimson Petal and the White*'s Romola Garai is Bel Rowley – producer of the BBC's first live hour of heavyweight news: bluestocking; Bakewell; bare-faced of make-up.

Freddie has loved Bel for years before we arrived – 'You've always been the only one for me,' he says, suddenly, in a moment of unusual candour.

But Bel has them nicknamed as 'Moneypenny' and 'James' – they are co-conspirators in revolutionising BBC news broadcasts; the progenitors of *The Hour*. They are not to be lovers. When the ripped, bullish Hector turns up – gifted the presenting job on their new show by well-connected relatives – Freddie hates him instantly. He spends all his time and fury constructing the most gratuitous, waspish insults for Hector.

'She [Bel] said you were witty,' Hector says, with the *noblesse oblige* of the posh.

'She's easy to make laugh,' Freddie replies, with the casual possessive-ness of someone close.

But while Freddie has the advantage of closeness, Hector has the advantage of chemistry. Bel knows he's a bumptious div – and a married bumptious div, at that – but there's something else going on here: they can't stand near each other without fidgeting; the eye-contact heats up at twice the normal speed. He's a terrible newsreader, but he allows Bel to criticise him – seemingly for the first time in his life.

'You have a certain … *gravity*,' he explains, as he bids her good night, in the rain, and it's clear he means both kinds: she's an intellectual heavy-weight, but she's also the planet both these moons-of-boys revolve around.

There's a thrill in watching a female character like this, and it's possibly the only parallel with *Mad Men*, other than the fact the men wear suits: Bel echoes Peggy Olson's bare-faced, bright industry: women in an era (*Mad Men* in 1962, *The Hour* in 1956) when they were getting the first glimpses of being allowed to play like the boys. Bel might not be allowed in the smoking room at Hector's private club, but she – along with den mother Lix (Anna Chancellor) – is dictating the BBC's hard-news agenda.

Perhaps it's writer Abi Morgan's way with a woman, but the dynamic of Freddie and Bel's relationship has a real poignancy: Ben Whishaw looks like a … boy … next to Garai's huge-eyed, solid-hipped stateliness. There's something rather lovely about how much *bigger* she is, in every sense, than him. It's almost as if the actors have been scaled up or down, to represent their future potential in 1950s Britain.

And 1950s Britain looks – as you would expect from a BBC drama – just wonderful: matching the soundtrack, there's a deft jazzy brush-work on all the period details – debutantes in foaming white cocktail dresses; cigarettes in rainy doorways; English Rose kitchens with a still-meagre collection of tins stored in rows. You can bet your ass every inch of parquet the heels and brogues tap across is date-correct.

But the period-porn is just a bonus. It's the three main characters – five feet up from the shoes sent over from Angels & Bermans in tissue-lined boxes – that make every hour of *The Hour* fly.

I'm jonesing for the third hour like a kid made to wait too long for Christmas.

Two extraordinary documentaries broadcast in the same week, meanwhile, asked very fundamental questions about death, and our response to it. I don't think I've ever cried more watching television. Not even when Maddie dumped David in Moonlighting.

A Week of Death, and All Its Faces

This week was a straight-up contest as to which programme could most emotionally destroy you. Would it be Jon Snow's *The Killing Fields of Sri Lanka* – widely being described, by those who'd seen it, as 'the most visceral war footage ever broadcast'? Or would it be *Terry Pratchett: Choosing to Die* – in which a man with motor neurone disease took his own life, leaving Channel 4 screening-rooms in tears?

The Killing Fields was presented by Jon Snow – straight-backed, angry-eyed, but very clear about what it was going to show, and why.

'This programme contains very disturbing images depicting death, injury, execution and evidence of sexual abuse and murder – much of it filmed on mobile phones,' he said, with quiet firmness. 'For the last two years, Channel 4 has been compiling its own dossier of war-crimes – evidence for bringing the guilty to justice.'

That it was down to a commissioning editor at Horseferry Road to do this was the first, shaming moment of *The Killing Fields*: for the opening footage showed the UN in 2008, evacuating from Sri Lanka. The government had reopened its attacks on the minority Tamil population, and told the UN it could 'no longer guarantee their safety'. With an obedience that blurred into complicity, the UN observers promptly packed and left, amongst scenes of Tamils gathered around their compound, weeping.

'We don't care about shelter, food or water – we can take care of ourselves if you leave,' a local Brahmin begged, as a stricken UN worker filmed him on his mobile. 'But if you leave, the truth is that everyone here will die. We have a knife to our throats.'

And he was right – within three months of the UN leaving, the Sri Lankan government were herding between 300,000 and 400,000 Tamils into a 'safety zone', to the east of the island. With no international witnesses left, these, then, became the killing fields of *The Killing Fields* – not fields at all, but a beach: a sandy spit of land that must have featured in thousands of tourist photographs. In a grotesque perversion of humanity, the military had considered the mechanics of human grieving, and come up with a novel way to kill tens of thousands: they would drop an initial shell on a village, usually killing those too old, weak or young to take shelter in time. Then they would wait ten minutes – until people had gathered around dead or dying loved ones, trying to save them, or weeping over them – and then shell for a second time; thus wiping out whole families in eleven minutes flat.

Soon, the Tamils learned to leave half an hour after a shelling before coming out into the open – 'In which time, many of those who could be saved would have bled to death, in the open, as their loved ones watched,' Snow noted.

This is a terrible, awful evolution for humans – not to go to your dead. To stay in the bunkers for a full half an hour, waiting for Death to finally pass over.

For those who wanted to know what this evil might look like in practice, we saw mobile-phone footage of three girls, in their teens, in bright dresses, standing together in a bomb-shelter of corrugated iron.

Ten feet away from them, in the open, were three adults and two children. You could practically see the ribbons that tied the hearts of the living to the hearts of the dead. But the girls were too afraid to go to them.

'The agony of not being able to leave the bunker is unbearable,' Snow said, in voiceover: not opinion but a single, endlessly heavy fact. The girls were writhing and clutching at each other. They had to wait for the half-hour all-clear – but they could not run, and they could not stay. Stuck between two moments, all they could do was hold each other and scream – each scream carrying on where the last one had left off; each scream as awful and unendurable as the last.

This is the kind of sadism that drives people mad. This is the kind of experience that drives whole countries mad: as a spokesman for Amnesty International explained – around the time you started asking yourself '*Why* am I watching this? I am just making myself anxious and useless' – 'Unpunished war crimes leave wounds that return, and prevent societies from moving on.'

Of course, there are always wars, across the world, calling out for international attention. If you took the Earth and marked them with splashes of red, the globe would look like it had a ferocious rash across its centre – like the after-effects of a cilice belt, recently removed. The awful, quiet fact is that it often takes a fresh, novel horror to make a conflict really come to your attention – to move from being background noise, to a conflict that is one of 'your' wars, a conflict you're 'keeping an eye on'. And *The Killing Fields* had that awful, novel thing, in the shape of the rape of the Tamil women. I have never seen footage like this before: dead women on the jungle floor – naked from neck to knee, like gifts torn open in the middle by greedy, evil children. The vulnerability of the hip-bone, and breast: women's anatomy is hard to defend. And here, they had all been put to one, last, awful use before they were shot in the head. Tens of them. Hundreds of them. This is how the women died.

As the mobile-phone camera – wielded by government soldiers – roamed across the jungle-floor, we came across a sight more shocking than any other. At the beginning of the show, we'd seen the famous Tamil newsreader Isaipriya Oliveechchu at her job – reading the news with the swanlike serenity of newsreaders across the world.

Now we found her here, on the jungle floor, dead: blood across her face like bad jewels, breasts naked, trousers torn down to her thighs. As an emblem of Tamil culture, imagining what she would have been put through was revolting. The crowing. The spite.

Sri Lankan soldiers filmed themselves loading the bodies of the women on trucks.

'If no one else was around …' one soldier grinned, lasciviously, to the camera, prodding a dead woman with his boot.

Behind him, another pointed at a dead woman – perhaps eighteen years old – being hauled into a truck by her ankles, and commented: 'She has the best body today.'

The best, dead, body today.

So that was death unwelcome – death from above, blowing the ground out from under your feet; death evil. Death with its skull face, and its hand across your face, like a claw.

But what about when death is kind – when it speaks with a gentle voice? When death is the boat you wait for; a door in a burning corridor; the friend you long to arrive from a journey that has taken so, so long?

Terry Pratchett: Choosing to Die was so controversial, *Newsnight* broadcast a special debate on it immediately afterwards. The BBC received over 900 complaints in less than twelve hours, and the Bishop of Rochester declared the show was 'one-sided propaganda'. The heat was understandable – in the hour-long programme, we watched seventy-one-year-old Peter Smedley die: drink what the employees of Dignitas unflinchingly referred to as 'the poison', gasp, beg for water, become unconscious, and then die.

Of course, if that were all that we had seen, perhaps the apoplectic columnists might have been justified in calling the show controversial merely for the sake of it. However, as *Choosing to Die* was a very good documentary, that wasn't all we saw at all. What we saw, instead, was Peter Smedley and his wife in a life that was melting like snow. Before Peter's motor neurone disease had struck, they had lived in love and ease: as Terry Pratchett toured their house, he noted the incredible wine cellar; photographs of months abroad. The Smedleys were posh, British bon viveurs: for forty years, he'd been her boy and she'd been his gal, and that was that.

But now, melt-water ran through their life: it was at the doorstep, seeping through the door. Peter struggled to stand – 'Sorry', he apologised to Pratchett, with a grimace. Motor neurone disease motors on – it never goes backwards. Soon, Peter would struggle to breathe. The water would be at the ceiling.

Flying to Dignitas in Switzerland, Peter was asked again and again if he understood what he was doing.

'I understand,' he said, with the quiet resolve of a boardroom. When the medical aide from Dignitas finally showed Peter how he must drink the barbiturate draft 'in one motion', Peter did not need her to show him how to drain a glass. He drank the poison in the same way he'd drunk his wines, and for the same reason: because he wanted to. He had the quiet certainty of a man who knows there is no point in mankind flying to the Moon if we still habitually die writhing in hospitals, next to medicine cabinets firmly locked.

But days later, it isn't Peter's death that I remember when I think of *Choosing to Die*. It's Peter putting his glass down, and saying 'Thank you to everyone. You really have all been first class' to everyone – Pratchett, the crew, Dignitas – in the room.

And, then: 'My wife is really very good at putting me to sleep by stroking my hands,' and his wife stroking his hands tenderly as he sat there, until he wasn't there any more.

I don't remember death, but love. What survived this show was love.

I've included the next TV review purely on the basis that David Baddiel tweeted me after he'd read it, to say he liked the line 'He smiles like a rabbit would in a field of foxes', and that it reminded him of a particular author. It's a measure of how ill-educated I am that I can't remember the name of the author he said – but yet, am so impressed that someone with a degree from Oxford (or is it Cambridge? No idea) liked what I wrote that I've put it in here above the column I wrote about heiress Tamara Ecclestone owning forty-two pairs of Ugg boots, wherein I made the point that this makes her 'basically the Uggenheim Museum'.

No More Journeys

I don't want to sound like I have some kind of … TV agoraphobia, but man alive, if I was never taken on another 'journey' on TV again, it would be too soon. Journeys, journeys – it's all about journeys. Documentaries, dramas, the sodding news – everyone's on a journey. It's as if television has been taken over by the Ramblers Association. The opening credits have barely finished before everyone's metaphorically putting on their anoraks and bolting out the door again, to discover some essentially microscopic truth about themselves they'll just forget by next week, anyway, if we're honest. Everyone cries, everyone learns, everyone hugs, and then 'Chasing Cars' by Snow Patrol wells up in the background, like some awful sign reading 'JOURNEY'S END, DIM VIEWER. YOU GO TOILET NOW'.

My problem is – I don't *want* to go anywhere. I'm tired. Can't we – just for one week – *not* go on any journeys? Just sit on the sofa and have a chat? I want to get to the end of an hour of TV fundamentally unchanged by some faux-revelatory pre-ad-break moments and mid-tempo alt-rock ballads.

And, so, to *Jamie's Dream School* – the latest instalment in Jamie Oliver's impossibly packed life, which apparently consists of wall-to-wall 24/7 world-improvement, punctuated only by the birth of a new child – Poppy Honey Rosie, Daisy Boo, Petal Blossom Rainbow, Buddy Bear – apparently named after specimen plants in the Thompson & Morgan bedding plants catalogue. Personally, I think Oliver's is a life lived wholly admirably. Four score years and ten devoted to philanthropy, slow-roast belly-pork and procreation? It makes the rest of us look like venal, lacklustre knob-ends. Yeah – I'm pro Jamie all the way.

This week's project – in between popping out Petunia Bedunia III, and making a Pukka Sandwich, out of layers of chorizo, micro-salad and bish-bash-bosh – is Jamie's attempt to rescue the entire British educational system. Having left school himself at the age of fifteen without A-Levels, Oliver is naturally sympathetic to the 47 per cent of British teenagers who hit sixteen without enough GCSEs to qualify for university, and so end their education immediately.

Oliver puts his poor academic performance down to being bored – and, so, to this end, has created the least boring school ever. Round-the-world yachtswoman Dame Ellen MacArthur gives sailing lessons! Sir Robert Winston gets out a circular saw, and cuts up a giant dead pig! McNulty from *The Wire* gives lessons on where crack dealers leave their stash! This school is amazing.

However, it's a school for television – and that can mean only one thing: every single pupil funnelled into this Amazarium needs to be a gigantically issued, querulous, ungrateful, borderline feral little shit intent on wasting everyone's time, including their own, and ours. I know I sound like Wackford Squeers here but, really – these kids are awful. Talking over each other and their teachers, texting, yapping out lame-ass wisecracks on both the in and the out breath: they don't need to be inspired. They need to be taught to shut up.

'ADHD isn't a disease – it's a description of an entire age group,' Simon Callow reels, after his first lesson. And no wonder. As the show goes on, it becomes clear these kids don't even know who, when he turns up, Rolf Harris is. Rolf! This means they haven't *even* been spunking their lives away watching *Animal Hospital* at 4pm, whilst doing hot knives round a mate's house. So what *have* they been doing? It's a genuine mystery.

Still – there are beneficial side-effects to having a fish tank of gorm-less, adolescent piranhas, into which you occasionally chuck a celebrity teacher. When 'controversial' historian David Starkey rocks up for his first history lesson, he is astounded by the wall of noise that drowns his lesson out. Riled, he eventually ends up in a slanging match with a sixteen-year-old boy, sneering, 'You're so fat, I doubt you *can* run.'

The class explodes in such furious indignation that the headmaster has to be called in to view the footage of the incident. Head in his hands, he sighs that Starkey's comment was so inappropriate than it would be a matter of possible dismissal, were Starkey *really* the children's teacher.

'But if he modified his attitude, he could have the kids eating out of his hand,' he says.

'We've got to help him, then,' Oliver replies, generously.

And it was at that point a massive klaxon went off in my head. PROFESSOR DAVID STARKEY IS ABOUT TO GO ON A JOURNEY. A JOURNEY IN WHICH HE LEARNS TO REACH OUT TO THE YOUNG. OH MY GOD NO. Going on a TV journey is the business of a young man, Channel 4! Someone of the post-Oprah generation. You can't get *Starkey* to go on a journey. His mind is so made up about immigrants (doesn't rate them), women (not too keen tbh) and fellow historians (all pussies) that you can't make him start hugging and sharing now! It would be the end of him! His head would just … fall off!

Seriously: if *Jamie's Dream School* ends with David Starkey wiping tears from his eyes while 'Fix You' by Coldplay cranks up in the background, then TV's journey-itis will officially have reached epidemic levels, and prime-time will have to be quarantined for a YEAR, minimum. I'm not joking.

The truism about incredibly poor people – and in particular, incredibly poor Africans – is that they still, despite their poverty, 'keep on smiling'.

'If you walk down Oxford Street, it's full of miserable-faced people who never give you the time of day,' people who've returned from a backpacking holiday will say, as they unload some bafflingly awful trinket, like a small hen made of old flip-flops. 'But when I walked down the street in Harare, everyone was smiling, and saying hello. Even the old man with no legs, being eaten by dogs a bit, in the gutter! Smiling away, he was!'

Famous, Rich and in the Slums with Comic Relief explored the phenomenon of poor people smiling. In the shanty town of Kibera, Kenya, over one million people live on a patch of land one and a half miles square. With the resourcefulness of all humans, everywhere, Kibera has built its own markets, food stalls, shops and community centres – but the lack of state infrastructure means everything takes place surrounded by lagoons of filth. The river looks like phlegm. Open sewers run past stalls selling chips, or toothbrushes. Child mortality runs at 20 per cent before the age of five. As Lenny Henry puts it, simply, 'There are turds everywhere.'

Comic Relief sent four celebrity volunteers to live, and work, as Kiberans for a week. Credit where it's due – this really wasn't a luxury celebrity charity junket. Radio 1 DJ Reggie Yates was put to work on the latrine-wagon – ladling lipid, roiling oomska from latrines shared by a thousand people a day. Even the Radio 1 2008 Big Weekend in Maidstone – starring Scouting for Girls, Nelly and The Hoosiers – must have been more fun than this.

Yates – who seems like a thoroughly decent fellow – is the grandchild of Ghanaian refugees, and saw his alternate future in every kid standing in cracked Crocs and tatty shirt.

'I can't even look at him. Jesus,' he said, eventually, turning away from a nine-year-old, who was just standing, listlessly, staring at the river.

Lenny Henry was with Sanusi and his family: eight children in a single bed, packed like dates in a box; all their wellbeing dependent on their dad's ability to sell handmade samosas, cooked in a cauldron by the roadside.

'You're always smiling,' Henry said, humbled by Sanusi's ostensible cheer. 'Always smiling.'

'I smile – otherwise, what will my kids think?' Sanusi said. 'They must think there is hope. But I,' he said, still smiling, 'have given up hope.'

And you suddenly saw what that smile was, as you looked closer. It's how a rabbit smiles in a field of foxes.

A book which intends to generally celebrate all there is in the world that is joyous and keen would look odd without a bit of David Attenborough in it. Attenborough – Nature Grandad – the voice of Earth itself, whenever we pull back, and consider our planet spinning, blue-ly, in the infinite dark.

First a review of Frozen Planet – a programme whose clear, sad, heavy message on global warming affected me so much I ruined a friend's dinner party by getting very drunk, then describing the entire first episode in detail, before weeping 'The polar bears! The poor, drowning bears!' until someone got me a taxi.

Frozen Planet: a World of Fatal Ice Cream

At the bottom of my garden is a brightness – the primroses are out; confused. The earth is still fidgety and mild, when it should, by now, be silent under frost. It still feels loud out there. There's a conversation going on. I can hear it every time I look out of the window at the lawn; the insanity of damask roses lolling on the pergola at Halloween. We've jumped straight from summer to spring. All that greenness is … shouting.

On *Frozen Planet*, Sir David Attenborough stands at the South Pole, in a red thermal jacket that makes him as wide as he is tall. Under a white lamp sun, 'that never rises high enough in the sky to warm my back', Attenborough explains that his final, epic series is about the frozen places of the world: 'Places that seem to be borrowed from fairytales.'

We are here 'to witness its wonders: perhaps for the last time'.

For as the opening credits of *Frozen Planet* rise on the screen – accompanied by low, slightly dissonant brass – there can scarcely be a viewer unaware of the context: the world is cooking. Even prominent sceptics like physicist Richard A Muller are worried: reviewing climatic meta-data to disprove global warming, Muller found that – contrary to what he had desired – the evidence proved it was alarming, and this week wrote a quietly terrified piece in the *Wall Street Journal* that concluded, 'You should not be a sceptic. Not any longer.'

The frozen planet that *Frozen Planet* covers, then, is smaller than the frozen planet we had even twenty years ago.

'What happens here – in these remote, ice-crusted caps – affects us all, wherever we are,' Attenborough says, braced against an Antarctic wind that, within our lifetime, has started to blow over lukewarm water instead of ice.

But facts like these would be focusing on the awful, drowning, catastrophic pity of global warming. What *Frozen Planet* does is even more affecting than that. It shows us what we will lose in terms of the awe and beauty of these places – the magic of being on a planet topped and tailed with these outrageous landscapes; white like teeth and cloud and pearl; wild like ecstasy, or the Moon. Heaped, blown, billowing snow: a world of fatal ice cream, punctuated by volcanoes and aqua melt-lakes, and penguins leaping out of wave-foam like girls out of a cake.

Christ, look at this! A break in the ice no bigger than the average municipal swimming pool – this could be the baths in Bexley, or Bilston – and six killer whales facing up out of the water, giant heads split with teeth, jostling for space like Year 5 kids at a swimming lesson. Their scale is dizzying – you could sit in their mouths. Their design is sharp: black and white, in simple curves, they'd look good on a record sleeve, or as a tile.

The orca are here for one of the natural world's signature manoeuvres – combining 'extreme play' with 'lunch'.

The menu consists of a seal on a raft of ice: as long as the seal is on the ice, the orca can't get it – however often their huge, toothed faces snap.

So, like the cast of *Reservoir Dogs* made out of wet PVC, they surge, black and white and fatal, rocking the ice until it flips. The seal looks like a mum on a lilo in Lanzarote, being hassled by the kids: it looks as if it's about to shout, 'Stop mucking around, Cameron – you'll get my hair wet!' before flip, snap – it's in the water, under the water, split between the pack: lunch.

You won't believe where they've got cameras filming this: on the ice, overhead, in the water, between the orca – at one point, a whale's tail slaps the camera as all six weave around. Anyone who'd ever seen killer whales like this before would have been very cold, and, six seconds later, very dead. It's like the kind of show they have at SeaWorld – but wild, live, in a landscape, a plain, white and potent as an empty page.

Frozen Planet roamed across both Poles, showing us new and astonishing things every six minutes – like an excited child showing off its toys on Christmas Day. Look! Another! And another! And another! Underground snow-crystal caves. Mountains crumbled to skeletons by Antarctic storms. Hundred-year-old pines bent double – swagged in never-melting, white fox-fur snow. And in the water – as bright and blue as the Pacific – creatures that looked like they'd fallen out of gothic fairy-tales: a sea-spider half a metre across, which looked like eight orange pencils. Ice fish. Woodlouse the size of dinner plates. Things that looked like winged babies, falling, downwards, into the dark.

In this white, wondrous world, Attenborough become rhapsodic. As Greenland thawed, an ariel shot showed a whole country turning into a gushing Olympic luge course, and he sighed in sated amazement: 'The water courses through an icy delta, like blood along the arteries of a cold-blooded monster. A monster that is … stirring.'

Attenborough is a vitaphile – life, all life – all energy and motion – fascinates him. As Van Gogh saw the night sky whirl above him, Attenborough sees the earth seethe and the ice grind, and the meat pulse under the fur. He knows so much – miles underground, millions of years back – that when we travel with him, we, too, become omnitemporal, 3D, thrilled. He has a way of hitting you with a thought that can leave you thinking for days. It might have been forty years ago Neil Armstrong first walked on the Moon, but it was only sixty years before that that Roald Amundsen first left his footprint at the South Pole – 'Coming inland over the highest, driest and coldest mountains on Earth,' as Attenborough puts it. Getting to the Pole was almost as hard as catapulting ourselves free of gravity, and onto another planet. The ice is as titanic, brutal, alien and kaleidoscopic as the sky. We press against the iron hardness, and know what we are.

Not that we even have to get to the Poles for this kind of wonder. Again, look – here is Attenborough showing us snowflakes as they form, in dazzling close-up; each blooming around a mote of dust. Crackling and feathering like a diamond etching on a windowpane, falling across the screen like frizzled stars. Attenborough claims there's no two alike, and whilst I'm going to have to call him up on that one – I've thought about it, and it's just not that likely, love – you are, once again, joy-struck: snow falls on Dudley, and dogs, and the seafront in Brighton. *Frozen Planet* comes here. And – while it still lies solid, and white, above and below us – we go to the frozen planet, with David Attenborough. While it still lies there.

Astonishingly, Frozen Planet *became the centre of some jumped-up contro-versy, which the following week's* Celebrity Watch *sought to tackle.*

Celebrity Watch Special: Attenborough vs. the Ass-hats

And so it came to pass that, in December 2011, humanity finally came up with a simple, sure-fire way of working out if another human being really is a genuine, copper-bottomed, 24-carat ass-hat: if they are 'outraged' about the 'faking' of David Attenborough's *Frozen Planet.*

Acting, as ever, like Cassandras for a terrible event that will never come – mainly because they made it up in the first place – the *Daily Mail* led the Charge of the Ass-Hat Brigade with a thunderous piece by A N Wilson, decrying the BBC's 'besetting sin' of 'offering up fakes to an innocent audience' and bewailing that the BBC – 'a body which receives its money from licence payers', lest the simple *Mail* reader confuse it with another BBC, such as BBC3 Hairdressers in Highgate, North London – 'so frequently fails to admit what it's up to'. Then the *Mirror* joined in and, suddenly, before you knew it, Britain looked like it was set for an Ass-Hat Christmas.

The hoo-ha centred round three pieces of footage on *Frozen Planet*: new-born polar cubs with their mother, caterpillars freezing solid and then regenerating, and snowflakes forming. The first was shot in a zoo, and the second two in the studio – not only wholly standard practice for nature documentaries, but also fully covered in the BBC's website. As 'failing to admit what you're up to' goes, 'making a documentary about what you're up to, then putting it on your website' isn't going to knock Watergate off the top spot any time soon.

Anyway, wilfully sloppy journalism in order to point-score in a decades-long ideological battle against public service broadcasting is neither here nor there, really. What CW objects to is the ... fundamental ass-hatism. It's *David Attenborough*, guys. CW just doesn't understand how you could watch something so outrageously, incandescently beautiful as *Frozen Planet*, and then start trying to pick holes it in. It speaks of a sickness of the soul. When CW watched those snowflakes forming – falling across the screen like cut-glass mandelas – it screamed 'COME IN HERE AND WATCH THIS, KIDS! IT WILL BLOW YOUR MIND! THIS IS ONCE-IN-A-GENERATION BROADCASTING THAT WILL ACTUALLY FORM KEY PARTS OF YOUR ADULT PSYCHE!' and then had a little cry over the beauty of the milky blue-green world we ride on.

To have watched it and started fretting about being, in some way, *screwed over* by this bounteously gorgeous stuff speaks of a sickness of the soul. Or maybe the ass-hats are just confused, instead. If this *is* the case, CW would remind them that filming naturally occuring phenomenon in a studio isn't like when Cheryl Cole got busted for having six million CGI eyelashes in the L'Oréal adverts, guys. Snowflakes do actually form. They're real. Do you, perhaps, need a 'red button' facility, wherein the voiceover guy from *The X Factor* shouts 'Snowflakes – REAL!' and 'Having six thousand eyelashes – NOT REAL!' during programmes, just to keep you on top of stuff? Because everyone else kind of ... gets it.

To commemorate this depressing, yet, ultimately, useful day, CW has now printed up 6,000 official 'Congratulations! You're Scientifically Proven to Be an Ass-Hat!' certificates, available on receipt of an SAE, which readers may now hand out to vexatious work colleagues, unloved family members and grudgingly included members of complex social circles, in the event of your hearing them say 'I can't believe they faked the *Frozen Planet*.'

Celebrity Watch generally tries to be supportive of our friends in the celebrity community, as the previous entry illustrates. But sometimes, even Celebrity Watch has to get tetchy, as the next two entries – two of my favourites – display.

Celebrity Watch Special: the Duke of York

The Duke of York. Bad times this week in the life of the Duke of York, who – in a week of relentlessly negative publicity about his role as 'trade envoy' for Britain – appeared to have pulled off the amazing coup of actually screwing up being paid to swan around the world, eating lunch.

As stories emerged of the Duke hosting the deposed Tunisian dictator's son at Buckingham Palace, privately visiting the corrupt President of Azerbaijan, and accepting cash gifts from convicted billionaire paedophile Jeffrey Epstein, many would be prompted to exclaim, 'What the hoo? All this guy had to *do* was walk through a door without smacking his face on the lintel, and he was on the gravy train for *life*. This is epic.'

It's hard to overstate just what a pickle the Duke is in. One of CW's favourites details in his Travailfest is the tidbit that the Duke often stayed at Jeffrey Epstein's 'sex' mansion, where topless teenage girls would cavort around the pool, Epstein paid underage girls to strip for him whilst he masturbated, and 'even the soaps [were] shaped like male and female genitalia'.

Pausing only briefly to imagine the man fourth in line to the throne washing his hands with a coal-tar-scented vagina, whilst saying to himself, 'Nothing wrong here. This house is perfectly normal,' CW notes that things are so bad, that even the *Daily Mail* – scarcely Robespierre-like when it comes to its position on the monarchy – are running headlines like 'How very different it might have been if someone had spanked Prince Andrew's bottom when he was younger'. They're essentially demanding that the Queen thump him. Amazing.

This, of course, throws CW into a terrible dilemma – as, by and large, if the *Daily Mail* object to someone, CW must approve of them, by default. Therefore, with an air of weary resignation, CW is going to throw its lot in with MP Ben Bradshaw, who called on the government to 'back or sack the Duke of York' – which, for one terrible moment, CW misread as 'back, sack & crack the Duke of York,' but still.

CW is going to put the case for retaining the Duke of York as our trade envoy as strongly as it knows how. Yes, it knows that the Duke comes across like a venal, boorish, arrogant, charmless freeloading twat – but dude, that's what international business needs. This is how these people roll. There's no point in sending … Bertrand Russell in to hammer out some controversial oil-rights deal with a bunch of repressive Arab dictators. These are people who like painting planes gold, and keeping cages of tigers in their dining rooms. What else have we got to throw at that kind of situation? Cowell's too busy, and Glitter's too controversial.

And Cocozza.

Celebrity Watch Special: Frankie Cocozza

Gigantic disruptions in the Showbusiness Force this week, as *X Factor* fired its first ever contestant, eighteen-year-old Frankie Cocozza. Cocozza – an over-confident underage drinker with a voice like a goose being kicked down a slide, and hair that looked like Chewbacca's arse – was thrown off the show on Wednesday, after having apparently 'broken the Golden Rule'.

At first, this gnomic statement from ITV1 flummoxed CW. There's quite a few 'Golden Rules' knocking around out there. The most obvious one is the ethic of reciprocity – 'Do as you would be done by,' which factors in every religion, and is the underpinning of all human rights. But this, surely, wasn't why Cocozza had been thrown off *X Factor.* Let's face it – Simon Cowell doesn't give a toss about the ethics of reciprocity: his management contracts for *X Factor* winners are binding for ten years, and threaten legal action for anyone who slags off *The X Factor* – which Cowell wouldn't like for himself at *all*. *X Factor* isn't a very ethic-y, reciprocal-ish show. CW's pretty sure that wasn't the Golden Rule Frankie broke.

Confused, CW researched other 'Golden Rules' Frankie might have transgressed. In fiscal policy, for instance, the 'Golden Rule' is a ban on leveraged investment for government spending-plans. Had Cocozza pre-taxed an electorate in order to kick-start a new funding initiative in education, or health? Observing both his lack of Parliamentary mandate and his stunned, blank eyes – like two Maltesers, rolling around on a plate – CW concluded not. CW also considered the classic *Saturday Night Live* musical parody *3-Way*, in which Justin Timberlake, Andy Samberg and Lady Gaga explain that if you've got two guys and one chick, the 'Golden Rule' is that *'It's not gay/if it's in a three-way/With some honey in the middle there's some lee-way'* – but that sketch went out in March and, let's face it, Frankie wasn't even born then.

Thank goodness, then, that an hour later, ITV1 clarified the 'Golden Rule' Frankie had broken: he apparently 'boasted about cocaine-fuelled sex sessions'. This, at least, made sense of last Sunday's show, where host Dermot O'Leary revealed that Cocozza had slept 'for just thirty minutes' following his performance on Saturday. Coincidentally, CW had only slept for thirty minutes after Frankie's performance on Saturday, too – haunted, as it was, by flashbacks of a man singing The Black Eyed Peas' 'I Gotta Feeling' as if someone were playing 'Bash the Rat' on his thorax.

But, here we are: just twenty-four hours away from the next instalment of *The X Factor*, which is now haemorrhaging both contestants and judges at such a rate that, if the exodus continues, ITV1 may have to look into beginning *X Factor* conscription by the end of the month. As it waits for its call-up papers, though, CW can only cast a glance in Frankie's direction – back at his mum's house, in Brighton – and issue a baffled 'Dude! Dude! Your job was singing just ONE SONG A WEEK, then doing the patented "Phone-Vote for Me" hand gesture! How could you screw this up? It's a working week even lighter than Prince Andrew's! Could you not just lay off the birds and the bugle until Christmas?'

Anyone of my generation – aged roughly 30–45 – will have a preternatural interest in pandas, thanks to the BBC's children's news-show Newsround. Our childhoods were punctuated by almost weekly reports on panda reproductive activity – what little there was – delivered by a solemn-faced John Craven, and in such a manner that suggested that the universe was made of equal parts matter, dark matter, dark energy, and pandas.

The success of pandas breeding in captivity was presented as one of the primary concerns of the age. All 1970s and 80s children were encouraged to obsess on the fertility of these particular animals – as if they were the real key to the future of the human race, rather than the development of renewable energy, or peace in the Middle East. Instead, to the average British ten-year-old, everything seemed to rest on Wang Wang and Lin Bing getting it on. There were breathless, daily reports on their horniness-levels; shuffling, monochrome attempts at coitus; and, then, eventual gestational failure – as some huge panda mother accidentally sat on her baby, or ate it.

Looking back, it was quite an odd subject for a children's news-show to dwell on. Imagine the equivalent now – CBBC endlessly banging on about whales humping; or chimps being pushed into what were essentially arranged marriages – then stared at, remorselessly, by a load of kids eating their tea off their laps in front of the telly, waiting for Jossy's Giants. Bizarre.

Even now, a small part of my brain still restlessly frets over the complete inability of pandas to get it on. Perhaps I should have sex with a panda, I sometimes think. Help them out a bit. Maybe that's what I was put here to do. Become the originator of the human/panda hybrid. Perhaps I am to be the last of the humans, and the first of the Panda People. Maybe that's what I am.

However. Pending my ability to schedule this evolutionary leap in around the school run and Christmas, this Celebrity Watch Special focused on the national hysteria that accompanied the arrival of two pandas in Edinburgh, at the end of 2011. One of them, perhaps, being my future husband.

Celebrity Watch Special:
the Edinburgh Pandas

Pandas. There was no doubt as to what the biggest celebrity story of the week was: the arrival of two pandas from China, to Edinburgh Zoo – the first pandas in Britain for seventeen years.

The BBC began its rolling, live coverage of the event at 1pm, as the pandas' nine-hour flight touched down at Edinburgh airport. By 2pm, however, the pandas still hadn't been unloaded off the plane.

As a consequence, the preceding hour was one of the all-time high watermarks of British broadcasting, viz: live padding of a massive non-event. It was the Padpocalypse. The Blahblahblahmageddon. For a solid sixty minutes, the BBC's heroic Colin Blane stood on the tarmac in an Arctic-provision Berghaus anorak, clearly freezing his knackers off – yet solemn and unswerving in his duty to cover the event in a manner befitting both the surreality, and importance, of the occasion.

The airport seethed with schoolchildren dressed up as pandas, and bagpipe players enthusiastically piping the confused and jetlagged monochrome creatures into Scotland – yet the advent of the pandas themselves was infinitely delayed. For the first twenty minutes, the plane – decorated with portraits of the pandas; in the manner of World War Two fighter planes with Betty Grable painted on the side, but more 'specialist' – taxied around the tarmac, aimlessly.

Blane – leaning at a 45-degree angle into the biting wind – urged us through this hiatus with a series of masterclass speculations on the possible love-lives of the pandas, once ensconced in the zoo. 'They're not just going to be … *thrust* together,' he explained. 'They will have separate enclosures, connected by a Love Tunnel.'

Blane also – with great formality – referred to the pandas as Tian Tian 'and her male colleague' throughout – making it sound like this whole thing was not a breeding project, but some massive, crazy team-bonding exercise by a paper-merchants from Slough, instead. Yet still the pandas didn't emerge. At one point, all we had seen for nine solid minutes was a shot of a massive shipping container – giving some viewers upsetting flashbacks to Season Two of *The Wire*.

And so the facts continued, with increasing levels of surreality. China, we learned, had once sent pandas to Nixon, as a gift. 'Pandas can be a Trojan Horse,' Blane mused, to the bafflement of the viewer. Trojan Horse? How could you use a panda as a Trojan Horse? They're only slightly bigger than a washing basket. What would you fill them with? Ants?

Finally – at 2.47pm – the cargo-door of the plane opened, to reveal: nothing. The plane appeared to be totally empty. Obviously, the panda's crates were just out of shot but – back in the studio – the anchorman panicked.

'Where's the pandas, Colin?' he said – voice both urgent, and slightly strangulated. 'WHERE'S THE PANDAS, COLIN?'

This keening, almost feral cry of 'WHERE'S THE PANDAS, COLIN?' will ring in CW's head for a long time. It was the call of every human being who has waited longer than most souls can endure – only to believe, for one awful second, that their vigil has been in vain. It may well become CW's go-to exclamation, in times of panic. This Christmas, should CW stagger over to the booze cupboard at 3am and discover that, alas, there really *is* no more Disaronno, it will turn its face up to the heavens and cry, 'Where's the PANDAS, Colin? WHERE'S THE PANDAS?'

One of the reasons I'm too busy to get pregnant by a panda is because I spent the day with Paul McCartney. I SPENT THE DAY WITH PAUL McCARTNEY!

My Day with Paul McCartney. From The Beatles

I didn't know I was going to start crying until I started crying.

We're standing side of stage of the Mediolanum Forum in Milan. Outside, a fog as thick as snow has reduced visibility to 15ft. The hardcore McCartney fans – here, despite the earliness of the afternoon – stand in long queues at each of the Mediolanum Forum's twenty-five gates. The fog merges them into single, huge, lumpen entities.

Approaching the arena in a taxi, the Mediolanum Forum looks like it's under siege by a series of dragons, or slow-moving brontosauri. They are singing 'She Loves You', damply, into the white-out.

One particularly large, looming one is nearly 50ft long. We drive past it, on our way to the backstage entrance.

'*Yeah yeah yeah,*' the Loch Ness Monster sings, mournfully, as it recedes in our rear-view mirror. '*Yeah yeah yeah.*'

Inside the Forum, and the whole building is also doing what the queues outside were doing: waiting. Waiting for Paul McCartney to arrive. He was expected at 4.30pm, but it is now 6.30pm – radios crackle with updates as to his location. His name is never really mentioned: it is just 'He'. Like when the animals talk of Aslan in *The Lion, the Witch and the Wardrobe*: 'He's going to be another half-hour.' 'He's doing a radio interview.' 'He is on the move, towards Cair Paravel.'

It is understood McCartney is the subject of all conversations. He is the purpose of everyone's presence here.

To while away the time while we wait for Him, John Hammel – McCartney's guitar tech for the last thirty-six years – takes me side of stage, to show me McCartney's guitars. Racked up at eye-level, in a line, it feels less like looking at some musical instruments, and more like being introduced to dignitaries, or royalty. They have a quiet presence. They have life stories better than most human beings.

'This is the "Yesterday" guitar,' John says, taking a slightly battered-looking acoustic off the rack. There's some scratching, and chips, by the fingerboard. 'This is the one Paul played "Yesterday" for the first time on, on *The Ed Sullivan Show*.'

There's a Wings sticker on it, I note. 'Yeah. Been there since 1973.'

It's a remarkably pristine sticker for one that's been there since 1973. McCartney is clearly no nervous picker.

'That's the Casino – Paul bought it while they were recording *Revolver*,' John continues, taking the next one off the rack with the air of a sommelier bringing out impossibly precious vintages from the cellar. 'He played the solo to "Taxman" on that. And wrote "Paperback Writer" on it. That ukulele's from George. That Les Paul is from Linda – that's probably around £400,000. And this – is the Hofner bass.'

We both fall momentarily silent as we look at it. This is the one that looks like a gum-chewing, back-combing violin – the one that Paul got for the 1963 Royal Variety: 'Rattle your jewellery', and neat bows to the Queen. The bass that started off making mono rock'n'pop'n'roll, and ended up on the roof at Apple. The McCartney Hofner bass.

'That is irreplaceable,' John says, needlessly. 'There was only one other like it and it was stolen to order – it'll be sitting in a private collection somewhere. It would never have been stolen on my watch,' John says, with the quiet certainty of a man who would leave any potential thief crawling around on his hands and knees, looking for his severed legs under a chair. 'I sleep with the Hofner in my bedroom. I put it in the wardrobe. I carry that, personally, with me everywhere.

'Paul uses them because they're the best,' John says, simply. 'He wants that sound on stage. He's not precious about them. He likes to throw them at me, head-stock first, like an arrow. I've never dropped one yet.' He pauses. 'Yet.'

I touch the Hofner bass with my forefinger. I imagine it left, carelessly, on the floor of Abbey Road as Paul and John sit next to it – smoking ciggies over it, scribbling the lyrics on a sheet of A4. That's when I start crying.

In a way, I'm not really surprised I'm crying. As a godless hippy, The Beatles are the grid by which I understand the universe. When I was ten and I heard my nanna had died, I ate a whole Soreen malt loaf, in misery, and then vomited it out of the landing window, on the shed roof, whilst singing 'Yesterday' in a mournful manner. Paul's words were the only thing I could turn to in that moment of childish sorrow.

In the next half-hour, I could now, finally, be in a position where I could tell Paul McCartney this fact.

I must not tell Paul McCartney this fact.

I palm the tears off my face with my sleeve.

'He's coming. Stage left.'

The radios crackle into action. A couple of phones beep. The attention of the entire arena is pulled to the access entrance, stage left, where a huge pair of double-doors are opened up, and fog swirls up the ramp.

As this is lit up gold by car headlights, a half-joyful, half-mournful cry of 'PAUL! PAUL!' comes from the serried diplodoci outside. A car comes up the ramp, security opens the doors, and, there, now, here: McCartney emerges. McCartney. Straight-backed, swagged in a beautiful, long, mid-blue coat.

He looks like a straight line – a straight line that always moves in a straight line, unimpeded in his intended trajectory for decades. He walks into the arena. He greets his crew. He comes to me.

'What's your name?' he asks me. I tell him.

'I'm Paul,' he says. He tells it like a joke. The idea of no one knowing who he is is absurd. Paul hasn't needed to give the actual information 'I am Paul' since 1963.

'Being backstage at a McCartney gig is amazing,' Stuart Bell, his PR, had been saying, earlier. 'Because you'll find, say, Bill Clinton sitting in the corridor. Waiting! Waiting for Paul. They'll all wait for Paul.'

Taking his coat off as he walks, McCartney walks straight onstage, where the band is waiting. Handed his guitar, he goes straight into sound-checking Carl Perkins' 'Honey Don't'.

For the next half-hour, he plays to an audience of thirty Italian competition winners with a set that most people would pull out to headline a festival. 'Something.' 'Penny Lane.' 'Things We Said Today.'

Halfway through 'Penny Lane' I think about how genuinely upset the world will be when Paul dies, and start crying again. We all want to believe in something we can regard with the awe and trust of a child. A Beatle is a man-made thing you can regard with the same astonishment you would the Moon.

'Oh, Paul!' I think, mournfully, as a perfectly hale and hearty McCartney bounds offstage, bidding the Italian competition winners 'Ciao!' with a cheery wave, and exuding the energy of a man in his late twenties. 'Paul! I will vigil *hard* for you when you die.'

And, so, to Paul's dressing room. Here is his wardrobe, including six handmade, collarless Nehru jackets – the classic Beatle-suit – and six pairs of jet-black, handmade Beatle boots. A brand new pair of Giorgio Armani socks sit next to them. A Beatle does *not* go on stage in pre-used socks. This is what we have learned today.

The room is in no way lavish – the walls are swagged with a few bright, Indian throws, a Diptyque Oyedo candle burns on the coffee table. Four bamboo trees, in pots, add what I'm sure interior designers refer to as 'room veg'. A pilates mat and ball sit under the gigantic TV, which is showing the Grand Prix. And that's it. The general vibe is 'London middle-class comfort'. We're basically in Islington.

'Hello!' Paul says, shaking my hand, and ushering us onto the sofa. He eats handfuls of chocolate-covered raisins, and occasionally glances up at the Grand Prix – 'Who's winning?' – as I settle in to ask him the main thing that puzzles me. After playing nearly 3,000 gigs in your life (2,523 with The Beatles, 140 with Wings, 325 solo): what's still in this for you, Paul McCartney?

'I like ... displaying the stuff,' McCartney says, eating another chocolate-covered raisin. 'I want to give people a good night out. I heard this story about Bob Dylan once – one of the guys in his band told me they were in the dressing room, going "That version of 'Tambourine Man' – we're doing great, Bob!", and Bob said, "Right, we're changing it tomorrow night." Well, I can see that, and that's cool, but I'm not like that.

'If I go to see Prince – I mean, I love his guitar playing, but I want him to play "Purple Rain". I'm probably going to be disappointed if he doesn't do it. If I went to see the Stones, I'd want them to do "Ruby Tuesday", "Honky Tonk Woman" and "Satisfaction". So I'm basically talking hits. Why are hits, hits? It's because we like them. They're the best ones.'

McCartney explains that his soundchecks – attended only by competition winners – are where 'I get to play the more obscure stuff; jam a bit. But I try to think about how I'd feel if I'd *paid* to see me jamming away. I think I'd think, "You miserable sod," and wouldn't want to see me again.'

Paul then goes on to tell three stories that suggest – in marked contrast to the disconcerting, alpha, tribal elder of Earth vibe he emits – that he is still insecure, after all these years.

The first about how he only announces the first two dates of any tour, 'To see how they sell,' so that – when they sell out in six minutes, as happened with this week's O2 gig – he can sigh and say, 'Well, people *do* still want to see me, after all.' He pauses, then adds, in the interest of balance, 'Although some of those would be to touts, obviously.'

The second is how he's only recently started playing a lot of lead guitar, 'Because the first time we ever played – pre-Beatles – I totally screwed up on the first night. The Co-op Reform, Liverpool Broadway,' he clarifies. 'Above a shop. I totally blew it – the nerves got the better of me. So I never played lead guitar again.'

'It's taken you this long to get your nerve back?' I ask, incredulously.

'Yeah,' he replies. 'I mean, I'm not really nervous now, but it was a big thing: when The Beatles did Wembley for the first time, I remember sitting on the town hall steps feeling physically sick. I thought, "I've got to give this up."'

He then goes on to talk about how even Paul McCartney gets the occasional 'tough gig'.

'Occasionally there will be a corporate gig you have to play. We did a corporate gig for Lexus, and we thought, "Oh my God, they're just standing there. They're so reserved." So I turned to everyone and said, "Hold your nerve! It's OK! Don't worry! We're good!" And we've learned to hold our nerve for the first few numbers because we get them. We always get them in the end. They always come back.'

People need to go to the toilet, I say. They might have just been going to the toilet. Paul looks horrified.

'My recurring nightmare is that people are leaving. It always has been. I still dream I'm with The Beatles, and we're going [sings] "If there's anything that you want," it's going great – and then people start getting up and leaving. And I turn to the others, and go, "Oh God! 'Long Tall Sally'!" I always call out that one, in my dreams. "Long Tall Sally" – that'll get them back.'

Having established that Paul is still quite a nervous performer, I decide that this is the time to give him some friendly advice for his forthcoming UK dates. He's recently added 'The Word' and 'Give Peace a Chance' to his set list, but there is still a glaring omission in a two-hour show that takes in 'Maybe I'm Amazed', 'Blackbird', 'A Day in the Life', 'Let It Be', 'Live and Let Die', 'Jet', 'Hey Jude', 'Day Tripper', 'Get Back', 'Eleanor Rigby', 'Penny Lane', 'Yesterday', 'Helter Skelter' and 'Golden Slumbers'.

'Paul,' I say. 'Do you know what I think people would go ape-shit for now? The Frog Chorus. "We All Stand Together" by the Frog Chorus.'

He looks at me suspiciously.

'Seriously,' I say. 'There is a whole generation that will have a massive Proustian rush when they hear it.'

'Oh my God,' McCartney says, looking thoughtful. 'Wow. I hadn't thought of that.'

'Go frog! Go frog!' I encourage him. 'Imagine when everyone starts singing "Boom boom boom/Biya!"'

I am singing The Frog Chorus's 'We All Stand Together' at Paul McCartney, in case he has forgotten it.

'You've planted a very dangerous idea there,' he says, still looking unsure as to how serious I am. But I am in deadly earnest. 'We All Stand Together' is as core-brand to McCartney's songwriting outlook as 'Penny Lane'.

From The Frog Chorus we move on to McCartney's recent wedding, to businesswoman Nancy Shevell. The newspapers widely reported that McCartney had played at the wedding reception at his house – 'I didn't' – and that neighbours had complained to the police about the noise.

'Well, our immediate neighbours were *at* the party,' McCartney says, 'and they loved it. But we did go on until 3am, it was Mark Ronson DJing loud rock'n'roll music, and, if I'd been someone further down the street, *I* probably would have complained. Three in the morning? I would have been Aggrieved of Ealing.'

I've only got three minutes left with McCartney, from my allotted twenty – I wasted five minutes trying to get his position on the current economic situation ('When the banks go bust, and we bail them out – OK, I can see that. But here's the bit I feel is missing – they didn't pay us back. I think everyone is like, "Wait a minute – did I miss something?" I am with all those people [protestors] in that respect. Pay it back') and whether the rumours of a forthcoming McCartney autobiography, or autobiographical documentary, are true ('Britney Spears has written hers aged, what, three? I've had Hewlett Packard digitise and index my entire collection of film and photographs, so I can find anything in seconds. Maybe I should, before I forget').

'The other big news story of the year has been hacking,' I remind him. 'You were hacked?'

'Yes,' McCartney says, looking serious. 'There would be stories about how I was going on holiday to the Bahamas, or whatever – and I would know I hadn't told anyone. And the worst thing is that then, you suspect *everyone*. Your PA, who you thought was a great girl – "What if?" At the time of the divorce, I realised there was quite a possibility of many people hacking me, for *various* reasons ...'

Paul raises his eyebrows here. Clearly he means Heather.

'So I just used to talk on the phone, and say, "If you're taking this down, get a life." It is a pity not to be able to talk freely on a private phone call. I tend not to say much on the phone now. If I leave a message, it's quite benign. You edit yourself according to the new circumstances of the new world. I think it really would be quite good to get some sort of laws. Actually,' McCartney continues, lightening, 'do you know what *really* annoys me? I'd like to be able to go on holiday and not have to hold my belly in for two whole weeks [in case of paparazzi]. I saw some guy on the beach the other week, playing in the sand, belly hanging out over his shorts, and I was so envious.'

McCartney goes back to musing on hacking. 'You know, I wouldn't mind a tabloid journalist's job. Obviously I've got the better job – but I like the idea of just ... making up crap. David Beckham. You could go *anywhere* with David Beckham.'

With McCartney's PR telling me my time is up, this is the point where I ask Paul McCartney the question about what he'd do if his face got mashed up in a horrific accident.

'Paul. If you had a terrible accident and your face got all smashed up – heaven forbid, obviously – would you rebuild it to look like yourself; or would you change it, so you could finally become anonymous again?'

I think it's quite a good question. It touches on fame, beauty, identity, ego, and the idea of living two lives in one lifetime. But Paul's actual, current face suggests he doesn't think so.

'I would rebuild it to look like David Cameron,' McCartney says, clearly thinking this is a shit question.

'Why?'

'Because I'm kidding. Silly girl.'

'Sorry – it's just, Cameron? It seems like a uniquely horrible idea.'

'I know. That's why it's funnier,' McCartney says, patiently. 'Imagine me singing "Yesterday", then people going, "Who is it? Cameron?" But, seriously, I'm from the "don't go there" school. I don't like visualising stuff like that. I like to visualise myself living a wonderful life, being very happy, and all my family making a wonderful old age. I don't imagine things like that.'

And that's it – my time is up with Paul McCartney, which I managed to end by bumming him out with visions of his face being mashed into a pulp. We have our picture taken together, then I go out into the corridor, where I make a low, sad, roaring sound, such as Chewbacca makes in *Star Wars* when things have gone wrong. Why did I ask McCartney about his face being mashed up? Why? Why? I am the worst Beatles fan since Mark Chapman.

An hour before show-time, and the unmistakeable sound of an American tour manager balling someone out comes from just outside the catering area. Anyone who has seen *Spinal Tap* will know what this sounds like.

'I've told you before – if they don't have a laminate, you KICK THEIR ASSES OUT!'

It appears that someone has been sneaking local chancers into the venue. It's not clear who, exactly, is responsible for this – but it's notable the Chief of Police and his sidekick are standing there, in their shiny boots and slightly-too-large hats, with faces like smacked arses. No one in McCartney's entourage is talking to them.

'There's no reason for them to be here – but you just can't keep the local police out if they insist they want to come,' someone explains.

When the shouting ends, the Chief of Police and his sidekick sit alone, in catering, and eat McCartney's tiramisu with a look on their face which is specifically the face angry Italian policemen pull whilst eating creamy puddings on their own.

Showtime, and, on stage, McCartney looks twenty years younger than he did in his dressing room. It's not the lighting – it's the music. Singing

'Penny Lane' is more effective than Botox or a facelift, if you are the person who wrote it in the first place. He piles into a two-and-a-half-hour set with all the attack of a man in his late teens. This is a *ferocious* gig. There's a moment in 'Jet' where he's playing that heavy, strobing, fuzz-edged bass with one hand, staring out at the crowd with a look that, for a moment, I can't place.

Then I recall an interview where he's asked, 'Does going to see other bands make you feel competitive?'

And McCartney replies, 'Actually, it works the other way. Without being too immodest, I tend to see shows and think, "Well, we rock out pretty well."'

And suddenly I know the answer to the question, 'What's in this for Paul McCartney?' All that stuff about being an insecure performer – yes, that probably is one part of the motivation. But the combustion comes from combining insecurity with the fact that McCartney is the best in the world at this, he knows it, and the quietly aggressive part of him wants to go out there and, in the most elegant way possible, smash his competition to bits.

At root, McCartney is still the quiffed-up rock'n'roll kid in the incongruous combination of black leather and cowboy boots in Hamburg in 1961, off his tits on speed at 4am, playing to sailors and whores. We might be in an arena which has spent all day waiting for a knighted global dignitary to turn up – but the set he blasts through is like the Death Star of rock'n'pop. Nothing can touch its fire-power. This old man is in the middle of the greatest pop show on Earth. Just with the opening '*Aaaah*' of 'Eleanor Rigby', he accelerates away from anyone who might come close.

As the two-and-a-half-hour gig comes to an end, I am confused as to why, joining us at the side of stage, is a whooping, dancing Kate Middleton, freaking out to 'Helter Skelter'. One always *presumes* everyone in the world is a McCartney fan – but I'm amazed at how little security the future Queen has. Then I realise this is, actually, Nancy Shevell – Lady McCartney – still-new wedding ring catching in the light. She has the extremely cheerful air of someone who came off honeymoon three weeks ago, and is really enjoying unwrapping all the diamonds off her John Lewis wedding list.

As Paul comes to the end of the 'Golden Slumbers' medley, Shevell fetches a red towelling robe and, when he comes off stage, sweating, she wraps it around him, with a kiss.

McCartney exits down the ramp with her – out of the Mediolanum Forum, and into his tourbus. His private jet is waiting: he'll be in bed in St John's Wood by 3am. The crew line his route to the tour bus – whooping and clapping. He high-fives each one as he passes them.

'Thank you!' he shouts to everyone. 'Thank you!'

And into the fog goes a blue-light-flashing motorcade, over which can be heard the half-joyful, half-mournful cries of 'PAUL! PAUL!' – the sound of his every entrance and exit since 1962.

I fly back to London with his plectrum in my purse.

The week after I interviewed Paul McCartney from The Beatles, I became the only person in a broadsheet proffering a solution to the Eurozone crisis. I'm not saying that I'm the template for some new manner of Renaissance hero. I'm not saying that at all. That's not for me to say. Excuse me whilst I go and look out of the window, in a noble yet romantic manner.

I Offer My Help in the Eurozone Crisis

All week I've been saying to people, 'In my next column, I'm going to try to tackle the schism in the Eurozone, then solve the boom/bust cycle of international banking crises,' but no one believes me.

This seems a bit unfair given how little there is in it for me to sort the whole thing out in the first place. My in-laws are Greek, and I've been able to use Greece's current economic predicament for great personal and domestic leverage.

'That's my decision, and I'm sticking to it, love,' I will say, in the show-room, as we try and choose new flooring for the front room. 'I am now committed to my choice. Unlike your lot.'

Personally, if I stop the Greeks crashing out of the Euro, I will no longer be able to use mild economic xenophobia to remain top-dog in our house. It will be a massive power-shift away from me.

But, still – my principles compel me to sacrifice my own happiness in order to save the world. For it's become clear in the last year that being cheerfully and wilfully dismissive of the subject of economics is a decadence we can no longer afford.

Previously, popular historians have suggested you can tell how buoyant an economy is from the length of the skirts (short = we're rich), or the state of pop music (mass unemployment = great music). But I think we need a new measure – a population's general political ignorance. While the economy's booming and there's Tropicana for everyone, you can say things like 'I don't vote – whoever you vote for, the government gets in!' and 'The EU? The N.O., more like. Booooring,' because everything's fine, so, whevs.

But when most of the people you know who graduated from university this year still don't have a job, the New Year sales start in mid-November and everyone on *Newsnight* looks like they're about to burst into tears, then we, as a populace, can't afford to be, to give it the scientific term, 'thick' about economics any more. We have to go into those huge news stories with headlines like 'EUROZONE ON THE BRINK' and 'COMPLEX GRAPH AREA' and just *read right through to the end,* however unhappy and irritable it makes us.

For the first few paragraphs, you'll be thrashing around on your chair like a dog in a bath – but if you keep going, right to the end, you'll usually find a bit where you stop going 'UGH UGH UGH UGH I HATE doing this, can't … I dunno … NIGEL LAWSON sort it all out?', and start going, 'Hang on – Berlusconi seems like a total dick,' instead. And, before you know it, being politically up to date on the tribulations of the Eurozone is as second nature as knowing who's in and who's out on *Strictly.*

And because you've not read much about international financial crises before – but you now note there's famously been quite a few of them – you put the paper down and go: 'Hang on. Why don't we ever have official inquiries into gigantic economic collapses?'

After all, it's not a random Act of God that's pushed Western economies to the brink of panic. It's an Act of Rod. If it was someone called Rod who screwed this all up, of course – which we don't know *yet,* but an inquiry would tell us: because this is all specific people's fault, and I think we need to know who they are. After all, if a tree falls over in a park at 3am and smashes into the swings, the local council have an inquiry about it. This is considerably bigger than a tree. Imagine, for a moment, how satisfying it would be if we knew exactly *who* had made these terrible decisions that now affect millions and millions of people – decisions that will make whole years seem toxic, anxious and dreary when we come to look back at them.

Imagine if we knew the backstory to the choices they made, the emails they sent, the buttons they pressed. Presumably they were put under pressure by other people – so let's find out who *they* are, too. Until the personal shame of bringing down the global banking system outweighs the fear of under-performing for some end-of-year report; which it clearly doesn't now, and never has before – because we've *never* known who triggers these things, when, really, they should be as infamous as Typhoid Mary, or the captain of the *Titanic*.

Obviously I'm still new to all this, and I still sometimes confuse Angela Merkel with Ann Widdecombe when she did the tango that time, but, so far, there's only reason I can think of for never having held an official inquiry into massive, economic collapses. And it's that the conclusion would be that, in the long-term, this system *always* collapses. It's fundamentally unstable.

And if I can somehow blame that on Greece, too, then I won't have to go to my in-laws for Christmas.

By the time you read this, the London 2012 Olympics will have happened. Great races will have been won and lost; reputations will have been gained, or exploded. There will have been sobbing, and fireworks, and sweat, and triumph.

Most notably, people will have stopped going on about the sodding Olympics – something that was most definitely not the case when I wrote this.

The Good News and the Bad News About the Olympics

If there were an event called Things That, in 2011, Already Annoy Me About the 2012 Olympics, this is the order they would cross the finishing line:

1) People going on about how rubbish the Olympics are going to be. This is just stupid. STUPID. It's the Olympics. There has never been a rubbish Olympics. Ever. That's because [assumes patient face] IT'S THE OLYMPICS. Even when the Nazis ran it, it was amazing: a load of African American athletes rocked up and kicked their fascist white-supremacy asses. If the Nazis can run a good Olympics, then Sebastian Coe certainly can. Please don't be ridiculous, Olympic haters. It's going to be four weeks of heart-bursting human endeavour, just like it always is. And, besides. Even if Sebastian *does* completely balls it up, there's no getting away from the fact that, for a month, the Canadian Men's Swimming Team are going to be on the Central Line, a little bit lost and a whole lot buff, letting me stare at them for free. Bring the honey to the MILFs, IOC. Bring the honey to the MILFs.

2) People going on about how brilliant the Olympics are going to be. Whoa there! Whoa there, bud! It is still a way off yet! Do not shoot your excitement bolt too soon! Getting excited months in advance works out badly! Remember that year you started to get excited about Christmas in September? By Christmas Day you'd pre-milked all your Yule Adrenaline so badly, you woke with a blank, grey, deflated feeling that led directly, in later years, to you getting into The Cure, walking on the bleak beaches of Northumberland thinking 'This is how I feel inside', and watching yourself in the mirror, crying. It's gonna be like that. Stop thinking about the Women's Curling until AT LEAST February. Your adrenal glands just don't have the juice for a nine-month campaign. I say this as a fully qualified medical professional. Buy my leeches.

3) The 'legacy' of Westfield shopping centre. As East London still bustles to the ferocious construction programme necessary to hold a world-class sporting event, just one of the projects has already been completed, nine months ahead of the Games: the new Westfield shopping centre in E20. Victoria station might still be poleaxed at rush-hour, St Pancras might be a living nightmare, and half the streets of London coned off and gridlocked – but if you want to lose eight hours wandering around a new Primark so large, it registers across two different postcodes on your GPS, Westfield Stratford City is now GO GO GO! Now, I am no anti-consumerist – I have silicone twelve-hole muffin trays still in their wrapping, ladies. I know my compulsive shopping chops when I see them – but why is the legacy of any gigantic event *always* a shopping mall? They reinstate the majesty of Birmingham's Victorian civic centre – AROUND A GIANT SELFRIDGES. Manchester is bombed by the IRA – then reconstructed as a million shiny shops. Sometimes I think that, in the event of aliens landing on Earth, our first response will be to cordon off the area their opalescent time-pod docked onto – then put up a massive replica of Gateshead Metro Centre, called 'Intergalactica (Including John Lewis)'.

4) Sexy Olympic Ladies. As someone who is both technically and legally a woman, I always like to keep an eye out for my sistahs out there on the athletics field. With the history of the Olympics originating in a male-only event, and a residual distaste lingering for the idea of women becoming dementedly determined muscle machines – pounding down the track like the Terminator – it's just that little bit harder to be a female Olympian, all told. So – with all the sacrifice involved – what is the best possible outcome for a medal-chasing chick? What is the ultimate prize on offer for all those years of sweating, crying, doubting, growing and standing, doubled over in pain, and hyperventilating? It's being photographed kit off, hair shiny, arse up in the air, butt naked on a bicycle! Yes, that's right – being part of a Sexy Lady Olympians photoshoot for something like *Grazia*, or the *Mail*. Because however steely and inspiring these women are, deep down, they still won't feel fulfilled until a bloke in IT has seen a picture of them and masturbated over it. At least, I *presume* that's what the women said to their agents. It's the message I pick up from those features.

N.B. the only exception to this Sexy Lady Olympian trope is gold medallist Rebecca Adlington. As she has spent all her working life in – and I paraphrase the thinking of others here – one long Bikini Round, when *she* did the Sexy Olympic Lady photoshoots, the magazines were all falling over each other to put her in a long ballgown and white sateen elbow-length gloves: as if she were tremblingly awaiting Mr Darcy's arrival, so that he might lead her in a quadrille.

In 2009, I 'celebrated' having been a columnist for sixteen years, by consider-ing just what a 'columnist' is for.

The Nutter Box

When I was eighteen, I grandly believed that, in exchange for the cost of a newspaper, a columnist should provide some useful or diverting opinion that the reader could, if they so wished, drunkenly pass off as their own in the pub that night. It's certainly what I used to do with Katie Boyle's agony column in the *TV Times*.

However, as, over the years, I've resolutely failed to ever achieve this, even once, I've now retrospectively become far more unambitious about the whole affair, and boiled the raison d'être of the columnist down to this: they exist for mad people to write letters to, once they've finished writing mad letters to local newsreaders.

Obviously not all the letters I get are mad: some of them are abso-lutely delightful. Kind, courteous people who just liked, or were puzzled by, something I said, and simply wanted to send a note marking the fact. That these people almost invariably have lovely handwriting and beauti-ful notepaper only drives home that, in many instances, a column in a newspaper can work by way of bringing like-minded and civilised people together. Sometimes, a column is like a party to which everyone is invited.

But then there are, of course, unavoidably, the mentalists. The curly-wurly thinkers. Apostles from the Church of Woo Woo. I collect the really outstanding ones in what I respectfully refer to as the 'Nutter Box', and as I leaf through it I can see the whole span of the human condition, every permutation of communication, and a lot of fonts from mid-nineties daisywheel printers that you just don't see any more.

By and large, they roughly divide into four categories:

1) People with theories. A man called Anthony was absolutely convinced that there are only 8,000 people in Britain. 'I fail to see how it could be more,' he said. David had discovered Tony Blair's secret – 'He's really Irish! Tony O'Blair.' Vince believed women need to start wearing corsets again – 'being tight-laced to nineteen inches, bewitchingly close to the magic eighteen, waiting to be unpinned'. Ben knows that there is an incredible hoard of gold buried in a field in Sussex, which we could find together, and enclosed a map to that purpose: an otherwise blank piece of paper with a fence drawn across the top, and a cross in the bottom right-hand corner, with 'HERE' marked, helpfully.

And there are so many people who believe the Queen is an evil lizard that I am genuinely starting to wonder if she actually might be. Can you call it 'coincidence' when your third communicant in as many months tells you that Prince Philip has no idea about his wife's true form, and that Princess Anne is the only wholly human royal offspring? I'm no statistician, but I suspect you can't. At that level of recurrence, it stops being paranoia that the anti-psychotics still aren't touching the sides of, and becomes, surely, the first chilling indication that something is very, very wrong with the British monarchy, instead. There's an early warning system going off all over the place in the Nutter Box. We should take heed.

2) Sex cases. Hey look. I can't be picky. I'm obviously delighted if I inspire Feelings du Sauce in a gentleman. We are but a short time on this Earth, and if you can't metaphorically wink at as many people as possible, you have, clearly, missed out on a whole heap of fun. It has to be said, though, I appear to have an appeal that is very 'niche'. Do you know who likes me? Who's really, really into me? Men in their seventies, writing dirty letters when their wives are out for the day. 'The door has closed behind her, and so I turn to you, again, fountain pen in one hand – and

in the other, my cock.' I've got dozens and dozens of these – all indicative of a generation who didn't need the internet, and could just make their own amusement. Well, by 'amusement', I mean 'hardcore pornography', obviously.

'Oh! You are splendid! I wish there had been more girls like you in the war!' James wrote. I actually quite liked James. Even when he told me he wanted to 'make holes' in my petticoats. Thanks to the regular correspondence of my silver foxes, I now know I could tear through a post office pension-day queue like wildfire.

I do occasionally attract the attention of the under seventy-fives, though. Edward, who was forty-seven, offered to build me 'a gazebo or pergola of your choice' in exchange for the hand of me 'or a similar-looking sister, should you have one' in marriage. Alas for poor Ian, though, who wrote, with admirable candour, 'I am obsessed with your nose' – fatally oblivious to the fact that the word 'nose' is impossible to use in a lubricious context, because it's just always funny.

3) Advice. As a writer, I have dealt with most work-related photoshoots by pulling a jolly, Muppet-inspired gurn. Andrew is very down on this: 'You are now a woman at the peak of her power and looks – so it does you no favours to be pictured pulling faces. Chaplin didn't! Harold Lloyd didn't! Buster Keaton didn't!' Paul, meanwhile, thought I would do well to reconsider my wardrobe: 'Have you ever bought and worn a Libidex latex catsuit? I think you would enjoy the experience. Wear one to the office, walk around and notice how you are being flooded with a lot of tactile information.' Yes. The information that I am being urgently bundled from the building by security, I suspect.

4) Really very angry. 'If you are going to make acidic comments about a person's career, at least be armed with the FACTS! Chris de Burgh doesn't not need to make a comeback – because he NEVER WENT AWAY.' 'How DARE you refer to Delia Smith as having eyebrows like Ming the Merciless. YOU can talk.' That is, to be honest, fair enough.

My all-time favourite Nutter letter, however, came only three weeks ago. 'Madam,' it started. 'Just to let you know, I am sending Photostats of your column to the Press Complaints Commission, the Lord Chief Justice, some Members of Parliament and, of course, the Human Rights people.' This was in response to something I wrote about how I thought the Queen looked rather bored.

Well yeah. Good luck with taking your defence of the Queen to 'the Human Rights people', Bob – because when the rest of the Nutters wise them up to the fact that the Queen's really a lizard, they'll drop your case like a ton of bricks.

The old music industry truism is that every male singer-songwriter will, at some point, write a song about a prostitute. They cannot help it. Every man has a yearning, heartfelt power-ballad about a streetwalker 'giving their love away'. We could call it 'the Roxanne Rule'.

Similarly, every media commentator must, at some point, write a column about the BBC. Love it or hate it – work for it, or be actively conspiring to bring it down – the fact remains it is the evolutionary imperative of every columnist to knock out 1,000 words on how they feel about the BBC at some point in their lives. You're not actually allowed to die until you do.

I thought I'd get mine out of the way nice and early – leaving my forties free for more gardening, and lunches.

I Love the BBC

OK, I'm going to start with everything that's wrong about the BBC. It's over-staffed. Its management appear rudderless and timid. There are so many layers of bureaucracy and compliance that thousands of great ideas get slowly choked to death under piles of paperwork and fear. The amazing wardrobe department got sold off. They keep firing women over the age of fifty (Moira Stuart, Arlene Phillips, that bird off *Countryfile*). They've got far too many panel shows where a bunch of male comedians essentially shout 'YOUR AGENT IS INFERIOR TO MINE!' at each other. BBC3 is still embarrassing. The afternoon dramas on Radio 4 never fail to sink the spirits. But, none the less, the afternoon dramas on Radio 4 are works of genius compared to the comedy shows on Radio 4, which emit a palpable grey mist of dolorousness that can, over time, cause mildew in the houses of listeners.

So that's the bad stuff.

Pretty much all the other stuff about the BBC, though, is good stuff. Really. Even the things people currently think is bad stuff is actually good stuff.

Take, for instance, BBC wages. Much has been made, over the last couple of years, about the BBC's escalating talent-bill – hiked in order to keep up with competitors. Graham Norton, Jonathan Ross – before he left – Chris Moyles, Anne Robinson and Jeremy Paxman have all had their wages revealed, discussed and roundly criticised; mainly in the *Daily Mail*, but also by some sane people, too.

The argument seems to be that it doesn't matter what the 'market rate' is on ITV1, C4 or Sky – if you work for the BBC, you should be prepared to do it at a massive discount, out of principle; and that a commensurate part of running the BBC should be to make your talent accept as small a fee as possible.

Well, that's not the way I think-roll. I *like* the BBC paying big wages. I like that we pay creative people lots of money to make things for a public service broadcaster. I think it makes us, as a country, look cool. It's like when we have top surgeons working for the NHS; or bishops who like gays. I don't want the BBC to end up only employing talent prepared to work for below the market rate, because then the BBC will consist only of a) pinko liberal bleeding-heart Marxist sandal-wearers or b) upper-middle public-school toffs sitting on a nice trust fund. EVEN MORE THAN IT IS NOW. Imagine.

Similarly, there are arguments that the BBC website is crushing the competition. That – being funded by the licence fee – it poses an unfair rival to commercial broadcasters. The BBC must take that market-leading website down, and stick to their proper job – making *Teletubbies*, and documentaries about sharks – instead.

But the way I look at it, that's a *good* thing about the BBC. Haha! They've won the internet! Not only are they the most respected broadcasting organisation in the world – but they knock out a market-leading website on the side, to boot! A bit like how Paul Newman was one of the sexiest men in the world – *and* made great salad dressings, as well. I *like* their polymath hotness. I don't get the arguments against it. I know I'm just a woman, in a cardigan, in North London, but my understanding of global, market-driven capitalism is that we're kind of generally *pro* massively successful organisations crushing the competition, in whatever way they can. That's just kind of … the game.

I even have a favourite bit of irony about the success of the BBC being 'bad': when politicians, pundits or businessmen appear on *Question Time*, to have a go at the BBC.

As they sit there, going 'rah rah rah', one can't help but reflect that there just aren't political debate shows on any other channels, where some of the most powerful people in the country can be quizzed by the general public, live, on an unfailingly entertaining programme. IF IT WEREN'T FOR THE BBC, YOU WOUDN'T BE ABLE TO SLAG OFF THE BBC. JUST THINK ABOUT THAT FOR A MINUTE.

I know the BBC is often creaky, smelly, objectionable, wrong-headed, embarrassing, dull, mad, and apt to repeat itself – but so was my grandmother, and I love them both. Talk to anyone from another country, and they're genuinely astounded that anyone in the UK would ever slag off the BBC. I think they think it might actually be treason – like trying to kill the Queen.

'But – but – David Attenborough!' they will say, staring at you like you're dangerously insane. '*The Thick of It! Doctor Who! EastEnders! Bleak House! Newsnight! Life on Mars! Sherlock! In the Night Garden!* BBC4! Radio 4! The Olympic coverage! iPlayer!'

'I know,' I say – so in love with the BBC that I can even forgive them for brutally rejecting my startlingly brilliant sitcom proposal last year. 'I know.'

Wow – I can do a power segue here! For the rejection from the BBC I mention in the last column – during a painful meeting – led directly to the column below. Oh, I love a good segue. It makes you feel you're fitting your entire world-view together like an extremely satisfying round of Tetris.

My First Meeting

Until last week, I had never been to a meeting before. I know. But it's true. When you work from home, they just never arise. The nearest I'd previously got was the family's Christmas Day's traditional 'debate' over which element of the meal is the most disappointing ('Chipolatas!' 'Duff crackers!' 'The old, dry bird!') and should, therefore, be bitched about until we met again next year.

Having never been to a meeting, I had formed a ridiculously idealised view of them. I thought it would be full of people wearing huge glasses, like Janine in *Ghostbusters*, storming into the room and saying, 'Those figures are INCORRECT, Dr Anderson!', and bringing about some manner of corporate revolution. Or flip-charts on which there would be a picture of a psychic robotic dog, with 'BEHOLD, PEOPLE – THE FUTURE!' written underneath it.

In the event, this turned out not to be the case. For starters, I found the meeting room very disappointing – it did not have a chair with 'THE CHAIR OF POWER' written on it; and no one seemed to be considering psychic robotic dogs at all. On the up side, there was a wide-ranging selection of snacks – grapes, croissants, salmon pinwheels – on the table which, at first, gave the illusion of us all being at a party, until you realised that a) most people here just wanted to die, literally die, rather than be in this room a second longer and b) there were no balloons.

This being my first meeting, I was surprised that no one was doing anything about all the people who didn't want to be here. It seemed obvious to me that they should be allowed to leave immediately – just as you would push a bunch of whales back into the sea, if you found them stuck on the shingle. This meeting was no place for these people. They were emitting subsonic distress sounds. Their baleen was drying out. They needed to get back to frolicking with octopuses, and being on Twitter.

Their departure would then immediately double the available budget for refreshments – thus ushering in an era of higher-end pastries and sandwiches, which would motivate the remaining participants to new levels of productivity and creativity.

In the absence of this realisation, however, we were just in a room of reluctantly corralled people eating lacklustre carbs, i.e., Christmas all over again.

As the meeting began, a second faction became apparent: those who were clearly inappropriate ingredients in a meeting Five-A-Day, due to lack of thinkamins. I think you know what I mean. The people who, twenty minutes in, were still 'experimenting' on balancing their chairs on two legs, and/or pretending their pencil was a gun.

The meeting proceeded to play itself in a way that seemed sighingly familiar to everyone present – with the people who were most obviously stupid saying something which was immediately vetoed by the people who were most bored.

Sometimes this dynamic would reverse – the bored people suggesting something that was then shot down by the stupid – but the main tactic appeared to be using a potent smorgasbord of passive-aggression, unwarranted authority and psychotic ennui to make the idea of 'getting something done' seem like the suggestion of a hopeless and deranged loon.

The few people in the room who actually seemed either willing, or capable, of doing anything looked as incongruous and doomed as croutons in Div Soup.

Getting into the lift two hours later, I was wholly bewildered as to how anything in the world has ever been achieved, ever.

'The freaks on the internet were right, after all,' I thought, sadly. 'The Moon landings *were* faked. Unless the *Eagle* was built by a single freelancer working from home, there's no *way* human beings could collaborate to the point of getting a vehicle on the Moon. I've just watched twenty people fail to agree if a meeting was actually over or not.'

Then I noticed two people from the meeting – the clever, harassed woman in the cuffy-looking Next trouser-suit, and the man who'd involuntarily mouthed 'for fuck's sake' whenever someone said 'liaise' instead of 'talk about' – were briskly concluding the entire purpose of the meeting in a minute-long conversation between the twenty-fourth floor and the lobby.

In many ways, the whole meeting – all those people, all those carbs – had been a way of getting these two people annoyed enough to finally send three emails to the one person who hadn't been there, and could actually sort things out. The stats on the enterprise were sobering. This was the effort-equivalent of it taking 7,000 litres of water to make a single hamburger.

Don't get me wrong. My first meeting was not a wholly unenjoyable experience. I welcomed the opportunity to leave the house, and it's always good to have access to an unguarded stationery cupboard. I'm now all good for liquid paper corrector and multi-size neon Post-Its until Christmas. But I can't help but think there are better ways than these 'meetings' to a) decide upon the various futures of mankind and b) get croissants.

Meetings and snacks lead into this meditation on celebrity weight loss – a subject which, in Google returns, brings up more results than 'potential nuclear holocaust' and 'Charlie bit my finger' combined.

Celebrity Weight Loss: the Truth

Over the years I've been very fat (size 24 – try getting *that* through the turnstiles at Regent's Park Zoo in a duffel coat) and I've been very thin (actually I haven't, but all articles on weight have to start with this sentence, I have noticed) – and all through these vagaries of heftiness I have observed one thing: women have to lie about how they lost weight; and the more famous you are, the greater the lie.

If a non-famous person loses a stone and is asked to comment on it, they'll say, 'Oh, I ate a bit more salad, and went running a couple of times,' in a slightly awkward 'Let's drop this' manner.

The reality is, of course, that they've been running up hills at 8am in the morning with 'Don't Stop Believin'' on repeat on their iPod, weeping with the searing pain that is manifesting, mysteriously, in one buttock only, only to return home to a great big plate of cold beetroot mash, and would rather die than tell you.

This reticence to fully disclose the reality of the endeavour stems from a) an unwillingness to become a Weight Loss Bore (returning from the toilet: 'Hey – everybody! Guys! Listen up! I lost an OUNCE!') and b) an awareness that if you – as is statistically likely – end up putting the weight back on, you don't want everyone casting pitying looks at you, and saying 'All that effort – and then she blew it all on a ten-day holiday with an all-you-can-eat savoury crepe buffet. Oh, the humanity.'

No – as regards the circumference of your arse, as far as everyone else is concerned, you want them to think it's 'easy come, easy go'. An air of studied casualness about your weight is the aim. It's no biggie.

However. When it comes to celebrity weight loss, this 'studied casualness' is taken to absolutely absurd extremes. As someone who spends half their life reading glossy gossip mags – and therefore doesn't miss a single post-baby/new album/new boyfriend weight-loss story – I can confidently announce that we are currently living through an Imperial Phase of celebrity lies about weight loss, and have duly collated my favourite ones here:

1) First post-baby photoshoot: Mom's looking HOT! She's at a premiere in a Hervé Léger bandage dress – just SIX WEEKS after pooing out a human-child! How, Celebrity – HOW?

'I've been so busy running around after the baby, the weight just dropped off!' celebrity mom reveals, giggling.

Whoa here, missy, whoa! 'I've been so busy running around after the baby, the weight dropped off'? But how can that be? Your experience is so very dissimilar to mine! When *I* had babies, I seem to remember most of that time being spent pinned under a fractiously half-sleeping colicky infant: unable to move in order to carry out even the most basic of human functions, like breathing particularly deeply, or finding the TV remote.

The first nine months of a baby's life are an infamously non-mobile period. Their notable stasis has been the inspiration for a number of high-profile inventions – such as the buggy, and the sling. How – six weeks after birth – anyone could be 'running around' after something with all the motility of an ancient tumulus is an absolute mystery to me. Perhaps celebrity dads strap the babies to remote-control helicopters, and get the celebrity moms to chase them around the house. Yes. That will be how Victoria Beckham lost all that weight after having Cruz.

2) 'I've been so busy with work, I just forgot to eat!' Again, celebrities, your experience is so very different to mine. I work on the fringes of entertainment/the media, and one thing that I have noticed about enter-

tainment/the media is that, in these fields, every single work-thing you could do – meetings, photoshoots, aftershows, filming – is accompanied by AT LEAST three of the following: a plate of cheese and ham slices, brioche, crisps, massive 'platter' of assorted Pret sandwiches, miniature burgers, meat on a stick, selection of stupidly dandy cupcakes, spendy chocolate biscuits, twenty-four 'deli-style' Scotch eggs, some salady shit that no one touches, and as many milky lattes as would take to fill a putative and revolving Lactose Hot-Tub. You can't 'forget' to eat in these conditions. Everyone *else* around you is medicating their constant, low-level media anxiety by troughing refined carbs, interspersed with fags smoked outside whilst texting their boyfriends about how everyone else they're working with today is a neurotic bitch. Just copy their behaviour. You'll soon 'remember' to eat again in no time!

3) 'I went to see this amazing woman, and found out I am allergic to wheat/that my blood-type means I can't eat cheese/that my face-shape means bananas make me fat – and since I cut them out of my diet, I've never been more toned!' The truth: 'As you can see, since I started mixing up all my prescription drugs in a big bowl by my bed and eating them like Dolly Mixtures, I've lost my mind and I'm not terribly hungry. Life is GREAT!' *falls asleep for twenty-six hours straight.*

Nearly the end of the book, now, and a couple of obituaries to finish things off. We will stumble towards the end-piece through death, and loss. Black-veiled and attendant at the graveside, thoughtful. Thankful. Confused.

Two of my favourite women died in 2011 – Amy Winehouse, and Elizabeth Taylor. Two lush-lipped, hard-drinking British women – broads made of eyeliner, grace and balls.

In my dreams, as a fan, I would have been on casual, cheerful email terms with both – enjoying the very great pleasure of seeing their names in my inbox, in black pixel; when they're more usually up on billboards, in lights. Asking questions not for quote, but from curiosity. Trying, in some manner, to amuse a pair who – Cleopatra-eyed, both – had seen everything by the age of twenty-five.

In the end, the only thing I ever said to them was these obituaries – the worst letters, never sent; but posted up under headlines, instead.

Elizabeth Taylor: Heavy, Like Wet Roses

They were the greatest eyes, and now they have ended: violet, violently beautiful and lush-lashed, Elizabeth Taylor's extraordinary eyes have passed from fact to artefact. Man, she was awesome – my favourite, my most watched. The best of all the legends. A star in an era of dames and broads, Taylor out-damed and out-broaded them all – even fabulous Ava Gardner, who once, when her then-husband Frank Sinatra was described as 'a 119lb has-been', replied, 'Yes. And 19lb of it is cock.'

But Taylor topped that, effortlessly – with a private jet called *Elizabeth*, two Oscars, skin like milk and the ability to drink any man under the table, she could walk into any gathering like the commander of a star fleet. No one was superior to her – but then, no one was worthy enough to worship her properly, either, until Richard Burton came along, for the first and then the second time, and kissed her right out of her shoes. Their relationship was like a bomb that kept going off: they were condemned for 'erotic vagrancy' by the Vatican at the start of their affair, but carelessly racketed around the world collecting Van Goghs, Pissarros, Rembrandts and diamonds, arguing, drinking and trashing big beds.

Burton was lost the moment he met her – his description of their first meeting is one of the most astonishing declarations of love ever written. It twangs with holy lust, even forty years later.

'She was so extraordinarily beautiful that I nearly laughed out loud. Her body was a true miracle of construction – the work of an engineer of genius. It needed nothing except itself. It was smitten by its own passion. She was unquestionably gorgeous. She was lavish. She was a dark, unyielding largesse. She was, in short, too bloody much.'

In a world where women still worry that they are 'too much' – too big, too loud, too demanding, too exuberant – Taylor was a reminder of what a delight it can be, for men and women alike, when a woman really does take full possession of her powers. Burton's nickname for her was 'Ocean'. Sometimes, it seemed too small.

On my wall, I have a shot of Taylor in her late forties. She is with David Bowie – outdoors in LA, at a guess. Bowie is emaciated – at the height of his cocaine addiction, but still, clearly, both powerful and beautiful. He has his arms around Taylor's waist – a thicker, rounder waist than her corseted days in *Cat on a Hot Tin Roof*; she is heavy, like wet roses. She looks like a banquet. As she puts a cigarette to Bowie's mouth, her face is both lascivious and maternal – her lips are half-open; you can practically hear her coo, 'Here you go, baby.' In that one shot, she makes David Bowie – *David Bowie* – look like a helpless teenage boy.

She was a storm front of a woman, in sapphires. Tonight, I will drink cold, cold champagne in her memory. Then eat a diamond.

And Winehouse.

Winehouse: Jump on Your Voice, Like a Lion, and Run Away

In a way not morbid or maudlin, all I can do is YouTube Amy Winehouse. I watch her in the kitchen, in the bedroom; in the garden, on the laptop, while I hack back gloomy loops of summer hops. Her voice seems unsuited for the outdoors, but I want her propped up on a garden chair. In the sunshine, now.

In my head I call her 'Winehouse', like a cartoon character or a punky kid: Winehouse with her tattoos and her stapled-on beehive; Winehouse with her long ankles, bottle in hand, tottery and roaring. A post-apocalyptic Marge Simpson; Betty Boop in charge of a pirate ship. Winehouse on *Never Mind the Buzzcocks*, shrugging off host Simon Amstell's jokey, awkward concern, with the downbeat timing of Joan Rivers or Denis Leary.

Would Amy like to collaborate with MOR chanteuse Katie Melua, Amstell wondered.

'I'd rather get cat Aids,' Winehouse replied tartly, funnier than any comedian on the show, but still Winehouse – Amy Winehouse with the voice, with the astonishing voice, like Billie Holiday scared, angry, hot; tooling up. When she sings in 'Back to Black': a tendon-tight song that, halfway through, just dissolves into its own awfulness – leaving only the tolling of a church bell, and Winehouse singing 'Black.../Black...' like it's the only direction she has left. One of the best singles of the twenty-first century, Winehouse wrote it when she was twenty-three. In the video, she dresses for a funeral. Sharp. Tight skirt. Eyeliner. She puts her gloves on, tearless. By the age of twenty-four, she has five Grammys. By twenty-seven, she's dead.

I can't stop watching her because I can't work out exactly how I feel about her dying. Her death is not something unexpected, after all – it had been coming down the tunnel for a long time. And yet it still rattled everyone – our preparedness is no preparation at all.

'This is how we will feel when polar bears finally become extinct,' I think, 'after all that sad waiting. Or when the last tiger dies.'

We still won't quite understand why – even though we watched almost every minute of it happen. I'm not the only one puzzled – friends, particularly women, keep fretting over Winehouse's death. It's not some wailing, pent-up boo-hoo, like when Diana died. Rather, it's like when woodland animals circle another woodland animal who has died, uncomprehending as to why they have gone. How they could have gone.

Perhaps part of it is that we didn't see who Winehouse really was, at the time. Like everyone, I'd always thought her problem was alcohol and drugs: those years of being photographed in bloody shoes, bleakly marauding at 3am. When the Hawley Arms in Camden – epicentre of the drunken world at that time – burnt down, everyone joked Winehouse had done it, by accident. Winehouse, with an unfortunate combination of crack pipe and Elnett hairspray.

But when a friend said, 'What if her biggest problem wasn't drink or drugs, but her eating disorders?', the YouTube footage suddenly felt like it was being played again; but now, with new subtitles.

So here is Amy Winehouse at the Mercury Awards in 2007, coming on stage to gasps, the bright neons of her dress playing badly against the pint-sized hollows of her collarbone. Everyone thinks it's the crack – but she gives interviews where she says she spends all morning running on a treadmill. She wears hotpants and cut-off shirts, revealing that tiny, knotted belly – even in winter, even in snow. She cooks for everyone, but doesn't touch anything herself. 'All she eats is Haribo,' a friend reveals to the *Daily Mirror*. With an eating disorder like that, you'd have all the tolerance for drink and drugs of a newborn baby.

And because eating disorders are all about trying to regain control, it solves the biggest confusion I have had about Winehouse, since I heard she'd died: how you could have a talent – such a once-in-a-generation, seemingly gravityless, endless talent – and let it get so battered by your addictions that your big album, in 2006, is also your last. Surely you'd want to protect it as you would a child, serve it as you would an empress? Couldn't she discipline herself? To keep her very Winehouseness safe? Well, she was. She was very busy disciplining herself. She wasn't eating.

For anyone without a talent like Winehouse's – and that's all of us – we just stare, like unjealous Salieris, and wonder how someone could have something so astonishing move through them – yet not have it elevate them at the same time. We become like children. Couldn't that talent, somehow, have saved her? Couldn't a song as astonishing as 'Back to Black' vouch for her against demons? Couldn't Amy Winehouse just climb on to her voice, like it was a lion, and jump out of the window, and ride far, far away?

But then, perhaps that's what she did.

I suppose we love celebrities because they seem like quite a certain thing: their 'brand' stands for something; they encapsulate an aspect of humanity more vividly than any other. They seem like raised, fixed points in the washing sea of people – landmarks. Immoveable.

I was torn – deeply torn – as to which piece to end this book on. I loved the idea of it being the obituaries for either Winehouse or Elizabeth Taylor – ashes to ashes, dust to dust, close the book and we're all over.

But then, if the protestors piece was the last piece, the book would conclude on the words 'Asking questions is beautiful. Asking questions is enough' – which feels all kind of profound, and like something Kevin Costner would say in one of his Big Films, when he's being noble, or ethnic, or half-fish or something. Were the eternal question 'What would Kevin Costner do?', the answer would be: 'End this book with the piece on protestors, wait six months – then issue a "Director's Cut" version of the book that's nine times longer, and has a lot of wide-shots of buffalo sweeping majestically across the plains. That's what Kevin Costner would do.'

But, in the end, I had to find my own way. I had to be true to what I believe. I had to end with an urgent missive on how much fish hate us. Particularly a fish called 'Colin'.

A Fish Called Colin

Last week, the variety of white fish known as 'pollack' was renamed 'Colin' by Sainsbury's.

Apparently, over many sad and fearful years, customers have just been too embarrassed to say the word 'pollack'. So they have continued to play it safe, and request cod instead – despite it being both six times more expensive than pollack, and on the endangered list. They asked for cod, that is, until Sainsbury's stepped in, with their 'Colin' solution.

'We want to highlight that there are species to eat other than cod and haddock, which are just as tasty and often cheaper. We urge everyone to try "Colin and chips" on a Friday,' Alison Austin, environment manager at Sainsbury's, said.

The accompanying press release later revealed than 'Colin' is French for pollack, and actually pronounced 'Co-lan'. Initially, the logic of effortfully dumping the name 'pollack' – presumably because it sounds a bit like 'bollock' – and then drafting in the name 'Colin' – which sounds a bit like 'colon' – is baffling; but I'm sure Sainsbury's have some high-level long-game we're not yet aware of. Perhaps it is just part of what seems to be a growing campaign to slowly name everything in Britain after an extremely normal man in his late thirties/early forties. With pollack now called 'Colin', and UK Gold 2 renamed 'Dave', I fully expect to be riding around in an Ian, drinking mugs of hot Malcolm and filling in my online Tim forms with my Mikes before breastfeeding my newborn with my Bobs before the year is out.

Of course, this isn't the first time mankind has gone all Istanbul/Constantinople on a fish. Until recently, monkfish used to be known as 'headfish', until someone realised that this was really playing up the delicious beast's gigantic weak-point: it looks like George Melly six weeks after he died. Similarly, the popularity of the pilchard was suffering a severe decline in fortune, until someone scrapped the whole 'pilchard' thing (sounds like mushy tomato-ey bone potion in a tin), and started re-marketing it as 'the Cornish sardine' (noble darting silver fish from holiday-land), instead.

And of course, why shouldn't we rename other species, as and when we chose? After all, we named them in the first place. It's not like they leapt up out of the sea, shouting 'I'm a prawn!', and then jumped back in again. We could wholesale rename every creature on the Earth and not only is there literally nothing they can do about it, but they wouldn't even care, either. We're playing this 'naming the animals' game totally on our own. Scientifically speaking, they just don't give a shit.

And what we name the fish of our planet reveals one of the great truths of our species. Dealing only with English for the moment – I'm still struggling with Cantonese, tbh – this is a language that has given us the words 'corybantic', 'opalescent', 'smite', 'sesquipedalian', 'bosky', 'wedding-cake' and 'zoo'.

Taking this into consideration, let us now peruse a list of names given to fish: 'Gudgeon.' 'Gurnard.' 'Pilchard.' 'Smelt.' 'Daggertooth pike conger.' 'Mullet.' 'Lungfish.' These are, without a shadow of a doubt, horrible names. More than horrible – disturbing. Just typing the word 'Lungfish' has made me retch a little. We might just as well have fishes named 'Headcrust', 'Gutbug', 'Oozehole' and 'Brown Illness'.

The majority of fish-names were bequeathed by those who deal with them most – fishermen. And the names the fishermen have chosen articulate what we all know, deep down in our hearts, to be true:

WE HATE FISH. Humans hate fish. We are scared of them. They alarm us. When it comes right down to it, we just don't really want to be near them. Whilst there might be the odd fresh-water fish that looks quite noble – few would slight a mighty silver salmon, say; or object to the blameless life of a beck trout – the ones in the sea are just total bastards. British maritime waters are stuffed with hideous bone-cages covered in eyes and slime, rendered in various, dreich streaks of brown, brown and grey; faces torqued by the pressure of the deep sea. They are terrifying. There's things down there that make Picasso look like a photo-realist, trying to cheer up a sad child.

Further afield, in the tropics, the fish may become more colourful – blue, say; or that one off *Finding Nemo* – but this small bonus is immediately nullified by the fact they are studded with poisonous spikes, have teeth in their urethra, or wish to devour you by luring you into a gigantic clam. Whilst I allow that this might not be totally true, on the other hand, it very well might be. Ultimately, we don't know. We never really get a proper look at them, because we only ever get to encounter them when we're underwater, i.e., drowning.

Periodically, during debates on the future of the Space Programme, someone will mention that whilst we consider voyaging light years to other planets, over 90 per cent of our planet still remains unexplored: the oceans. A few hundred miles off our coastlines, there are vast mountains and uncharted chasms – seething volcanic vents, bubbling soup-warm nutrients – that we have never charted. What that means in a nutshell, then, is that those finned bastards could have developed hundred-mile-wise, animatronic killing Robot Krakens, and fish-bombs full of potent fish-essence – that clings to the skin of the victim for ever, rendering them wholly isolated by society – and we wouldn't have a clue about it. Fish could be up to anything. It's not like they don't have the motivation to attack – we've filled their world with poo, nets and rusting Russian nuclear submarines, turned half their population into catfood, and seem to go out of our way to be offensive even to the underwater creatures with good PR, like whales. Plus, no shark ever saw a penny of copyright for *Jaws*. It's an emotional, moral and legal minefield.

If you talk about this with a group of people for more than ten minutes, you realise that we quietly regard the oceans with borderline hysteria. What goes *on* down there? What are they all *doing*? Even though lions and mosquitoes and, as we know now due to *QI*, donkeys, kill millions of people a year, there's something ultimately less terrifying about them compared to fish. At least they have the decency to breathe air. Fish don't even do that, the demented, heinous, bewildering items.

Yes. There is one thing that is quite clear. It is not embarrassment that has caused us to rename the 'pollack' something cheering, and human, like Colin. It is fear.

Actually, I lied. This is the last piece in the book. Ending where we began – in bed, with my husband unwillingly dragging himself out of unconsciousness to deal with the kind of issue which looms large in the heads of women the world over, but seems like an outright declaration of insanity to all men.

My Tragically Early Death

It is 11.48pm. We are just about to go to sleep. I can hear the dishwasher downstairs come to the end of its self-aggrandisingly named Superwash. Otherwise, the house is silent.

Beside me, Pete's breathing changes down three gears – into early, stop-motion dreams. It has been a long day. He deserves his rest. Today is now ended. Sleep well, sweet prince, I think. Sleep well.

'Pete?'

'M.'

'What would you miss most about me if I died tragically young?'

'Whrrr?'

'If I died – tomorrow – perhaps brutally – what would you miss most about me?'

'Not now. Please. So tired.'

'When the sad, young policeman appeared at the door with his *Casualty* face on, and said, "I'm so sorry – there's been an accident," what would be the first thing that popped into your head, that started you crying?'

'This is happening? Oh God, this is happening.'

Pete turns over. I sit up in bed.

'It's just, I know what upsets *me* most about me dying tragically young,' I say. 'Not being there for the girls the first time some fifth-form bitch is catty about their shoes. Never having learned French. Never having written that BAFTA-winning sitcom set in a lookalikes agency, called *Cher & Cher Alike*. But what about you? What would be making you feel utterly destroyed and helpless?'

Pete sighs. He is now totally awake. He does also look a bit sad. Talking about death in bed appears to be a bit of a downer. He finds my hand under the duvet, and takes hold of it.

'The total loss of companionship, love and sex,' he says, with a squeeze.

Pause.

'That's a bit broad,' I say.

'*What?*'

'I wanted more specific things.'

'What?'

'I wanted to be able to imagine the exact points, during a day, you would suddenly go "She's gone!" and collapse on the floor, sobbing.'

'Why. On. *Earth*. Would you want to do that?'

I think this is a bit of an odd question.

'All women wonder it,' I explain, patiently.

'Why?'

'We just do. It's a woman thing. It's a thing we do. You just have to accept it, as part of sharing the Earth with us – in the same way we accept you will come into the kitchen and show us a book on the history of service stations, from 1920 until the present day, going, "Look at the pictures! Every single one is a gem!", whilst waving around a shot of three men in Sta-prest trousers smoking a fag outside a cafe on the A6. *You* do that. *We* like to imagine the after-effects of our tragic early deaths on our menfolk. So. What, *very specifically*, would leave you feeling hopeless and broken?'

'Splinters,' Pete says.

'What?'

'Splinters. When the girls get splinters. You can go in there with the pin. Jesus. I can't do that. Splinters.'

Pause.

'OK,' I say, 'now you're being *too* specific. Can you take the focus of your Mourning Camera at some midway point between "total loss of companionship" and "splinters"? Something in the middle?'

Pete thinks. He thinks for quite a long time. His breathing catches a bit. Oh God! He's crying. I have a massive stab of love for him – crying for me, his dead wife, in the dark.

'Is it upsetting you?' I ask, squeezing his hand.

'Blarrrr. Fell asleep again,' he says. 'Did I start snoring? So tired.'

'I'm DEAD,' I say. 'DEAD at thirty-six. Fucking tell me what the worst bits are! Now! Do it now! Now!'

'OK,' Pete says, totally awake now, sitting up in bed. 'I would miss you when I wake up. I would miss you when I go to sleep. I'd miss you when I'm scared, and you say "Everyone can screw themselves" and it seems to make things better. I'd miss you every time our kids laughed, or cried. I'd miss you every time I looked at that tree at the end of the garden that you love, or smelt your perfume on a woman walking by, or saw someone laughing so much they made piggy snorting noises and lay on the floor, crying. I'd miss you all. The. Time.'

It's a beautiful list. So full of love, and memory, and pride. I am a lucky woman. I pause.

'What about my bread-and-butter pudding?' I say. 'No one else's bread-and-butter pudding is as good as my bread-and-butter pudding.'

'Yes,' Pete says, still emotional. 'I would be sad to eat someone else's bread-and-butter pudding.'

' … and punning,' I say. 'Your second wife would never be as good at puns as I am.'

'That is, also, true,' Pete says, slightly brisker.

'And I think one of my real strong points has always been my ability to absorb large amounts of information, then render it down to the essential parts in a really easy-to-understand way …'

'Just so you know,' Pete says, turning over to sleep, 'this is definitely another memory that will make me cry. A lot.'

acknowledgements

This book would have nothing in it were it not for the fact that, over eighteen years at *The Times*, I have had a series of parodically clever and lovely editors, who made being a columnist for them a dream job, which I would willingly have done for free. Thank you, a million times, to Sarah Vine, Alex O'Connell, Emma Tucker, Shaun Philips, Mike Mulvihill, and particularly the properly demented and brilliant Nicola Jeal, for making my job something where I might, on occasion, find myself at 4pm in February at Cliveden, in a massive wedding dress, wearing a Kate Middleton wig, and pretending to kiss a Prince William lookalike. And James Harding – you are the Gentleman Editor of Fleet Street, and I am proud to work for your paper. I know how lucky I am to deal with you all. Thank you.

At Ebury, I cannot spade enough appreciation onto the head dude, Jake Lingwood, who dreams BIG and then makes it all come true, and Liz Marvin, for being wholly indomitable. And there's a reason why Ebury's PR, Ed Griffiths, wins awards – he's scientifically and provably the best. I love you, Mr Jeff Pigeon.

Georgia Garrett – if you ever stop being my agent, I will end myself. You've got a mind for business, a body for sin, and the heart for long lunches.

To all the people who let me come and hang out with them for features – thank you. I hope I was reasonably accurate. It was a proper thrill to meet you all. Gareth Dorrian – thank you for replying to my panicked, anxious Tweet of 'I AM THREE WEEKS OVER DEADLINE AND WILL GIVE CHAMPAGNE TO SOMEONE WHO CAN THINK OF A TITLE FOR MY BOOK' with the perfect, elegant, pun-ny and Beatleish 'Moranthology'. Enjoy your champagne. I've never been happier to put three first class stamps on a bottle of blanc de blanc.

As with the last book, I must thank all the people I hang around with all day on Twitter, in the saloon bar of my virtual *Cheers*: @salihughes, @gracedent, @Martin_Carr, @DavidGArnold, @heawood, @Hemmo, @pgofton, @laurenlaverne, @traceythorn, @alexispetridis, @Dorianlynskey, @porksmith, @mydadisloaded, @mattpark, @nivenj1, @indiaknight, @victoriapeckham, @jennycolgan, @mrchrisaddison, @evawiseman, @emmafreud, @scouserachel, @julianstockton, @zoesqwilliams, @EosChater, @sophwilkinson and @stevefurst. Thank you for being my friends in my laptop.

To my daughters – Mummy lied. 'The Man' has *not*, in fact, closed down Disney World, all the rides *didn't* get melted down to make more useful things, like school chairs – and YES! We *can* go there, now mummy's finished all the typing! The Guys – Caz, Weena, Eddie, Col, Henri, Gezmo, Jimmy and Jofish – BOOM!

And, finally, to my husband, Pete: thanks for letting me make up all those ridiculous conversations with you, over the years; just to fill up column-space. We know I'd never *really* say stuff like that – and your current silence on this issue is a legal acceptance that I really am *not* like that, and I am finishing the book now so you can't argue back yes yes thank you byeeeee.

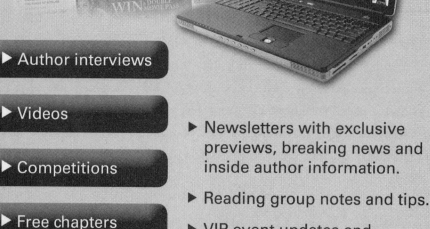